Chitra

Chitra

Cities and Monuments
of Eighteenth-Century India
from French Archives

Jean-Marie Lafont

Liberté • Égalité • Fraternité
RÉPUBLIQUE FRANÇAISE

The Embassy of France in India

OXFORD
UNIVERSITY PRESS

OXFORD
UNIVERSITY PRESS

YMCA Library Building, Jai Singh Road, New Delhi 110001

Oxford University Press is a department of the University of Oxford. It furthers the
University's objective of excellence in research, scholarship, and education
by publishing worldwide in

Oxford   New York

Athens   Auckland   Bangkok   Bogota   Buenos Aires   Calcutta
Cape Town   Chennai   Dar es Salaam   Delhi   Florence   Hong Kong   Istanbul
Karachi   Kuala Lumpur   Madrid   Melbourne   Mexico City   Mumbai
Nairobi   Paris   Sao Paolo   Shanghai   Singapore   Taipei   Tokyo   Toronto   Warsaw
with associated companies in   Berlin   Ibadan

Oxford is a registered trade mark of Oxford University Press
in the UK and in certain other countries

Published in India
By Oxford University Press, New Delhi

With the assistance of the Cultural Section of the
Embassy of France in India
as part of the
French Sources of Indian History Series

ISBN 0 19 565731 4

Designed and produced by Tulika Print Communication Services
35 A/1 (third floor), Shahpur Jat, New Delhi 110 049
and published by Manzar Khan, Oxford University Press
YMCA Library Building, Jai Singh Road, New Delhi 110001

Contents

List of Plates   vii

Foreword by Bernard de Montferrand, Ambassador of France in India   xi

Acknowledgements   xiii

Map of India (eighteenth century)   xiv

Cities and Monuments of Eighteenth-Century India from French Archives   1

Centre des Archives d'Outre-Mer (CAOM) (plates 1 to 45),
Archives de France, Aix-en-Provence   2

Album Gentil (plates 46 to 50), Département des Estampes
et de la Photographie, Bibliothèque Nationale, Paris   9

Reflections   14

Conclusion   21

Dépôt des Fortifications des Colonies (DFC), Centre des Archives
d'Outre-Mer, Archives de France, Aix-en-Provence   23

Département des Estampes et de la Photographie, Bibliothèque
Nationale, Paris   25

Institut Géographique National, Paris   26

Plates   27

Glossary   137

Select Bibliography   143

Index   156

List of Plates

PLATE 1   Maritime Map. Gujarat, Konkan, Deccan. Artist unknown, *c.* 1756.

PLATE 2   Plan of the City of Surat and the 'French Garden' done in 1758 under the supervision of Sir Anquetil de Briancourt, then Chief of the French Nation at Surat. Artist unknown, 1758.

PLATE 3   Plan of Daulatabad drawn on the orders of Monsieur de Bussy, Commander General of the Auxiliary Army sent to Salabat Jang, 'Suba' of the Deccan. By Frédérick Tiinzch, 2 May 1758.

PLATE 4   Island of Bombay, Coast of Konkan. Artist unknown, no date.

PLATE 5   Map of Bombay Island in 1777. By Lafitte de Brassier, 1777.

PLATE 6   Plan of the Port and City of Vijaydurg, Malabar Coast, belonging to the Marathas. By Lafitte de Brassier, 1778.

PLATE 7   Plan of Mangalore, on the Malabar Coast, belonging to Nawab Hyder Ali Khan. By Lafitte de Brassier, 1778.

PLATE 8   Plan of the City of Cochin, Malabar Coast, belonging to the Dutch. By Lafitte de Brassier, 1778.

PLATE 9   Plan and cross-section of the Fort of Mahé, of the Battery des Roches and of the Redoubt of the Green Mountain. By Ranger, 17 January 1770.

PLATE 10   Magazine in the Settlement of Mahé. By Bellanger, 1770.

PLATE 11   Plan of the City of Trichinopoly, drawn in 1755. Artist unknown, 1755.

PLATE 12   View of Trichinopoly. Artist unknown, *c.* 1742.

PLATE 13   Plan of Great Srirangam. By Gérard, *c.* 1755.

PLATE 14   Plan of Small Srirangam. By Gérard, 1755.

PLATE 15   Plan of Tanjore, a Town in the Indian Peninsula, Coast of Coromandel. Artist unknown, no date.

PLATE 16   Maritime Map, Coast of Coromandel. Artist unknown, *c.* 1756.

PLATE 17   Plan of the City of Tranquebar, belonging to the Dutch, in 1778.
By Lafitte de Brassier, 1778.

PLATE 18   The City of Negapatnam on the Coast of Coromandel. Artist unknown,
post-1656.

PLATE 19   Plan of the Fort and City of Negapatnam, belonging to the Dutch.
By Lafitte de Brassier, 1778.

PLATE 20   Plan of the Fort Saint-David and of the City of Cuddalore [as they stood
in 1754]. Artist unknown, 1754.

PLATE 21   Map of the City and Fort of Ginji, in the Carnatic, Coast of Coromandel.
Artist unknown, no date.

PLATE 22   View of the Chandraine Rock. Artist unknown, no date.

PLATE 23   View of the Rajagiri Rock, Ginji. Artist unknown, no date.

PLATE 24   General plan of Pondicherry Territory in the East Indies, on the Coast of
Coromandel, showing the works done and to be done in 1702 and 1703.
By Nyon, 9 February 1704.

PLATE 25   Particular plan of Fort-Louis at Pondicherry, ground-floor section.
By Nyon, 15 February 1709.

PLATE 26   Front view of the Governor's Palace at Pondicherry.
By Champie de Fontbrun, 1755.

PLATE 27   Cross-section and back view of the Governor's Palace at Pondicherry.
By Dumont, 1755.

PLATE 28   Plan and cross-section of the 'Blanchisserie', Pondicherry. By Bourcet,
28 February 1768.

PLATE 29   Internal and external elevation of the Gate of Villenour, Pondicherry.
Artist unknown, 1788.

PLATE 30   New methods of fortification. By Bourcet Junior, 1 February 1776.

PLATE 31   Pondicherry, 1771. Fortifications. Project for protecting the southern sector.
Artist unknown, 1771.

PLATE 32   Plans of the buildings constructed at Pondicherry during the years 1785
and 1786. By La Lustière, *c.* 1786.

PLATE 33   Plans of the buildings constructed in 1785 and 1786 by orders of
M. the Viscount de Souillac. Artist unknown, *c.* 1786.

PLATE 34   Fort of Arcot, belonging to the Nawab. By Valory, 1777–78.

PLATE 35   Plan of the Town of Madras. Artist unknown, post-1688.

PLATE 36   Plan of Fort Saint-George of Madras and the Black Town with its surroundings in 1780. By Lafitte de Brassier, 1780.

PLATE 37   Plan of the Fort of Chinglepet, belonging to the English. By Lafitte de Brassier, 1780.

PLATE 38   Maritime Map. Gergelin, Orissa, Bengal. Artist unknown, *c.* 1756.

PLATE 39   Plan of Vizagapatnam, settlement of the English East India Company in India, taken by the French on 26 June 1757. Artist unknown, *c.* 1757–58.

PLATE 40   Plan of Fort William and the Black Town and its surroundings in 1779, belonging to the English, Calcutta. By Lafitte de Brassier, 1779.

PLATE 41   Plan of Chandernagor and its territory, belonging to the French Company in the Kingdom of Bengal, 1722. By Riftierre, 1722.

PLATE 42   Plan of Chandernagor and Fort d'Orléans, the French settlement on the western side of the Hoogly. By Bourcet, 1762.

PLATE 43   View of the Loge of Chandernagor, from the King's Gate, from the Garden. By Riftierre, *c.* 1722.

PLATE 44   Plan of the Loge of Kasimbazar, belonging to the French East India Company. Artist unknown, *c.* 1729.

PLATE 45   Cross-section of the Loge of Kasimbazar. By Lavabre, 3 September 1729.

PLATE 46   Palace of Nizam ul-Mulk at Delhi, from the bank of the Jamuna, 1774. By an architect working for Shuja ud-Daula, 1774.

PLATE 47   Palace built in Old Delhi by Salim Shah, who also built Salimgarh, used as a prison for the Mughal princes. Drawn in 1774 by an architect of Wazir Shuja ud-Daula.

PLATE 48   Palace of the Great Mughal, Delhi, from the bank of the Jamuna. By an architect working for Shuja ud-Daula, 1774.

PLATE 49   Mahtab Bagh. Garden made by Aurangzeb for his wives inside the Red Fort at Delhi. By an architect working for Shuja ud-Daula, 1774.

PLATE 50   Residence of Shuja ud-Daula at Faizabad. By an architect working for Shuja ud-Daula, 1774.

Foreword

*I*n France there is a rich, but largely unexplored, documentation on seventeenth- to early nineteenth-century India in the fields of political, social and economic history. It also covers cultural aspects, for example, collections of Sanskrit manuscripts, miniature paintings and cartography.

This superbly illustrated book shows plans and views of eighteenth-century cities and monuments of India. These drawings, made by French and Indian architects, reveal a very dynamic continent with political entities open to the external world and modernizing themselves according to the pace and means decided by their governments.

Dr Jean-Marie Lafont's book describes Indo–French relations at that time, not only on the official level through the French Compagnie des Indes Orientales and the French settlements, but also through the number and competence of the Frenchmen who served the Indian States.

At a time when some European powers were trying to impose their hegemony over huge colonial empires, it is interesting to note that the policy of France, initiated by Choiseul after 1763 and partly implemented by Vergennes in 1783, was to maintain or restore a balance of power, whose purpose was to preserve (in India) or create (in North America) great political units independent from the dominant European States. On many occasions Vergennes reaffirmed his commitment to the rule of law in international affairs and to the principle of the balance of power. Would it be anachronistic to call it a 'multipolar' policy ? Whatever the local success or failure in implementing that policy, one of the best manifestos of French intellectual and political perception of India can be found in Anquetil Duperron's *L'Inde en rapport avec l'Europe* (1798). In this perceptive book the equality of these two political entities is proclaimed, and the author advocates the development of commercial exchanges based on respect of each other's rights and legislations.

The fifty documents reproduced in the present volume are a small selection from the hundreds of maps, plans and views of Indian cities and monuments in French archives. It invites the reader to an unusual travel to eighteenth-century India, an India all the more fascinating because it is an *Inde des Lumières*, an independent India on the path of change and modernization.

New Delhi
11 December 2000

BERNARD DE MONTFERRAND
Ambassador of France in India

Acknowledgements

H.E. Bernard de Montferrand,
Ambassador of France to India

H.E. Claude Blanchemaison, *Former
Ambassador of France to India (1996–2000),
Ambassador of France to the Federation
of Russia*

Mr R.V. Vaidyanatha Ayyar, *Secretary,
Ministry of Culture and Tourism, Government
of India*

Mr Philippe Bélaval, *Director General, Archives
de France, Paris*

Mrs Françoise Durand-Evrard, *Director,
Centre des Archives d'Outre-Mer,
Aix-en-Provence*

Mr Jean-Pierre Angrémy, *President,
Bibliothèque Nationale de France, Paris*

Ms Catherine Fournier

Dr R.D. Choudhury, *Director General,
National Museum, New Delhi*

Dr R.S. Chauhan, *Assistant Director–
Exhibitions, National Museum, New Delhi*

Mr Frédéric Grare, *Director, Centre for Human
Sciences, New Delhi*

Mr Bernard Malauzat, *Councillor for Culture,
Science and Technology, Embassy of France
in India*

Mr Laurent de Gaulle, *Cultural Attache,
Embassy of France in India*

Direction Générale des Relations
Culturelles, Scientifiques et Techniques,
Ministère des Affaires Etrangères, Paris

Bibliothèque Nationale de France

Centre des Archives d'Outre-Mer

Institut Géographique National

Mr André Bourgey, *President, Institut
National des Langues et Civilizations
Orientales (INALCO), Paris*

Cultural and Scientific Cooperation Service,
Embassy of France in India, New Delhi

Service Historique de l'Armée de Terre,
Château de Vincennes, Paris

Mr Christophe Beyeler

Mrs Catherine Bizot

Mrs Colette Caillat

Colonel Chinailh

Mr Serge Dubuisson

Mr Jean-Claude Jacq

Ms Indu Chandrasekhar

Ms Purnima Joshi

Mrs Béatrice Khayat

Mrs Réhana Lafont

General Gurbir Mansingh

Mrs Francine d'Orgeval

Mr Alexis Rinckenbach

Mr Klaus Roetzer

Mrs Barbara Schmitz

Colonel Henri Switzer

Mr Nicolas Wuest-Famôse

Mrs Laure Beaumont-Maillet

Mrs Hélène Fauré

Mr Jean-Yves Laigre

Mr J.P. Tessandier

Mr Rukun Advani

Mr Gaurav Ghose

Mrs Nitasha Devasar

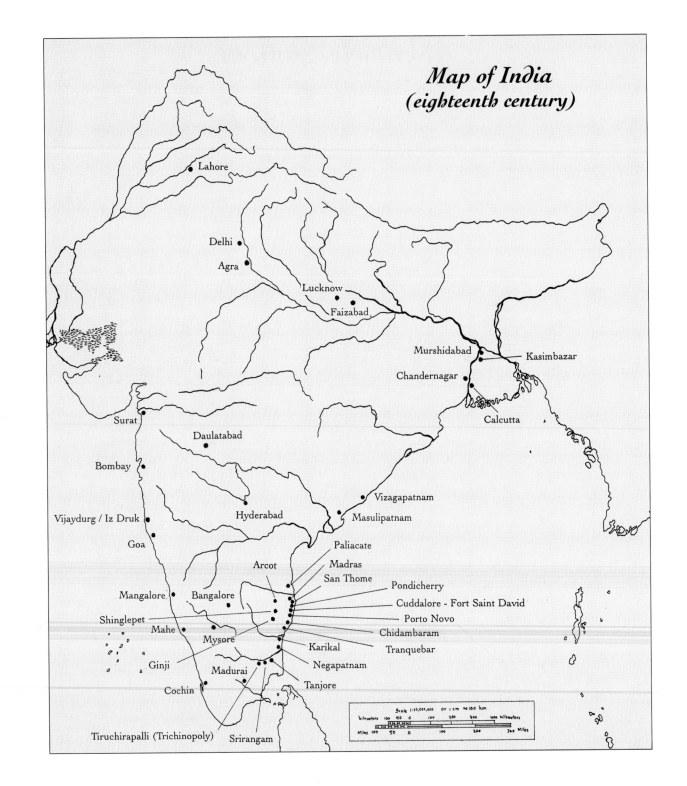

Map of India
(eighteenth century)

Lahore

Delhi

Agra

Lucknow

Faizabad

Murshidabad

Kasimbazar

Chandernagar

Calcutta

Surat

Daulatabad

Bombay

Vizagapatnam

Vijaydurg / Iz Druk

Hyderabad

Masulipatnam

Goa

Paliacate

Arcot

Madras

San Thome

Pondicherry

Mangalore

Bangalore

Cuddalore - Fort Saint David

Shinglepet

Porto Novo

Mahe

Chidambaram

Mysore

Karikal

Tranquebar

Ginji

Negapatnam

Madurai

Tanjore

Cochin

Tiruchirapalli (Trichinopoly)

Srirangam

Scale 1:10,000,000 or 1 cm to 100 km

kilometers 100 50 0 100 200 300 400 kilometers

Miles 100 50 0 100 200 300 Miles

xiv

Cities and Monuments
of Eighteenth-Century India
from French Archives

Recent researches by French and Indian scholars have uncovered many new aspects of the exchanges that took place at multiple levels between France and India during the seventeenth and eighteenth centuries. Libraries and archives in France contain rich and as yet unpublished documentation on this subject. The Centre des Archives d'Outre-Mer (CAOM), Archives de France, Aix-en-Provence, is one such institution that houses more than a thousand documents, including various memoirs, on India and Sri Lanka. Forty-one of the drawings and maps presented here come from the CAOM. Five other drawings included here have been sourced from an album of the Gentil Collection in the Département des Estampes et de la Photographie, Bibliothèque Nationale de France, Paris, and are being reproduced for the first time. The Institut Géographique National, Paris, possesses instruments used in cartography and a copper plate of the plan of Pondicherry.

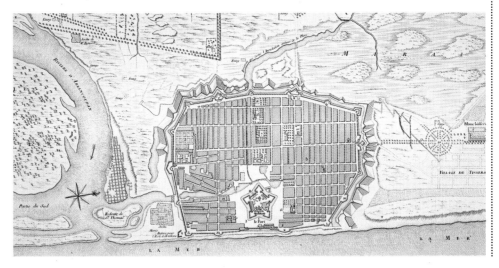

Plan of the city of Pondicherry, dedicated to the memory of Monsieur Dupleix. Courtesy: IGN, Paris (from a copper plate)

1

Centre des Archives d'Outre Mer (CAOM) (plates 1 to 45)

Archives de France Aix-en-Provence

French cartographers of the eighteenth century. Courtesy: IGN, Paris

DRAWINGS, PLANS AND MAPS

The drawings and maps from the Archives de France show plans and views of Indian cities and forts in the eighteenth century. They also show French settlements (*loges*) and trading posts: Surat (the oldest *loge*, going back to Mughal Emperor Aurangzeb's *farman* of 1666) and Mahé (1721, with seven *loges* added in the 1750s) on the west coast; Chandernagor (permission for which was granted in 1674 and which came into being with the Mughal Governor of Bengal's *parvana* of 1693) and Pondicherry (1674) in the east; and Karikal (1739) south of Pondicherry. There was a cluster of other *loges* around Chandernagor, from Patna to Kasimbazar, Dacca and Chittagong, where French traders ordered and received goods for France. Between 1700 and 1754, the prominent settlements witnessed the construction, in a distinctly French architectural style, of splendid monuments and buildings. These included civil buildings like the Governor's Palace in Fort-Louis, Pondicherry and the *Loge* of Chandernagor in Fort d'Orléans, commercial buildings like the Great *Blanchisserie* just outside Pondicherry, the *Loge* of Kasimbazar and the magazines of Mahé. Political instability and the growing rivalry between the European companies in eighteenth-century India impelled the principal settlements to build fortifications or simple *redoubts* (Fort-Louis and Gate of Villenour in Pondicherry, Fort Mahé, Fort d'Orléans in Chandernagor). All of these are represented in the drawings from the Archives de France. Chandernagor and Pondicherry, in their heyday, were considered amongst the most beautiful European-style cities of India. When they were captured by the British East India Company, in 1757 and 1761 respectively, their splendid monuments were razed to the ground.

Besides France, other European nations were also attracted by the riches of India, the expertise of its artisans and the quality of its merchandise. They too established trading posts, and the Archives de France possesses several documents that bear testimony to their histories. There are magnificent views and plans of the Portuguese settlements in Goa; the Danish in Tranquebar; the Dutch in Negapatnam, Cochin (with its Villejuif), Colombo and Trinquemale; and the British in Madras, Cuddalore, Calcutta, Vizagapatnam and the Island of Bombay. Some of the monuments, such as Fort William in Calcutta, are represented in great detail. The cities are usually

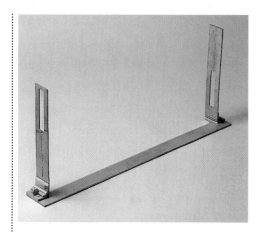

Instruments used in cartography.
Courtesy: IGN, Paris

shown with their territorial extensions and official limits as fixed by treaties with Indian authorities: the Mughal emperor or his representatives in the north, sovereigns like the ruler of Tanjore in the south, or other provincial rulers who had jurisdiction over their territorial boundaries.

In addition, the Archives de France has a series of drawings and plans of Indian cities and fortresses that are invaluable in any attempt to trace the local and national history of eighteenth-century India. The Fortress of Ginji, seventy kilometres west of Pondicherry, with its three peaks (including 'Chandraine' and 'Rasegadou'), was one of the strongest defences in the subcontinent. It played a very important role in the various conflicts of South India before and during the Mughal period, as well as at the time of Anglo–French rivalry in the Carnatic. Two other South Indian towns that fascinated European travellers were Trichinopoly with its formidable rock, and Tanjore with its fort and great temple. Near Trichinopoly, on the island of Srirangam in the midst of the Cavery river, two major temples enclosed by high walls attracted the curiosity of Jacques Maissin in 1754. He gained information about the local rites and rituals from the religious authorities there and, based on this, made voluminous notes on the customs and traditions of the Hindu religion which are conserved to this day. He also had drawings made which unfortunately have disappeared. The Fort of Arcot, of which nothing remains today, was once the seat of a powerful *nawabi* with authority over Madras and Pondicherry. The plan of Chinglepet Fort shows a splendid residence and gardens that one can hardly imagine today.

The plan of the city and port of Izdruk (Vijaydurg, Gheria) on the Malabar coast is of special interest. An erstwhile stronghold of the Angrias, this place used to be the base for a powerful naval force before it was bombarded and captured by an English fleet in 1756: several ships, including one with forty guns, which were under construction, were burnt during the attack. Naval maps before 1756 mention Iz Druk, or Gheria, as *'aux Angrias'* ('to the Angrias', along with other coastal ports), while later maps cite it as *'aux Marathes'* ('to the Marathas'), for it was to them the authorities in Bombay delivered the city after its capture.

Another fascinating map is that of the city and port of Mangalore, which brings to us memories of Hyder Ali's navy and Tipu Sultan's plans for

3

Meeting of Hyder Ali and Bailli de Suffren near Cuddalore, July 1782. Private collection

building a new and more modern blue-water fleet. The English captured Mangalore in 1783 and it was recaptured by Tipu Sultan, with the help of the French, in 1784. The details of the monuments and the names on some of them in the Mangalore map are particularly interesting. Another map of this city gives an indication of the depth of the water at the entrance of the two passes. Together, the plans of Iz Druk and Mangalore are an excellent pointer to the maritime vocation of the subcontinent in both the trading and military fields.

THE ARTISTS

Fifteen of the forty-one maps from the Archives de France are anonymous. Twenty-six are signed by the artists who drew them, most of them engineers or military officers in the Corps Royal d'Artillerie. Denis de Nyon was *ingénieur du roi* (king's engineer) in the French army for ten years before he began, in 1700, to draw up plans and oversee the construction of Fort-Louis in Pondicherry (it is modelled on the Fort of Tournai, a city now in Belgium). Paul Gérard joined the Compagnie des Indes in 1753 as an engineering officer. In 1756 he was posted in Chiringam (Srirangam) as an artillery major and was asked to draw maps of the regions conquered by Lally from the English in 1757. Gilbert de Ranger served in the Artillery Corps of India from 1752 to 1758. He was appointed an engineer in Pondicherry in 1756, promoted as second engineer in 1759, and served under Law (with a stay in Mahé) from 1764 to 1778. François Bourcet, younger brother of Jean Bourcet, who was one of two engineers who rebuilt the ramparts of Pondicherry between 1763 and 1778 (the other was Desclaisons), was an artillery officer attached to the battalion of India. He served as an engineer in Pondicherry during the siege of 1778. Touchant de la Lustière, an *ingénieur ordinaire du roi* (commissioned engineer), was named captain of engineering in Pondicherry in 1782. He then spent some time in Ceylon before returning to Cherbourg, where he worked on the fortifications of the new port during the French Revolution. We have very little information on some of the other artists whose signatures are on the maps. Frédérick Tiintzch is indicated as an artist; Champie de Fontbrun was a sub-lieutenant of artillery; and Dumont, who drew the elevation and plan of the new Governor's Palace in Pondicherry, continuing the work begun in 1738 following the plans prepared by the architect Gerbault, commanded in Villenour for some time.

4

Instrument used in cartography.
Courtesy: IGN, Paris

Ginji Fort (1750–61), Rajagiri, as it stands today. The modern bastion can be seen in the foreground. (Photo: Lafont)

Three of the French officers who drew maps had rather eccentric and interesting careers. Pierre Basile de Sornay, educated by his own father who had been a chief engineer in Ile de France and constructed many buildings there, arrived in Pondicherry in 1750. Having joined the army as an engineer and infantry officer, he served under Dumont in Villenour, under Glatignac in Ginji and under Maissin at Trichinopoly. Bussy then took him into the Deccan army and Lally used his engineering skills during the siege of Fort Saint-David in Cuddalore. In 1764 Law appointed him captain and engineer at Karikal. In 1759 he married Jeanne-Madeleine Sinan, daughter of Joanis Sinan (an Armenian trader born in Persia) and Catherine Elias (descended from a Jewish–Portuguese family living in the Carnatic). It is recorded that in 1784 Jeanne-Madeleine apprised Minister de Castries about how useful her family had been to Dumas, Dupleix and de Leyrit because of the special relationship it enjoyed with 'the princes of the land, our family being the only one invited to their private celebrations of festivals and marriages in their palaces'. De Sornay drew or supervised the drawing of several maps which are now in the Archives de France, including that of the new *Blanchisserie* built by Dupleix outside Pondicherry. He was befriended by Bailli de Suffren, commander of the French fleet in the Indian Ocean, in 1780. In 1784, when de Sornay's wife travelled to Paris to present to the Academy of Sciences an instrument to measure the longitude at sea invented by her husband, Suffren took her and her sons under his protection.

Two other engineers, Valory and Lafitte de Brassier, helped prepare the French expedition to India at the same time as the French intervention in North America (1778–83). The evolution of the French policy towards India involved a reticent acceptance of Dupleix's policy of 1741 ('indirect' government of the Carnatic and the Deccan) initially, and later, abandonment of this policy (Dupleix was recalled in 1754). There was an effort to destroy English power in India (Lally's expedition in 1757–61), as also attempts to liberate territories acquired by the East India Company and return them to their legitimate sovereigns (the expeditions of Suffren and Bussy from 1780 to 1783). This last strategy, an interesting mixture of pragmatism and idealism, was analogous to the French policy with regard to the revolting colonists in North America, as elaborated by Choiseul right from 1763. In order to

Montigny, *Agent de France*, at the Maratha *darbar*, Pune. Private collection. (Photo: Lafont)

implement this the French government appointed or confirmed Agents such as Gentil, Pallebot de Saint Lubin, Montigny and Piveron de Morlat at the Indian courts of Mysore, Poona, Hyderabad, Awadh and Delhi. Their task was to collect information on the willingness and ability of the Indian rulers to form alliances against the East India Company. The reports made by these French agents form a rich and detailed source of Indian history. It was also necessary to have up-to-date information on the state of the cities and ports, European and Indian, for Indo–French naval and military operations as in North America. This task was performed by the French engineers who drew plans and maps of harbours, cities and forts. The maps drawn by Valory and Lafitte de Brassier, which have survived the passage of time, serve as a valuable record of Indian urbanization during the 1770s and 1780s.

Louis Marc-Antoine, Marquis de Valory d'Estilly, was a captain of the Grenadiers, an elite troop. In January 1776 he was given permission by Ternay, Minister of the Navy, to visit his relative Chevalier who happened to be the Governor of Chandernagor. Valory took leave for a year but extended it to three years. During this period he spent seven months in Hyderabad with the Nizam and his sons, and six months in Madras copying English maps of the coast and making plans of the new fortifications of the city with tracings of the mines defending the *glacis*. He did so at great risk because this amounted to nothing less than military spying. Valory was gifted with a strong political acumen and in 1777 he warned Sartine, Minister of the Navy, about the impending English plan to conquer India at any cost if the American colonies got their independence. He returned to Paris with a rich harvest of maps and plans that were signed by him; today only a few unsigned copies remain preserved in Aix-en-Provence. On his return to France he wrote a book titled *On the Attack and Defence of Colonies, Coasts and Maritime Places of the Continent*, where he incorporated all the information that he had gathered. However, its publication was prohibited by the French government due to the sensitive nature of the information it contained. Valory's military superiors misunderstood the reasons for his long absence from service, attributing it to commercial motives, and refused his reintegration into the army.

Nine of the twenty-six identified maps bear the signature of Louis-François-Grégoire Lafitte de Brassier. At the age of twelve Lafitte de Brassier

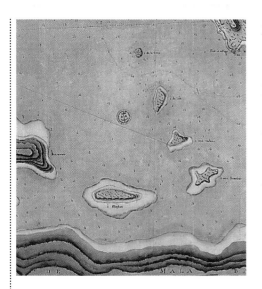

Detail from map of Bombay Island, 1777, drawn by Lafitte de Brassier.
Courtesy: CAOM, Paris

joined the famous regiment of Lorraine which set sail for India in 1757 with Lally. He participated in numerous battles, some glorious (the capture of Fort Saint-David and the siege of Madras in which his father, also in the army, was killed) and some disastrous (Vandivash and the siege and surrender of Pondicherry in 1761, during which he was taken prisoner). We are not sure where he acquired his skills as an artist, possibly at the Compagnie d'Ouvriers de la Mer of Ile de France, where he supervised some workshops in 1767. He joined the corps of engineers of that island in 1774, and embarked on a voyage on the *Union* in 1776 to draw maps of the Seychelles archipelago. In 1777 he sailed with Admiral Tronjoly's *Le Brillant* and drew up maps of the oriental coast of India extending to Pegu, Achem, Sumatra and Nicobar islands. In 1778 he mapped the Malabar coast. The aim of these exercises was certainly to improve the existing naval maps but also 'to give us the resources to keep a naval squadron in the Indian Ocean without having to send it to Ile de France'. That could be done by capturing enemy territory (eventually disembarking in Negapatnam) or by using an ally port such as Izdruk (belonging to the Marathas) or Mangalore (belonging to Mysore). Lafitte de Brassier did not have the time to put his maps in order before 1778, when he was once again taken prisoner in Pondicherry. Sailing on an English ship that was to take him from Madras to Europe via Bombay and Surat, the Detroits, China, Bali, the Cape and Saint-Helen Island, he 'bought the plan of Fort Saint-George of Madras as well as the black city from an Indian artist working for the English', drew maps of Surat and Calcutta, as well as of Macao and Batavia. For the English, he made naval maps of the islands of Pondi and Galion and the *détroit* of Bali. He returned a free man to Paris in 1781, with a total of twenty-six maps. Under instructions from the minister, he completed these maps and bound them in two large and splendid volumes, one of which (comprising twenty maps, some with commentaries) has survived intact. Lafitte de Brassier—an excellent servant of the king but timid and without a patron at court—staked a claim to the Croix de Saint-Louis but was denied the honour. His file carries the stern comment that 'his twenty years of service (as a subaltern officer) could only be counted for half' and therefore he did not have the number of years considered necessary to claim the decoration. He felt he had been 'forgotten and ill-treated, deprived of his normal advancement', and

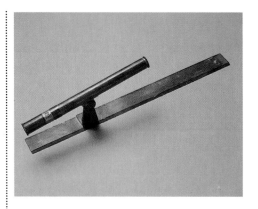

Instrument used in cartography.
Courtesy: IGN, Paris

Prince Tipu Sultan. Painting in Tipu Sultan's
summer palace at Srirangapatnam.
(Photo: Senthil Kumar)

left Paris in 1786 for Ile de France, where he drew maps and plans for the rest of his life.

In this introductory essay we have made a mention only of the engineers and geographers who were in India on official missions from France. But Valory's stay with the Nizam of Hyderabad is a pointer to a fact that is less known—that there were French officers at native courts who were either political refugees after the debacle of the Seven Year War or on secret missions. These men, three of whom we shall mention, are not represented in this publication because they worked in Indian territory and most of the archives relating to them have not reached us. Le Goux de Flaix, for instance, served Hyder Ali and Tipu Sultan as a civil and military engineer for many years. His monumental *Essai historique... sur l'Hindoustan avec un tableau de son commerce*, published in 1807, is a warm description of developments in the fields of Indian commerce and technology. Another engineer, Charles [de] Canaple, wrote about himself that 'he was dedicated to the service of princes friendly to the Nation [France], and he erected for them military fortifications and buildings which would enable them to resist the English'. In 1772 Canaple had started building a formidable hexagonal fortress with six bastions for Shuja ud-Daula on the Ghaghra river, north of Faizabad (Awadh), but it remained incomplete at the time of the Nawab's death in 1775. Gabriel Johet de Courcelles, after his multiple *péripéties* with the Marathas, 'offered his services to Nizam Ali Khan, Souba or Viceroy of the Deccan, who took him on as an engineer and artillery officer. His skill in mechanics and physics particularly attracted the attention of the prince who had an interest in these subjects.' He was chosen to go on a mission to Delhi, but it did not materialize and Courcelles returned to France. His file in Aix-en-Provence contains no further information on his career.

All these engineers, who are practically unknown today, played a major role in developing a modern system of fortification for the emerging Indian states of Awadh, Hyderabad and Mysore, aiding them in their quest for secure borders amidst an increasingly dangerous political environment. The nawabs of Awadh alone built fifty-one new forts during the short period of political independence of their principality. Besides Canaple, three other well-known 'French' officers at the Awadhi court, Gentil, Polier and Martin, played an important, if not entirely clear, role in their construction.

Album Gentil
(plates 46 to 50)

Département des Estampes et de la Photographie, Bibliothèque Nationale, Paris

Portrait of Colonel Jean-Baptiste Gentil.
(Photo: Lafont)

Portrait of
Marquis de Bussy.
Private collection.
(Photo: Lafont)

There is no doubt that Jean-Baptiste Gentil (1726–99) was one of the most well-known French officers to have served an Indian state. We have substantial documentation on him, for a large part based on his *Mémoires sur l'Indoustan ou Empire Mogol* published posthumously in 1822, which gives an account of his activities first in the Deccan and then in Awadh, Lucknow and Faizabad. His notable collection of Persian manuscripts and albums of Indo–Persian miniatures are preserved in two sections of the Bibliothèque Nationale, Paris: Manuscrits Orientaux (Suppléments Persans) and Département des Estampes et de la Photographie.

Gentil arrived in India in 1752 with an infantry regiment and was immediately put under the command of Bussy, who initiated him in the policy he had drawn up for implementation in the Deccan. The remarkable work of Bussy's engineers and map-makers is known to us only through the magnificent plan of Daulatabad drawn by Frédérick Tiintzch in 1758, which is included in this publication. But, as Susan Gole observes in her significant book, the French contribution to Indian mapping becomes obvious when one observes the difference between the maps published before Bussy's expedition in the Deccan of 1750–59 (the *suba* was shown as an empty space where one placed *cartouches*, titles and scales) and after it (numerous names of cities and forts were included). Gentil contributed substantially to this work. His passion for Indian geography is evident in his *Empire mogol divisé en 21 soubas ou gouvernements tiré de différents écrivains du païs*, a forty-three-page manuscript, of which twenty-one are maps (55 cm x 38 cm in size) made in Faizabad in 1772. As Susan Gole aptly puts it, Gentil's work included information not only from Abul Fazl's *Ain-i-Akbari*, but also from other, far less known sources.

Bussy had a keen interest in Indian history, archaeology and painting, and it was perhaps from him that Gentil acquired a taste for these subjects. Anquetil Duperron, in his introduction to *Zend Avesta*, acknowledges the 'services essentiels' which Gentil, 'an artillery officer', offered him at Aurangabad in 1758, especially when he decided to visit the Ellora caves. According to Modave (1776), of all the Frenchmen, including Bussy, who visited these caves, only 'M. Gentil appreciated their value and could make a correct assessment' of them. On the top of Gentil's map of the *suba* of Aurangabad, there is a long frieze representing the Ellora caves, painted by a native artist of Faizabad.

Nawab Shuja ud-Daula. From Gentil's *Mémoires*. (Photo: Lafont)

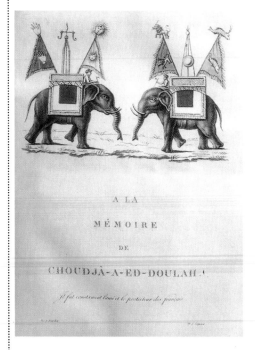

Title page of Gentil's *Mémoires*, with dedication to Shuja ud-Daula. (Photo: Lafont)

Gentil's stay in the Deccan came to an end in 1759, when the English recaptured Vizagapatnam. We know that he had by then already begun to collect manuscripts and miniatures which he later developed in Faizabad. It turned out to be a remarkable collection.

Then began Gentil's 'Indian' career, which took him to Mir Kasim Ali, Nawab of Bengal and, after the latter's downfall, to Shuja ud-Daula, *Wazir* of the Mughal empire and Nawab of Awadh. After the defeat of Buxar (1764), Shuja ud-Daula nominated Gentil to negotiate with the English to save what he could of the *nawabi* of Awadh. Gentil obtained such favourable terms—Awadh remained independent till 1855—that Shuja ud-Daula decided to retain his services. Setting up his headquarters in Faizabad, Gentil proceeded to enrol six hundred of the numerous Frenchmen who were fleeing from the English attacks on Bengal. Pursued relentlessly by the English, Frenchmen such as Sombre, Madec and their followers were helped by Gentil to seek refuge in Mughal territories. The Nawab of Awadh's relationship with Gentil was one of mutual trust and friendship. Till his death in 1775, Shuja ud-Daula refused English demands to expel Gentil from his state, and Gentil dedicated his *Mémoires sur l'Indoustan ou Empire Mogol* 'to the memory of Choudjâ-a-ed-Doulah'.

While in Faizabad Gentil continued to build an extraordinary collection of Persian manuscripts. A large part of this was devoted to the history of North India. There were also Persian translations by Abul Fazl, Dara Shikoh, Banvali Das and others, of Sanskrit texts concerning the religion of the Hindus. We know from other sources that Gentil had a systematic scheme of getting copies made, at his own expense, of all the major works in Sanskrit in the libraries of Benaras. The project was abandoned because of the time it took (probably six years) and the money involved. Most of the Persian manuscripts in Gentil's collection came from Delhi: remnants of the great imperial and private libraries that were dispersed during the invasions of the Iranian Nadir Shah in 1739 and the Afghan Ahmad Shah Abdali from 1761 onwards. Gentil also collected Mughal miniatures of various schools—early Mughal, classical Mughal, Christian Mughal, 'late' (eighteenth-century) Mughal, provincial—and he employed several miniaturists to illustrate his various *Mémoires sur l'Indoustan*, to paint his *Recueil de toutes sortes de dessins sur les usages et coutumes des peuples de*

Colonel Polier and General Claude Martin.
Detail from *Colonel Mordaunt's Cock Match*,
mezzotint engraving (1792) after an
oil painting by John Zoffany.
(Photo: Lafont, with the kind permission of
Deepak Jain)

JULIANA.

'Juliana', from Gentil's *Mémoires*.
(Photo: Lafont)

l'Indoustan (Faizabad, 1774, unpublished), and to decorate his *Maps of the Subas of the Moghul Empire*. Three of these artists—Mounsingue (Mahan Singh), Mihr Chand and Nevasilal—were especially dear to him and he made a mention of them in the titles of his albums. By patronizing local artists, showing them European engravings freely and asking them to adapt subjects, settings and palettes to his taste, Gentil created a school of painting in Awadh that was later developed by Polier and Martin. Nowadays, art historians tend to assimilate this style of painting with the 'Company' school of painting but in actuality it preceded that school. In 1992 Mildred Archer, the great English specialist of the Company school, graciously acknowledged the existence of a 'French Company' school, but perhaps the original and more accurate Persian description—*'farenghi'* art—is to be preferred.

An event that propelled Gentil into the Indo–Muslim high society of his time was his marriage to Therese Velho, whose family had served the imperial court of Delhi since the time of Aurangzeb. The family's fortunes could be traced back to the famous Juliana to whom Aurangzeb had entrusted the education of his son Bahadur Shah, the future Shah Alam I. Among other gifts and honorary titles, Shah Alam I gave Juliana Dara Shikoh's palace in Delhi, which remained in her family's possession until Safdar Jang, the then *Wazir* of the empire and Shuja ud-Daula's father, acquired it forcibly for a ridiculous sum of money. Shah Alam I also assigned a specific place for Juliana in the imperial harem, a hereditary assignment that was known by her name and held by six young women of that family before the Afghan conquest of 1761. Gentil's wife, Therese Velho, was the daughter of Lucia Mendece, the last 'Juliana' of the imperial harem. After her husband was assassinated by the Afghans in Delhi, Lucia and her daughter sought refuge in Faizabad, where they caught Gentil's attention. He intervened in their favour with Shuja ud-Daula and eventually married the young Therese in 1772.

It was his attachment to his wife's family that impelled Gentil to commission the great album *Palais indiens recueillis par M. le Gentil*. Of the twenty-four large fold-out paintings in this album, two are dated: the 'Palace of Nisamoulmoulouk (Nizam ul-Mulk) at Delhi, from the bank of the Jamuna, 1774' and the 'Palace built in old Delhi by Salim Shah, who also built Salimgarh, used as a prison for the Mughal princes. Drawn in 1774 by an

General de Boigne. Private collection.
(Photo: Lafont)

architect of Wazir Sandjan Daula [Shuja ud-Daula]'. Three more drawings from the album are reproduced here: 'Palace of the Great Mughal, Delhi, from the bank of the Jamuna', 'Malab [Mahtab] Bagh. Garden made by Alemgir [Aurangzeb] for his wives inside the Red Fort at Delhi', and 'Residence of Soudjaat Daula [Shuja ud-Daula] at Faizabad'. The name of the Nawab's architect who worked on these drawings is not known. The other paintings show several palaces and details of monuments in Delhi, plans of Dara Shikoh's palace in Agra, and Shuja ud-Daula's residence on the bank of the river Ghaghra in Faizabad.

These were certainly not the only 'French' commissions of Mughal monuments in Delhi and Agra. The British Library has five plans of Delhi and Agra inscribed in Persian, Latin and French, including a street plan of the Chandni Chowk area in Delhi with identifications of houses and buildings written in French. French interest in the buildings of Delhi persisted even after the departure of Volton, Modave, Madec and Polier (who lived for a while in Dara Shikoh's residence) in the late 1770s and early 1780s. When Madhavrao Sindhia, the great Sindhia, took over the Doab and was entrusted the charge of administering it by Shah Alam II in 1784, he transferred part of its military and civil administration onto General de Boigne, who looked after the interests of the Mughal imperial family from his headquarters at Aligarh. De Boigne had a keen interest in Indian art and archaeology: he had the Taj Mahal renovated before he returned to Europe in 1796. Paintings from his personal collection were first exhibited in Chambéry and Paris in 1996 and these included a view of the Tomb of Humayun, of the Taj Mahal, and several miniatures. De Boigne's successor, General Perron, was more involved in the administration of the Mughal capital and he successively appointed some of his senior officers, Mars, Le Marchand, and then Drugeon, as *Préfets de Delhi*. They commanded a strong 'Maratha' garrison in the city and at the Red Fort. When Lord Lake and the English army advanced towards Delhi in 1803, they were challenged at Patparganj by two of the 'French' brigades of Hindustan commanded by Geslin and Bourquien. After severe fighting the British took over the city and Dara Shikoh's residence, or what remained of it, the Dara Shikoh Library, became the office of the first British Resident at Delhi.

After the death of Shuja ud-Daula in January 1775, the English

Tipu Sultan's ambassadors at Versailles, 1788. Gentil was invited by Louis XVI and attended the reception. Private collection.

government at Calcutta imposed a precondition on their recognition of the new Nawab of Awadh: the expulsion of Gentil (and Canaple). English connoisseurs of art offered to buy Gentil's collection of paintings and manuscripts for Rs 120,000, but Gentil declined the offer. Emperor Shah Alam II offered him a golden exile in Delhi, while the Nepalese sovereign invited him to his court. Turning down all these offers, Gentil returned to France, accompanied by his wife, three children, mother-in-law and young brother-in-law. When he was received in Versailles he presented most of his Persian and Sanskrit manuscripts to King Louis XVI. They are preserved today in the Bibliothèque Nationale, some of them bound in the royal coat of arms of either Louis XVI or of Napoleon. In Paris he met his friend Anquetil Duperron, the founder of Zoroastrian studies, to whom he had a long time ago offered Dara Shikoh's Persian translation of the *Upanishads*. Anquetil Duperron translated them into Latin and these were published in Strasbourg in 1798. Gentil, who was promoted to colonel and was a *chevalier* of the Order of Saint-Louis, retired to the countryside in Bagnols (southern France) with his family. In 1788, Louis XVI called for his services during the visit of Tipu Sultan's ambassadors to Versailles. Soon after, Gentil returned to his estate in Bagnols, where he died in 1799. His son, who wished to return to India, served in Napoleon's great army and, in 1822, published the *Mémoires sur l'Indoustan ou Empire Mogol* written by his father; he faithfully kept his father's dedication to Shuja ud-Daula.

The best tribute to Gentil comes from the pen of S.P. Sen, the great Indian historian who wrote on Indo–French relations in the eighteenth century: 'Apart from the political interest of his long residence in Awadh, Gentil has a claim to fame for another reason, perhaps more important: he was one of the earliest Europeans to attempt to make Indian civilization known in the west. He spent a fortune in purchasing Sanskrit, Bengali, Arabic and Persian manuscripts and presented them to the king of France. In fact, the beginning of Indological studies in France may be traced to the first collection of Indian manuscripts made by Gentil. For this reason alone Gentil deserves to be remembered in India more than any other Frenchman, more than Dupleix, Lally or Bussy, who played such an important part in the political history of the country.'

Reflections

The seventeenth- and eighteenth-century maps, plans and drawings of Indian cities, landscapes and monuments prepared by French engineers are comparable to contemporary Indian maps such as those published by Susan Gole in her pioneering book, or the collection of eighteenth-century plans of buildings and palaces kept in the City Palace in Jaipur. According to Muhammad Salih Kambo Lahori, Shah Jahan often looked at the plans of the palaces and gardens of his nobles during *darbar* and at the maps of his provinces in the evenings. The eighteenth-century drawings by Indian artists of monuments which have been preserved to this day are similar to the drawings prepared for Gentil by the anonymous Indian architect working for the Nawab of Awadh (plates 46–50). However, the maps of cities and provinces such as those published by Susan Gole—and even later, the maps of Kashmir prepared for Ranjit Singh or the map of Lahore drawn at Kangra in 1832—are very different from those made by the French engineers. They demonstrate that there were major differences in the perception of space and importantly, of man's mastering of space, as it existed in Europe and in India at that time.

The maps and plans reproduced here capture Indian and European cities in India at a crucial period in Indian history, and indeed in world history. The times were prosperous, assuring the cities of a strong political position which, in turn, led to further commercial development. It was a period of economic consolidation for the Indian and world economies as they adjusted themselves after the great age of discovery in the late fifteenth century. Up to the 1750s, the European settlements, which only partly connected the Indian economy to the outside world, followed a businesslike policy based on mutual respect and advantage. As Om Prakash observed in 1998 in his magisterial *European Commercial Enterprise in Pre-Colonial India*, the 'bullion for goods' character of European trade in India brought a huge amount of gold and silver to this country which in turn brought a growing level of monetization, one of the basic factors for the expansion, stabilization and grandeur of the Mughal empire. The growth of precious metal in the Indian coffers directly affected the levels of income, employment and production. It percolated the entire social structure and even agricultural productivity as revenue farmers invested their benefits in land. Land revenue was increasingly paid in cash, not in kind or share of crop as was formerly done. The monetization of Indian society led to

Detail of Mahtab Bagh, a garden made by Aurangzeb for his wives, within the Red Fort, Delhi. Courtesy: Bibliothèque Nationale, Paris.

Nadir Shah. From Gentil's *Mémoires*. (Photo: Lafont)

the establishment of banking firms, which helped manufacturers to respond to the growing European demand for cotton and silk textiles. The demand for goods always exceeded the supply, giving a bargaining strength to the Indian agencies dealing with the European East India Companies. It also benefited the weavers in their relations with local employers. As Om Prakash correctly observes, by 1700 India was the 'premier trading and manufacturing nation of Asia' and the 'largest and most competitive textile-manufacturing country in the world'. This not only brought prosperity to the people but also enhanced India's status considerably.

However, the Mughal political structure, which St Blake has called a 'patrimonial–bureaucratic empire', was weakened at the centre by the crisis of succession after the death of Aurangzeb in 1707, and was further eroded by the devastating raids of Nadir Shah in 1739 and of Ahmad Shah Abdali in 1761. The great 'provincial' units (the future 'successor states') stopped sending the *khalisa* revenue to Delhi, thus depriving the Mughal emperor of his main source of political power—money. There was indeed decadence at the centre because of its impoverishment. But riches started accumulating in the 'provincial' capitals. One is reminded of Clive looking at the captured treasures of Bengal at Murshidabad in 1757, or of Arthur Wellesley and his officers upon their discovery of the treasury of Srirangapatnam in 1799. As late as 1849, British officers taking charge of the Punjab were amazed at the amount of money they were able to divert to Calcutta 'for imperial purposes'.

Contrary to widespread European stereotypes, these riches did not lie idle in the hands of feeble or imbecile rulers lost in bigotry or unspeakable cruelty. The emergence of new states around new capitals—some of them were old centres that suddenly grew and developed a number of 'modern', or 'pre-modern' activities—is one of the most fascinating aspects of the history of eighteenth-century India. It is true that these local sub-imperial governments often had imperial pretensions or at least wanted to achieve a kind of hegemony over neighbouring states. In order to achieve this hegemony, the states on the eastern coast tried to implicate the European settlements in their local struggles and political conflicts from the late seventeenth century onwards. The Danish, Dutch, English and French settlements on the Coromandel coast were not only a source of regular financial surpluses for the rulers of Tanjore, Ginji and

15

Arcot: they could—or would not—supply loans, arms, ammunitions, troops for military operations, and even refuge in case of military disaster, as when the Nawab of Arcot's family escaped to Pondicherry in May 1740. The European communities were a source of highly trained specialists, from military engineers to surgeons, that was used to develop a particular sector by the local Indian governments. Such solicitations by the Indian powers for European assistance to help them resist aggression or achieve local supremacy are a largely forgotten aspect of 'precolonial' history. That such politics misfired on some occasions is of course another matter.

In the 1740s, the military superiority of European armies in the use of infantry, discipline, tactics, strategies and their technologies of artillery, fortifications, siege and seafaring were identified by a number of Indian rulers as the main reason for European power. By the 1760s, rulers in the south of the subcontinent had decided to introduce European methods and innovations in their respective states. This the rulers did based on their personal convictions, sometimes haphazardly and sometimes against the advice of political advisers in the *darbars*, by using their monetary surpluses. It so happened that the disastrous campaigns of Lally in 1758–61, ending in the capture of Pondicherry and Chandernagor by the English, left a few thousand French and French-trained officers and soldiers in India unemployed and looking for protection. They were also eager to thwart British expansion. From 1761 to 1803 most Indian rulers, including the important Hyder Ali and Tipu Sultan in Mysore, the Nizam of Hyderabad, Shuja ud-Daula in Awadh, the Sindhias in the Doab, Holkar in Indore and Shah Alam II in Delhi, employed French officers to raise and command modern military units on the European model. Many excellent Indian officers had been trained in the French army (hence their French title *kumedan*, 'commandant') and they too joined the Indian rulers or formed companies of 'mercenaries' whom they hired out. Just as monetization had percolated the wealth of Indian states, military modernization with its new concepts of discipline and 'industrial' production started percolating Indian society anew. We see 'French' military brigades in the armed forces of Indian rulers, and gun foundries, firearm factories and powder mills, as required by modern units.

These new military units were more expensive to maintain than traditional armies and the troops had to be paid regularly. When, in the 1780s

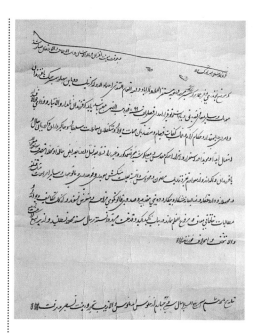

Madhoji Sindhia's gift of 52 *parganas* in the Doab to General de Boigne. Private collection. (Photo: Lafont)

and 1790s, India was hit by an unprecedented shortage of silver because of the monetary policy of the East India Company, some of the Indian rulers gave big plots of land as *jagirs* to their French generals. For example, Sindhia gave fifty-two *parganas* in the Doab as *jagir* to General de Boigne, and the Nizam of Hyderabad gave General Raymond huge estates that yielded an annual revenue of Rs 5,200,000 (Compton). On these estates the peasants' welfare was particularly well taken care of. And new commercial crops, especially indigo, were developed. This policy quickly increased the revenue from the land, brought more prosperity to the villages, and introduced another world-oriented trend to some of the major products of independent India. What can be seen at the micro level is a series of modifications, which might have gradually accumulated into the critical mass of (industrial) revolution, as did happen in Europe in the mid-seventeenth century.

In 1757 the English East India Company won a military success over the Nawab of Bengal at Plassey and soon after, seventy-five ships loaded with silver went down the Hoogly from Murshidabad to Calcutta where they were received triumphantly. In 1765 Emperor Shah Alam II officially invested the East India Company with the *diwanat* (revenue collection) of Bengal and from then on, as Om Prakash puts it, 'Bengal revenues provided an indirect subsidy to the British exchequer'. For a quarter of a century, till 1784, England stopped sending silver to India and the Bengal revenue surpluses were spent both in the purchase of Bengali goods to be exported from India and in developing a formidable army, 115,000 strong (90 per cent sepoys) in 1782. Hence the gradual drain of silver in northern India in the late eighteenth to early nineteenth centuries. When, in 1784, England started sending silver again to India, it was to further develop its military machine. The Treaty of Versailles of 1783 had just recognized the independence of the United States of America, and there was no question of England letting India go the way of the British colonies in North America. Lord Cornwallis, whose capitulation at Yorktown to Washington and Rochambeau in 1781 ended the War of Independence of America, was thrice appointed Governor General *and* (in 1786) Commander-in-Chief of British India.

The French, whom the East India Company thought they had wiped out of India in 1761 by reducing to dust their two main settlements,

17

Fortifications of Srirangapatnam.
(Photo: Lafont)

Pondicherry and Chandernagor, were aware—at least some of them—that English power rested on two main pillars: men and land in North America, and money from India. Right from 1763 onwards Choiseul and the French government prepared for a renewal of the fight, but with a singular difference. Because of the philosophical thinking of the *France des Lumières*, the policy of Dupleix in India had been widely condemned in Paris and Versailles. For the intellectual elite who held sway and their ready followers in *salons* and *académies* all over the country, India was a highly civilized country and not to be enslaved or governed by a body of European merchants and adventurers, including the French. Not everybody, of course, agreed with this analysis which was generally condemned as utopian and irresponsible by the propounders of the 'second' French colonial empire in the nineteenth and twentieth centuries. Strong lobbies and influential people pushed for a decidedly 'colonial' policy, but the fact is that the French government's decision was to help the Indian states maintain or regain their independence. Count Lally's expedition (1758–61) ended in disaster. However his instructions, which he himself drafted, clearly ordered him to liberate India from the East India Company and give back the freed territories to their legitimate rulers. Bussy's instructions drafted for the 1781 expedition were similar.

Meanwhile, several French agents, military officers and diplomats had been sent to India to verify whether it was possible for the major powers—Hyder Ali, the Nizam of Hyderabad, the Marathas, and Emperor Shah Alam II—to unite against the East India Company. Military officers were secretly sent to some of the Indian states to strengthen their defence capabilities. A few engineers were ordered to seek out places where French squadrons could anchor and locate friendly country where French troops could land. Some of the plans they prepared are published here. There was, of course, no specific reason for the Indian rulers to be particularly impressed by these moves, nor did they have any compulsion to trust the French any more than their English counterparts. Bengal was already a British colony in the true sense of the word, but the possibility that the East India Company could take over many other Indian states had not entered the minds of most Indian rulers in the 1770s, although it was a semi-certitude for most French observers of the scene. They prophesied that no Indian troop could resist the onslaught of the East India

Marquis de Bussy in his 50s.
Private collection

Company unless supported by a strong body of European (that is, French) troops. Concerning the possibility of forming a coalition with Indian powers against the British, the reports of the French envoys in India were not as enthusiastic as were the reports of their colleagues sent to North America who spoke, deceitfully, of the total disaffection the colonists bore towards the British government. Yet, in 1780, the French government decided to act both in North America and in India. The means were not exactly equal even though the military expedition to India was carefully planned: Bussy was to have 8000 troops (Rochambeau's brigade in North America was 6000-strong, plus the '*volontaires*' of La Fayette, Lauzun and others) and 10,000,000 livres (5,000,000 in cash, 5,000,000 in bonds on the VOC to be paid in India, a contract which was not honoured). The first detachment of this army sailed with the squadron of Admiral de Suffren, the best sailor France ever had.

This is not the place to elaborate upon the outcome and shortcomings of the French policy in North America and India during 1778–83. Let us remember that on 19 October 1781 Cornwallis and his 8000 men surrendered at Yorktown to Washington and Rochambeau, who captured 162 guns, 22 flags and 40 ships after a tremendous siege directed by French engineers and artillerymen who rained 3000 cannon-balls, shells and incendiary bombs per day on enemy positions. In India, the French squadron under Admiral de Suffren met with uninterrupted success against the Royal Navy. But Bussy, who sailed from France in November 1781, landed in India only in March 1783. He found himself trapped in Cuddalore with 4000 French troops, no money and no bullocks for pulling his field-guns and heavy artillery. However, he succeeded in repelling an all-out English attack on 13 June 1783. Although he failed in a limited action on 24 June, he still contemplated a move towards Madras after Suffren's naval victory at Cuddalore (20 June) when an English frigate brought from Madras the news of the signing of the preliminary treaty between England and France in Paris on 20 January 1783.

After the Treaty of Versailles (3 September 1783), the 'Americans' immediately assumed charge of the United States of America and framed the American Constitution (1787) which still stands today. Most of the Indian states were gradually incorporated into British India and remained so till 1947. A strong imperial administration, financed by India herself, substantially modified both the political and the economic structures of the subcontinent. The system of 'unrequited' exports, exports from India paid in bills of change in London, 'only meant that the payment in silver was now made in Europe rather than in India. But of course that silver never reached India', Om Prakash writes. The nature and scope of the economic development (or was it 'arrested development'?) of India under the British Raj in comparison to what it could have been under her own governance will probably remain a topic of heated political debate for a long time to come.

The story of the cities which are represented in the maps and plans of this book can be followed in the British Raj period through Hamilton's descriptions prepared in the early 1820s, Thornton's *Gazetteer* published in 1858, and the various *Imperial* and *District Gazetteers* published from the 1870s onwards and regularly updated till the eve of Indian independence. Some of them thrived, some of them merely survived, and in 1911 Delhi became the capital of British India. Scholars are not supposed to follow the path of José Saramago and write 'histories' of what might have happened. But there were other possibilities. The India which became independent in 1947 is certainly not the India that would have emerged had the Treaty of Versailles of 1783 done for India what it did for the United States of America.

Fort of Bangalore.
(Photo: Lafont)

Conclusion

In this publication we are presenting just a small part of the Indian collection of the Dépôt des Fortifications des Colonies (DFC), CAOM, Archives de France at Aix-en-Provence. Many of the maps are accompanied by *mémoires*, some brief, some more voluminous, which often touch upon subjects far removed from their primary military or political interest. They sometimes contain facts and analyses which throw fresh light on otherwise rather politically correct accounts—also easier to access and better known—of the officials of the Compagnie des Indes Orientales. These drawings show that the 'European' cities of India, although influenced by some indigenous techniques such as the foundations on wells, systems of ventilation, and so on, presented new ideas to the local populations. The Indian cities progressively adopted a military defence system that paralleled the development of the artillery in the native armies of the subcontinent. This happened in two ways: on the one hand, beginning with the early sixteenth century, numerous Indian soldiers and officers served in the armed forces of European powers who established settlements in India (the Portuguese, Dutch, Danes, French, English); on the other, a large number of Europeans chose to live in 'native' India and served Indian sovereigns. The first known Frenchman to do so, Augustin Hiriard from Bordeaux, lived in Agra, Delhi and Lahore from 1612 to 1632, and others followed him. The French were particularly numerous and active in India from 1750 to 1803. They worked zealously, if often in obscurity, to help the Indian rulers who employed them to modernize the (mostly military) structures of their states. Through this publication, we aim to unfold the story of that unknown, though very important, aspect of Indo–French relations before the British Raj.

Beyond their professional, civil or military commitments, these 'Frenchmen of India' almost always displayed a personal commitment that was marked by curiosity tinged with sympathy for the country, the persons and the monuments that surrounded them. In *Les Indes florissantes, Anthologie des voyageurs français aux Indes entre 1750 et 1820*, Guy Deleury brought together extracts from more than fifty books published between these two dates. The original publications contained descriptions that went beyond ethnographic inquiry to penetrate the heart of India, her cultures and civilizations. Anquetil Duperron, one of the founders of European Indology, whom even Edward Said has absolved of the capital sin of 'orientalism', wrote *L'Inde en rapport avec l'Europe* in

1782 (published in 1798), in which he presented the eight basic principles that should regulate economic exchanges between the two continents, and stated that they should be based on scrupulous and mutual respect. As many of these Frenchmen married in India, they were able to gain a richer insight into and understanding of the human values of the subcontinent. Jean-Baptiste Gentil was one such. His interest in Indian architecture, both ancient (Mughal) and contemporary (Awadh), is represented in this volume by only five large drawings. These are but a glimpse into the rich and original collection that we hope will be shown one day to the Indian public in its entirety.

French cartographers of the early nineteenth century. Courtesy: IGN, Paris

Dépôt des Fortifications des Colonies (DFC)

Centre des Archives d'Outre-Mer
Archives de France
Aix-en-Provence

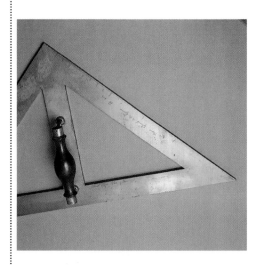

Instrument used in cartography.
Courtesy: IGN, Paris

Drawing a map is a way of understanding space. It leads man to an understanding of his position in a given geographical context. Between the sixteenth and eighteenth centuries France was mapped by its engineers and astronomers in a series of precise engraved maps. Louis XIV, it is said, congratulated his cartographers on being the only subjects who aggrandized his kingdom without waging war.

The interest in measured territories was linked to an interest in borders and their fortification. Under the direction of Vauban, many fortresses were built on the frontiers of France, particularly on the northern border, called the king's '*Pré carré*'—the Fort of Tournai, for instance, which was erected in 1668 and whose plan was later used for building Fort-Louis at Pondicherry. These early plans were two-dimensional since the *courbes de niveau* were not invented until the middle of the eighteenth century. Therefore, three-dimensional models of the fortified towns and forts of France—about 140 have been preserved in Paris and Lille—were made. Some of them still retain their *glacis* and systems of canals and *écluses* used for inundating the countryside as a defensive measure. The '*ingénieurs géographes du roi*' were usually entrusted with the task of levying and drawing these maps: to begin with they were civilian officers, but were later integrated into the French army in 1776. In addition, there were many military officers, artillerymen, specialists of engineering and mathematics who drew maps of sites, towns and fortifications.

Some of these engineers and military officers joined overseas expeditions and drew maps of the places they saw and plans of the buildings they visited or constructed. In 1680, Louis XIV's Prime Minister, Colbert, gave orders to collect and file all the papers of the Marine Department. In 1720, the '*Cartes et Plans*' (Maps and Plans) section with numerous memoirs and '*Journaux de Bord*' was given over to the Dépôt des Cartes et Plans de la Marine. Many similar documents were, however, scattered in various cities, in the residences of governors and headquarters of military commanders. Ministers in Versailles and Paris regularly complained about these high-ranking civil and military officers who, on retirement, took along with them, to their provincial *châteaux* and residences, the maps and plans of provinces and cities where they had been posted.

French officers of the early
nineteenth century.
Courtesy: IGN, Paris

In 1776, Louis XVI ordered his governors and military commanders overseas to collect and send to Paris their entire collections of maps and plans, either as originals or as copies. The Dépôt des Cartes et Plans des Colonies was created in 1778; its present name, Dépôt des Fortifications des Colonies (DFC), dates only from 1800. In 1914, the section was transferred from the Marine Ministry to the archives of the Ministry of Colonies, where the 'Plans des Fortifications' (archives of the Génie, Ministry of War) had already been transferred.

The transfer of the DFC (Indian section) to the Centre des Archives d'Outre-Mer (Aix-en-Provence) took place in 1986. There are 1229 documents in this section of the archives, with the following sub-sections: Indes Orientales (390 plans and memoirs), Pondicherry (717), Mahé (60), Karikal (34), Chandernagor (21) and Yanaon (7). A catalogue, Dépôt des Fortifications des Colonies. I. Indes, prepared by Alexis Rinckenbach, provides information on the maps, plans, drawings and accompanying memoirs. In his introduction, Rinckenbach details the historical background of the collection. A chapter of thirty-six pages, 'Sources Complémentaires', gives a list of the plans, maps and drawings of India kept in other major French collections—the Ministry of Defence, Archives Nationales (Paris), Bibliothèque Nationale (Paris), and Bibliothèque de l'Arsenal (Paris). The chapter also includes information on documents in the National Archives of India, Pondicherry, that were left behind in 1954.

In 1994, the National Archives of India sent a photographer to Aix-en-Provence to take pictures of 74 plans at the DFC . These are now stored in the National Archives of India, Janpath, New Delhi. The Archives graciously allowed some of these slides to be reproduced in the book Reminiscences: The French in India, published by INTACH and the Embassy of France in 1997–98.

Département des Estampes et de la Photographie

Bibliothèque Nationale Paris

The quest for, and the subsequent purchase and conservation of drawings and prints collected separately from illuminated manuscripts, was begun by the King's Library in France a long time ago. In 1661, Louis XIV entrusted the care of the Royal Library to Colbert, his Prime Minister. Colbert, himself a bibliophile, had been trained by Cardinal Mazarin, who owned a magnificent personal library. Colbert quickly acquired for the King's Library 2000 paintings of plants and flowers on vellum which belonged to Gaston d'Orléans, Louis XIV's uncle. This collection, which Louis XIV, Louis XV and Louis XVI continued, grew to 6000 paintings by the 1780s. Colbert also purchased the Marolles collection, consisting of 123,400 items bound in 400 large and 620 smaller volumes, and the Gaignères collection which contained, among many other items, 7752 engraved portraits. The prints market (*marché des estampes*) witnessed rapid development in Europe in the seventeenth century. Louis XIV himself established a print unit in his library and its splendid productions were offered as diplomatic gifts to the sovereigns of Siam, China and other countries, and to ambassadors accredited to Versailles. In 1721, the Département des Estampes had 200,000 prints. Abbé Bignon, who was the king's librarian from 1719 to 1731, purchased 80,000 prints from the Marquis de Béringhen in 1731. The collections continued to increase till the French Revolution.

French curiosity about and interest in people—their portraits; 'costumes and manners'; masterpieces of paintings and sculpture; lands, as expressed in plans and illustrated maps; buildings and grounds of cities, residences, palaces; and so on—were remarkable. The curiosity was not limited to the various provinces of France and other European countries. It extended to other continents and cultures. Paintings and prints of Asia and Africa as well as of the Americas are an important part of the collections of the Département des Estampes today. For Asia, there is a rich sixteenth-century collection of paintings and coloured prints representing the Middle Eastern peoples and dresses. This includes 61 plates depicting the 'diversity of the Levantine nations' as described by Nicolas Nicolay, that was published in Lyon in 1568 and contains engravings by Danet; 127 colour plates of 'Modes' of Asiatic Turkey that had belonged to Gaignères; an album of portraits of the Turkish sultans dating from the late sixteenth or early seventeenth century in a binding bearing the coat of arms of Gaston d'Orléans; and 150 coloured drawings depicting the dresses at the court of the Great Seignor dated 1630.

The oldest Persian and Indo–Persian paintings were probably purchased in Constantinople in the late sixteenth century, as were the two oldest Indo–Persian manuscripts in the Oriental Section of the King's Library, and most probably the Sancy diamond, 'the very Sphinx of diamonds', which entered the king's collection in the 1570s and is now in the Louvre Museum. However, the French were present in Persia and in India in the seventeenth and eighteenth centuries, and the Département des Estampes has a rich but little-known collection of Indo–Persian miniatures. These include the collection of Colonel Gentil during his stay in Awadh in 1765–75. There are also many albums commissioned from Indian artists by French patrons who were employees of the Compagnie des Indes, travellers, merchants, missionaries or individuals settled in India in the service of local sovereigns during the years *c.* 1750–1803. Many drawings and prints were also made in the first half of the nineteenth century by Indian artists for French residents in Pondicherry. French and French-trained artists like Solvyns and Mr and Mrs Belnos lived in India or travelled in India up to the time of, and immediately after, the Great Revolt of 1857 (Sepoy Mutiny of 1857). Of these prints and drawings from India, most of them coloured, which are housed in the Département des Estampes, the most beautiful and valuable documents are kept in a special *Réserve*. They can be examined with permission from the curators.

Institut Géographique National (IGN) Paris

Heir of an ambitious enterprise begun under Louis XIV, the Institut Géographique National was commissioned to represent French territory. It aims to produce and maintain the map of France as well as to set down guidelines for all cartographic products. Its strength lies in the blending of state-of-the-art technology and craftsmen's skills. The IGN's mission, in France and abroad, is to meet the needs of local authorities and the general public. Using its maps and geographic database, managers of public and private enterprises are able to improve their management and communication skills. With its detailed and innovative tourist maps, IGN fulfills the traveller's basic needs, of finding one's way and planning an itinerary. It also contributes to a better understanding of space, thereby playing an important role in our changing society.

Plates

PLATE 1

Carte Marine Gusurat Concan Decan

Maritime Map
Gujarat, Konkan, Deccan

Artist unknown
c. 1756
Collection: Private
Courtesy: Colonel Chinailh
480 mm x 645 mm

This map shows the western coast of India from Pointe des Géants to the city and territory of Goa. It includes Gujarat, the Gulf of Cambay, the city of Surat and its harbour Swali, which were the main centres for export of Indian goods to Europe till the late seventeenth century. Surat, the 'blessed port' of the Mughals, who also called it 'the door to the House of God', was synonymous with fabulous riches in seventeenth-century European literature.

The map shows how difficult navigation was in the Gulf of Cambay, with its many sandbanks on which the heavily loaded European ships could be wrecked: 'the road outside the bar is very dangerous in the spring, when southerly and westerly winds prevail', wrote Thornton. The numbers off the sea-shore indicate the depth of the water in '*brasses*' (1 *brasse* = 1.60 metres).

It is interesting to see the profiles of the Bombay islands—Ile des Pères Jésuites (Island of the Jesuit Fathers), Ile Salsette, Ile Bombaye and so on, and of the Goa islands—Ile de Goa, Ile Salsette Marmagon, Ile aux Serpents (Snake Island) and Fort Agoado. The captions on the map reveal the names of some of the European settlements: for example, *Daman aux Portugais* (Daman belonging to the Portuguese) and *La Compagnie de France avait un comptoir à Geitapour en 1683* (the French Company had a settlement at Geitapur in 1683).

Of greater interest is the fact that the captions allow us to approximately date the map. They refer to two major Indian maritime powers of the time: the Angrias and the Sidis. Four places on the map are indicated as '*au Sidi*' (belonging to the Sidis)—the ports of Seurden, Quelci, Mahar, Sangueser. The Sidis were of Abyssinian origin and came to India as Muslim mercenaries. In the fifteenth century they established naval supremacy over the western coast of India. The Portuguese captured Daman and Diu from them but the Sidis fortified themselves along the coast between Bombay and Goa. Their main strongholds were Janjira-i-Mahrub and Dabhol. They engaged in constant warfare with the Marathas. They were finally defeated by the English in 1759.

The Angrias were scions of the Marathas who established themselves on the western coast. Their main stronghold was the city and fortified harbour of Gheria-Izdruk. On the map the places shown as '*aux Angrias*' (belonging to the Angrias) are: Harny, Geitapour, *Port des Angrias nommé Izdruk* (Port of the Angrias called Izdruk), Achera, Malivane. In 1756, the combined English fleet of Bombay and Madras, under the command of Admiral Watson and with the help of a marine corps commanded by Clive, destroyed Gheria, which was then given to the Marathas. On later maps Gheria is therefore shown as '*aux Marathes*' (belonging to the Marathas).

Going by the facts mentioned above which are revealed by the captions, the map can be dated *c.* 1755–60.

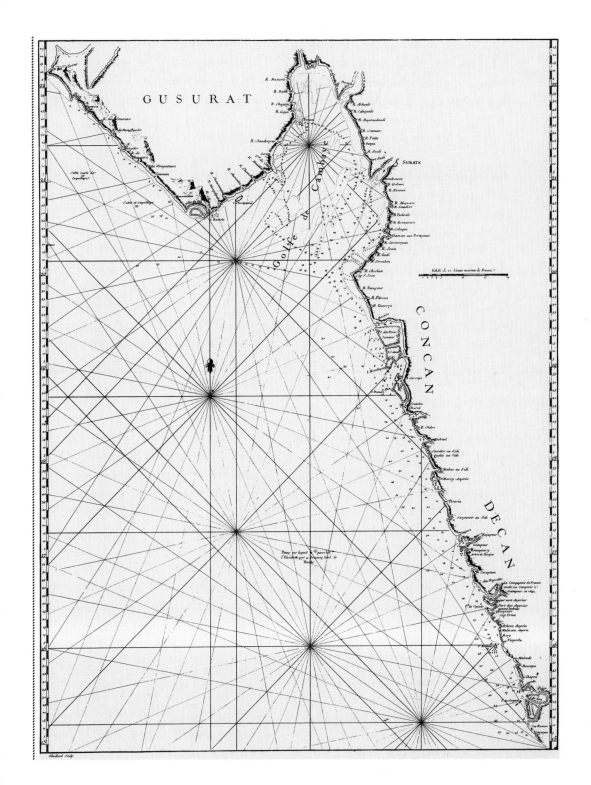

29

PLATE 2

Plan de la Ville de Surate et du Jardin Français dressé en 1758 sous l'inspection du Sieur Anquetil de Briancourt, alors Chef de la Nation Française à Surate

Plan of the City of Surat and the 'French Garden' done in 1758 under the supervision of Sir Anquetil de Briancourt, then Chief of the French Nation at Surat

Artist unknown
1758
Collection: CAOM, DFC 30 B 162
Scale [1/38320]
650 mm x 470 mm

Most of the European commerce of the sixteenth and early seventeenth centuries passed through the city of Surat, the principal port of the Mughal empire. The Portuguese arrived there in 1515, the English in 1612, the Dutch in 1616 and the French in 1668. An incredible quantity of goods was exported from Surat, and an equivalent value in gold and silver that came from the Americas was used as payment. This trade gave the Mughal empire the financial means to exist and indeed flourish. In western literature Surat became a symbol of unlimited riches. Its impressive ramparts, 6 miles long with twelve gates, date back to the period of conflict between the Mughals and the Marathas (1664, 1670, 1702 and 1707). Within these ramparts lived the densest urban population of India. A French factory containing some handsome and convenient apartments still existed outside the ramparts in 1820. However, the city itself began to decline in the late seventeenth century. The English left Surat for Madras, they acquired Bombay in 1661, and finally founded Calcutta in 1690. The Frenchman François Martin left Surat to found Pondicherry in 1674.

The plan reproduced here was drawn in 1758 on the orders of Anquetil de Briancourt, then chief of the French enclave in Surat. His brother Anquetil Duperron joined him there; Anquetil de Briancourt and the director of the English factory facilitated his entry into the local Parsi community.

Anquetil Duperron took with him to France numerous Indian manuscripts, including a copy of the *Zend Avesta* that was published in a French translation in 1771. Later, his friend Colonel Gentil presented him a Persian translation of the *Upanishads* done by Dara Shikoh. Anquetil Duperron's research and publications covered topics as diverse as philology, geography and political economy. They can lay claim to being the first systematic examination of the languages and literatures of India. His *L'Inde en rapport avec l'Europe*, published in 1798, pleads for economic exchange based on respect for others.

Anquetil de Briancourt spent twenty years of his life in Surat, and he managed to establish a French consulate there in 1773. In 1778 he was arrested by the English authorities in the city and sent back to Europe. His official papers are housed in the Archives Diplomatiques (Ministry of Foreign Affairs) at Nantes, and a very interesting autobiographical *Mémoire*, still unpublished, is preserved in a private collection in France.

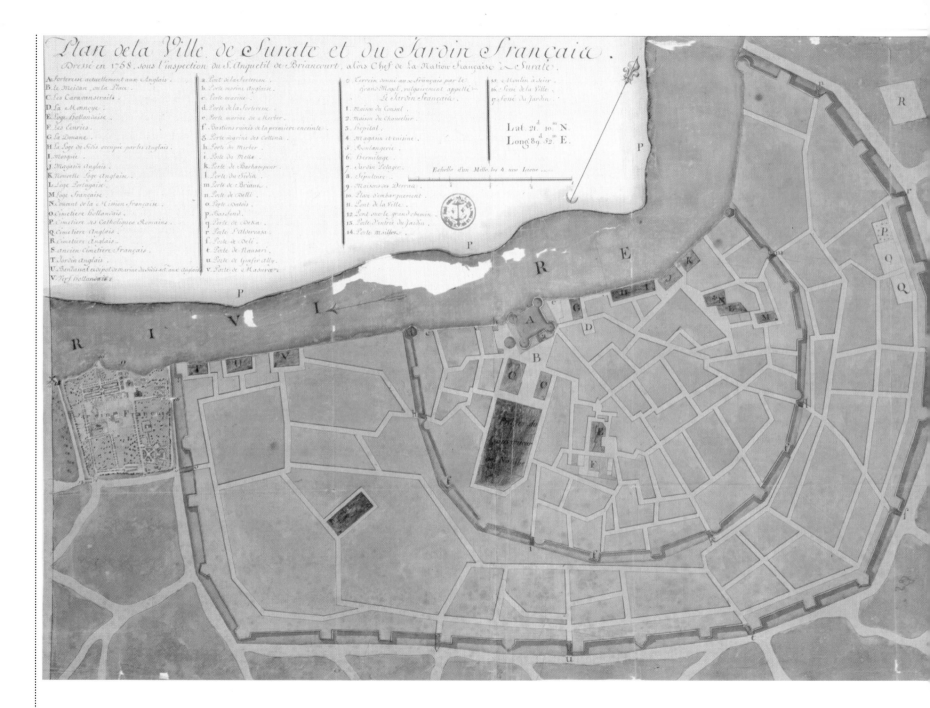

Plan dela Ville de Surate et du Jardin Françaies.
Dressé en 1758, sous l'inspection du S. Anquetil de Briancourt, alors Chef de La Nation Française à Surate.

A. Forteresse actuellement aux Anglais.
B. le Meidan, ou la Place.
C. les Caravanserails.
D. La Monnoye.
E. Loge Hollandaise.
F. les Ecuries.
G. la Douane.
H. la Loge du Tiois occupée par les Anglais.
I. Mosquée.
J. Magasin Anglais.
K. Nouvelle Loge Anglaise.
L. Loge Portugaise.
M. Loge Française.
N. couvent de la Mision Française.
O. Cimetiere Hollandais.
P. Cimetiere des Catholiques Romains.
Q. Cimetiere Anglais.
R. Cimetiere Anglais.
S. ancien Cimetiere Français.
T. Jardin anglais.
U. Bastion et ci-opel et marine du Tiois et aux Anglais.
V. Tref Hollandais.

a. Port de la forteresse.
b. Porte marine anglaise.
c. Porte marine.
d. Porte de la Forteresse.
e. Porte marine de Merber.
f. Bastions ruinés de la première enceinte.
g. Porte marine des Cottona.
h. Porte du Merber.
i. Porte du Meila.
k. Porte de Barhampour.
l. Porte du Tiois.
m. Porte de Briane.
n. Porte de Delli.
o. Porte Oatois.
p. Sans fond.
q. Porte de Deka.
r. Porte d'Aldervasa.
s. Porte de Oeli.
t. Porte de Nansari.
u. Porte de Giafer ally.
v. Porte de Masura.

o. Terrein donné au Français par le grand Mogol, vulgairement appellé Le Jardin Françaies.
1. Maison du Consul.
2. Maison du Chancelier.
3. Hopital.
4. Magasin et cuisine.
5. Boulangerie.
6. Hermitage.
7. Jardin Potager.
8. Sepulture.
9. Maisons ces Derviz.
10. Place d'embarquement.
11. Pont de la Ville.
12. Pont sur le grand chemin.
13. Porte d'entrée du Jardin.
14. Porte à villere.

15. Moulin à Scier.
16. Fosé de la Ville.
17. Fosé du Jardin.

Lat. 21.d 10.m N.
Long. 89.d 52.m E.

Echelle d'un Mille les 4 une lieue

R
P
E
R
I
V
R
O
U
V
P

31

PLATE 3

Plan de Doltabad tiré par ordre de Monsieur de Bussy, Commandant Général de l'Armée Auxiliaire auprès de Salabet-Jingue, Souba du Dekan

Plan of Daulatabad drawn on the orders of Monsieur de Bussy, Commander General of the Auxiliary Army sent to Salabat Jang, 'Suba' of the Deccan

By Frédérick Tiinzch
2 May 1758
Collection: CAOM, DFC 31 A 341
Scale [1/1400]
700 mm x 805 mm

Situated 10 kilometres north-west of Aurangabad, Daulatabad (formerly Deogir or Devagiri) Fort, like Ginji, was one of the strongest in India. The city was the capital of the Yavada kingdom in the twelfth century. Conquered by Ala ud-Din Khilji in 1296, it was Muhammad bin Tughlaq's capital from 1327 onwards. It then went into decline for almost three hundred years until it was conquered by Mughal Emperor Shah Jahan in 1636. Tavernier, who visited Daulatabad several times, wrote about its strong ramparts and the numerous Dutch and English gunners who manned the fort under Shah Jahan and Aurangzeb. Bernier described it as the capital of the Deccan. In 1707, after Aurangzeb's death, Daulatabad came under the rule of Asaf Jah, founder of Hyderabad's Nizam or Asaf Jahi dynasty.

The main fortress of Daulatabad was made of an insulated mass of granite, the perpendicular height of the hill above the surrounding plains being 170 metres. The lower part (one-third), scarped like a wall, presents a vertical cliff all round. It is isolated by about 3 kilometres from the nearest hills. An outer wall surrounds the city, and three other lines of walls and gates lead up to the main fortress. The governor's residence, a fine building surrounded by a veranda with twelve arcades, was situated in the lower fort, and the causeway across the main ditch between the lower fort and the main fortress did not admit more than two persons at a time. A building with a battlement defended it on the opposite side. After crossing the ditch, the ascent is through an excavation in the heart of the rock, 12 feet high and wide, and strongly defended with traps and recesses. At the top of the hill stood a large 24-pounder. The rock contained large reserves of water and if properly defended it could only be won by famine (Hamilton).

Bussy, as Commander of the French Auxiliary Army sent by Dupleix to reinforce the Nizam's forces in 1750, commissioned geographical surveys of the Deccan by officers who were asked to travel around the countryside. Some of the data collected by them were used by Jean-Baptiste Gentil in his maps of the twenty-one *subas* of the Mughal empire, completed at Faizabad in 1770. The blank spaces (places left unmarked) in previous maps, which d'Anville had used for writing titles and legends on his map, were filled with names of cities and forts in Gentil's map. Susan Gole, in her book on Gentil's *Maps of Mughal India* (1988), points out that although Gentil used Abul Fazl's *Ain-i-Akbari* extensively for his '*Essai sur l'Indoustan*' dated 1769, 'in addition, he used other untraced manuscripts for the southern part of India of which the *sarkars* and *parganas* had not been listed by Abul Fazl'.

Not many of the maps commissioned by Bussy have survived. The plan of Daulatabad is very precise and shows the main buildings and monuments as they stood in 1758. The twenty-five captions identify many of them. Several copies of this map are preserved in the DFC.

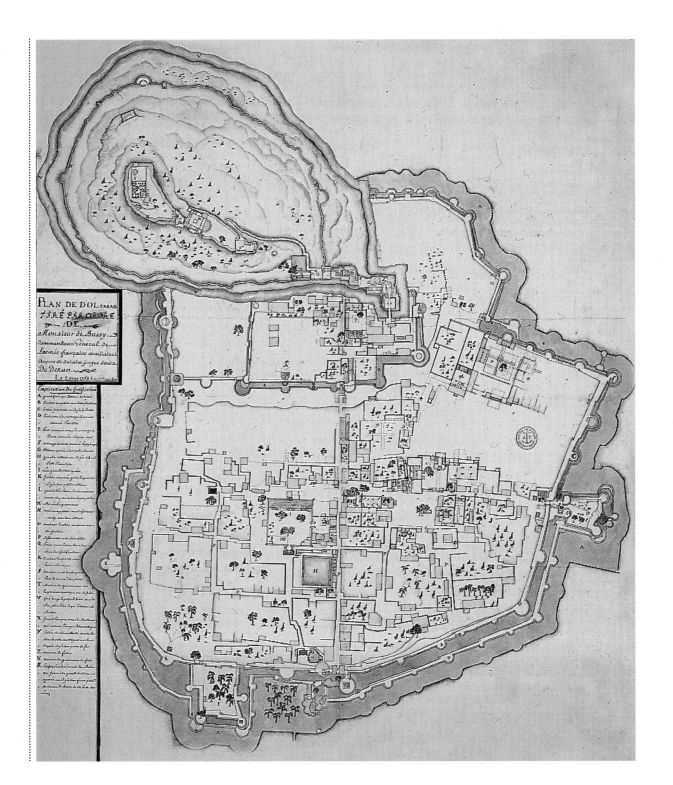

33

PLATE 4

Ile de Bombay, Côte de Concan

Island of Bombay, Coast of Konkan

Artist unknown
No date
Collection: CAOM, DFC 30 C 171
Scale [1/47540]
500 mm x 340 mm

Ptolemeus mentions a 'Heptanesia' (Island of Seven) on the west coast of India, perhaps a reference to the seven islands that jointly took the name of one of them, Bombay. In 1534 Bahadur Shah, Sultan of Gujarat (1527–36), was attacked by Humayun, the Mughal emperor. He signed a defence treaty with the Portuguese by which he ceded to Goa this cluster of islands and part of their coastal territory including Bassein, where the Portuguese established their government. The Portuguese retained it until 1665.

Part of these lands were given to deserving Portuguese officers. From about 1554 till his death in 1570, Bombay Island belonged to Garcia da Orta, the famous botanist who authored *Colloquios dos Simples e Drogas ... da India*. The cession of Bombay to the English Crown was signed at his residence. From 1534 onwards, large tracts of these islands were also given to religious Catholic orders, first the Franciscans, then the Jesuits who built and directed the College of Bandra ('Island of the Jesuits' on the map), and finally the Dominicans.

The English knew about the importance of Bombay as early as the 1580s through an English Jesuit Father who ran College Saint-Paul at Goa. In 1654 the Court of Directors directed Cromwell's attention to the importance of that station. Far from any Mughal influence, Bombay could control the west coast of India and act as a check on the Dutch VOC established in Ceylon and South India. On 21 May 1662 Catherine of Braganza, sister of King Alfonso VI of Portugal, married King Charles II of England. Bombay and Tangiers (Morocco) were part of the dowry the Portuguese king offered to Charles in exchange for British troops to reinforce Portuguese independence against Spain, and British assistance in the event of a Dutch attack on Portuguese territories in India. The transfer of authority took place at Bombay Island on 18 February 1665. De Mello de Castro, Governor of Goa, wrote a personal letter to the King of Portugal on 6 January 1665, protesting against the transfer, 'because I foresee the great troubles that ... will result to the Portuguese, and that India will be lost the same day in which the English nation is settled in Bombay'.

In 1668 the East India Company rented Bombay from the King of England for 10 pounds a year. In 1683–84, the military governor of Bombay revolted, a bizarre episode mentioned by François Martin in his *Mémoires*.

In the early eighteenth century Bombay's population comprised Portuguese and English residents, an important Muslim community of Bohras, Khojas and Memons from the Persian Gulf, rich Gujarati businessmen and, from 1740 onwards, an active community of Parsis. By 1780, with the building of a harbour and the creation of a powerful merchant fleet, Bombay had become the main centre of the opium and cotton trade to China, and the first port on the west coast of India.

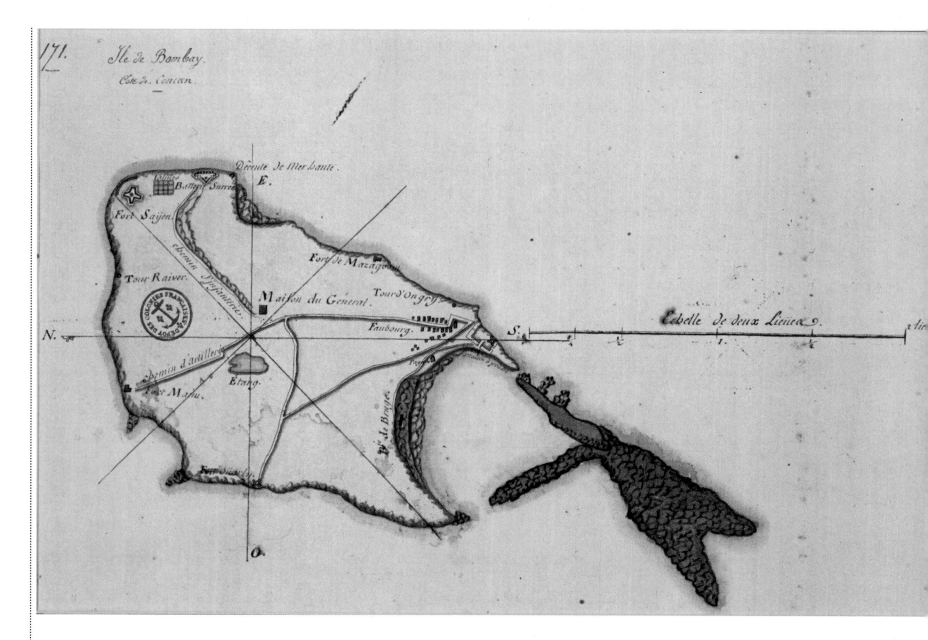

Ile de Bombay.

Côte de Concan.

Décente de Mer haute.

E.

Batterie Surée

Fort Saijen.

Fort de Mazaigou

Tour Raiver.

Tour d'Ongry

DÉPOT DES COLONIES FRANÇAISES

Maison du Général.

chemin d'infanterie

Faubourg.

Echelle de deux Lieües.

N.

S.

Lieüe

chemin d'artillerie

Fort Mahu.

Etang.

B.ie de Brege.

Fort Ouseby.

O.

35

PLATE 5

Plan de l'Ile de Bombay en 1777

Map of Bombay Island in 1777

By Lafitte de Brassier
1777
Collection: CAOM, DFC 30 A 170
Scale [1/1400]
1110 mm x 785 mm

In 1686 the seat of the British government on the western coast was moved from Surat to Bombay. However, because of the threats posed by external attacks the English settlement at Bombay did not develop as quickly as might have been expected. The thinly populated island was invaded in 1688 by the Sidi fleet who occupied its northern part—Mahim, Mazagong and Sion—until 1690. The plague struck Bombay Island in 1694 and again in 1702, with devastating effect. Nor did the existence of a powerful fleet of English pirates on the high seas in the late 1690s—against whom Aurangzeb retaliated by threatening the East India Company at Surat—help Bombay develop smoothly.

Hamilton wrote in 1828: 'Bombay appears for many years to have been left to itself and individuals were allowed to occupy what land they pleased. [...] In 1703 the greater part of the present limits of the fort had become private property, but by subsequent purchase and exchange between that date and 1759, it became the property of the Company, yet was subsequently transfered to private persons. It is certainly an extraordinary fact that the principal, if not the whole of the landed property which the Company now possesses within the walls of Bombay, has been recently acquired.' And it had been acquired for Rs 737,927!

The Bombay government had three residences, the first of which was within the fort. Another, at Malabar, was described as 'a cottage in a beautiful situation, on a rocky, woody promontory, and actually washed by the sea spray'. The third was at Pareil: 'The interior of the house is very handsome, having a fine staircase and two noble rooms, one over the other, about 80 feet long, and very handsomely furnished. The lower of these is said to have been an old desecrated church belonging to the Jesuit's college which had fallen into the hand of a Parsee, from whom it was purchased by the government about sixty years ago.'

Parsis, Europeans and a number of Armenians lived within the fort. According to Hamilton, 'the town within the fort was built by the Portuguese, and even the houses that have been since built are of a similar construction, cased in wood, with wooden pillars supporting wooden verandas shut up with Venetian blinds, the roofs sloped and covered with tiles. The floors are planked with wood.' In the native town north of the fort, Hamilton said, there was 'a floating population' consisting of 'Carnatas, Ghautis, Carvas, Marathas, Arabs, Persians, Goa Portuguese, Parsees and a large proportion of seafaring men'. In the 1800s Bombay Island belonged almost completely to the Parsis. As shown on the map, a great part of the interior of the island was still empty, either planted with coconut trees or occupied by swamps. However, 'the rage for country houses' had already set in among the Europeans.

In 1761 ten French officers captured at Pondicherry were sent to Bombay as prisoners of war. Their observations are summarized by Folnay in a letter to the Minister of the Navy on 5 January 1780:

COTE DE MALABAR.

37

'The island is almost flat and sandy, covered with coconut trees, with spare houses of Indians and some gardens and European residences. The place towards the land has only one rampart, with very small bastions without breast-works or covered-ways.' In the 1770s, when the French government was considering a military intervention in India, as in North America, Bussy advocated an alliance with the Marathas and preferred landing on the western coast of India with the intention of attacking Bombay. In 1777 Lafitte de Brassier spent eighteen days levying this map, which cost the French government Rs 40 (96 French livres).

The first instalment of 2800 of Bussy's men reached Ile de France in October 1781, and Bussy himself with 4000 more troops was expected to follow immediately (Rochambeau had 6000 troops in North America at this time). A third convoy consisting of a naval squadron and transport for marines was under armament at Brest. Bussy's plan of operation was kept secret even from Souillac, Governor of Ile de France, and Admiral de Suffren, who commanded the French fleet in the Indian Ocean. Bussy's unexpected and unavoidable delay made Suffren and Souillac decide to land the first instalment of troops at Cuddalore. When Bussy arrived at Ile de France in 1782, he had no choice but to go to the Coromandel coast, where he landed in March 1783. However, news of the preliminary treaty of peace between England and France which had been signed in Paris in January, reached the Coromandel coast in June.

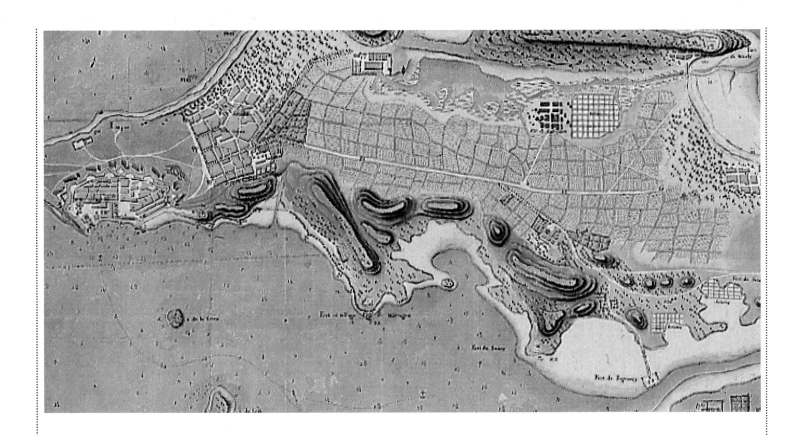

PLATE 6

Plan du Port et Ville Iz-Druk, Côte Malabar, aux Marathes

Plan of the Port and City of Vijaydurg, Malabar Coast, belonging to the Marathas

By Lafitte de Brassier
1778
Collection: CAOM, DFC 30 A 204
Scale [1/14500]
1030 mm x 670 mm

Native navies have existed in the Indian Ocean since antiquity. In the sixteenth century the Portuguese imposed a pay-toll with passports (*cartaz*) on these navies, which led to conflicts with the Great Mughal at their main port, Surat. Under Shivaji, the Marathas developed their own navy; in the late seventeenth century two lesser powers, the Sidis of Janjira and the Angrias of Gheria, tried to build naval power with light fleets that docked at numerous ports along the Malabar and Konkan coast and sought protection from their forts. The French maritime map of this zone (Plate 1) distinguishes the places belonging to the 'Sidis' from those of the 'Angrias'. It also carries the title 'Port of the Angrias called Izdruk'. Izdruk is a French corruption of 'Vijaydurg' or Viziadroog. Mid-eighteenth-century cartographers were unsure of the identity of Izdruk, Viziadruk and Gheria (the names most often seen on English maps), whether they were two or three different places, and their precise location.

Gheria, or Vijaydurg, was a town and fort at the mouth of the river Kunvee, 170 miles south of Bombay. The fort was situated on a rocky promontory about one mile and a quarter broad. The rock is joined to the continent by a narrow neck of land and lies one mile from the entrance of a harbour formed by the mouth of the Kunvee, which flows west from the *ghats*. The harbour is excellent, the anchorage being landlocked and sheltered from all winds. There is no bar at the entrance, and the depth in the early 1800s was between 5 and 7 fathoms. Built in 1662 by Shivaji, the fort passed into the hands of the Angria branch of the Bhonsle family, and in 1707 Conajee Angria established an independent sovereignty at Gheria that possessed a numerous fleet.

In 1756 the combined English fleet of Bombay and the Gulf of Bengal, fourteen sails under the command of Admiral Watson, with the help of a marine unit—1800 men commanded by Clive—stormed the coastal fortresses of Angria, entered the harbour of Gheria, and burnt down the defending fleet which consisted of 3 three-masted ships with 20 guns each, 9 two-masted ships with 12 to 16 guns, 13 *gallivats* with 6 to 10 guns, 30 unclassified ships and 2 others on the stocks, one of them pierced for 40 guns. The bombing lasted twenty-four hours. After its surrender Izdruk was given to the Marathas, allies of the English at that time.

Instructions to Tronjoly, Commander of the French squadron in the Indian Ocean, on 3 February 1777 asked him to stop at 'Ixdruk (or Chiora)' during his cruise of the Malabar coast, to show his pavillion and establish contact with the commander of the port. This was to explore possibilities of docking an expedition to India similar to the one France was preparing for North America. Plans of the city and fort were made on this occasion by Lafitte de Brassier who was on *Le Brillant*, Tronjoly's flagship. Brassier made the map in twenty days, at a cost of Rs 36 (86 livres, 8 sols).

In March 1977 a missile-launcher corvette commissioned by the Indian navy was baptised *INS Vijaydurg*, in memory of the Angria stronghold and its history.

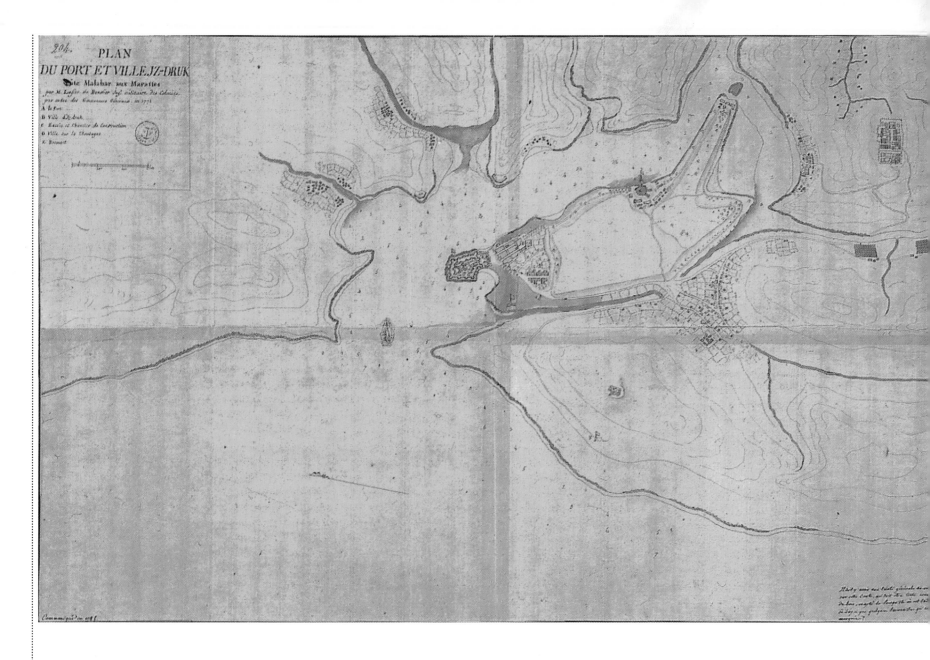

PLAN

DU PORT ET VILLE JZ-DRUK

Côte Malabar, aux Marattes

par M. Lafitte de Brassier Ingr. militaire des Colonies,
par ordre des Gouverneurs Généraux, en 1771.

A. le Port
B. Ville Jz-Druk
C. Bassin et Chantier de Construction
D. Ville sur la Montagne
E. Rempart

PLATE 7

Plan de Mangalor, à la Côte de Malabar, au Nabab Hyder Ali Kan

Plan of Mangalore, on the Malabar Coast, belonging to Nawab Hyder Ali Khan

By Lafitte de Brassier
1778
Collection: CAOM, DFC 30 B 175
Scale [1/7500]
715 mm x 480 mm

This ancient city on the Malabar coast was presumed to be the Greek and Roman 'Muziris'. Mangalore — or Mangalapura, the city of prosperity — was one of the great South Indian ports of the medieval period. It belonged to the Nayaks of Bednore before it was occupied by Hyder Ali Khan, Regent of Mysore, in 1768. Hyder Ali took a liking to this part of his kingdom and he devel-oped it actively, installing new industries — especially military ones — in and around the city, modernizing its fortifications, and renovating the port where he set up a military dockyard and shipbuilding facilities.

According to Portuguese sources, Hyder Ali had thirty warships in 1765, but by 1778 his fleet consisted of 80 three-masted ships carrying 20 to 40 guns and an equal number of merchant ships. This quick and systematic development of the Mysore navy, commanded by Desvaux in 1771 from his headquarters in Mangalore, was in response to several factors. Hyder Ali had to protect the coasts of his newly-conquered territories in the west. He also wished to acquire the means of projecting his military forces by sea and one of his fleets, commanded by Ali Raja, landed a Mysorean body of regular troops who captured the Maldive Islands. Further, Hyder Ali had to protect the sea-lines of the increasing commercial activities of his kingdom: his son Tipu Sultan developed trade with Egypt, the Arabic shores and the Persian Gulf.

The plan of Mangalore shown here, along with slightly differing copies of it in the DFC, Aix-en-Provence, shows the city and harbour of Mangalore as they stood in 1778, before being destroyed in 1781–84. Lafitte de Brassier prepared the map in seventeen days at a cost of Rs 40, or 96 livres. One of his plans gives in '*brasses*' the depth of the water at each of the two entrances of the harbour: the northern one only being fit for large ships.

The development of an Indian blue-water navy was unacceptable to the East India Company. In 1781 Admiral Hughes captured Mangalore and destroyed the dockyard with all the ships in the port. The British once again occupied Manga-lore in 1783, seized Bednore and instituted a systematic campaign of terror to compel Tipu Sultan to leave the Coromandel coast (where he was expecting the French expe-ditionary forces of Bussy). With the help of French units commanded by Lallée, Bouthenot and Cossigny, who commanded the Régiment de l'Ile de France with its gunners and heavy siege artillery, Tipu Sultan recaptured Bednore and laid siege to Mangalore. The British garrison capi-tulated in 1784 after difficult negotiations channelled through Piveron de Morlat, the French Agent accredited at the court of Mysore. The *Mémoire des Indes* by Piveron de Morlat, written in 1786 but unpublished (English edition forth-coming), contains fascinating information concerning the campaigns of Hyder Ali and Tipu Sultan between 1780 and 1784.

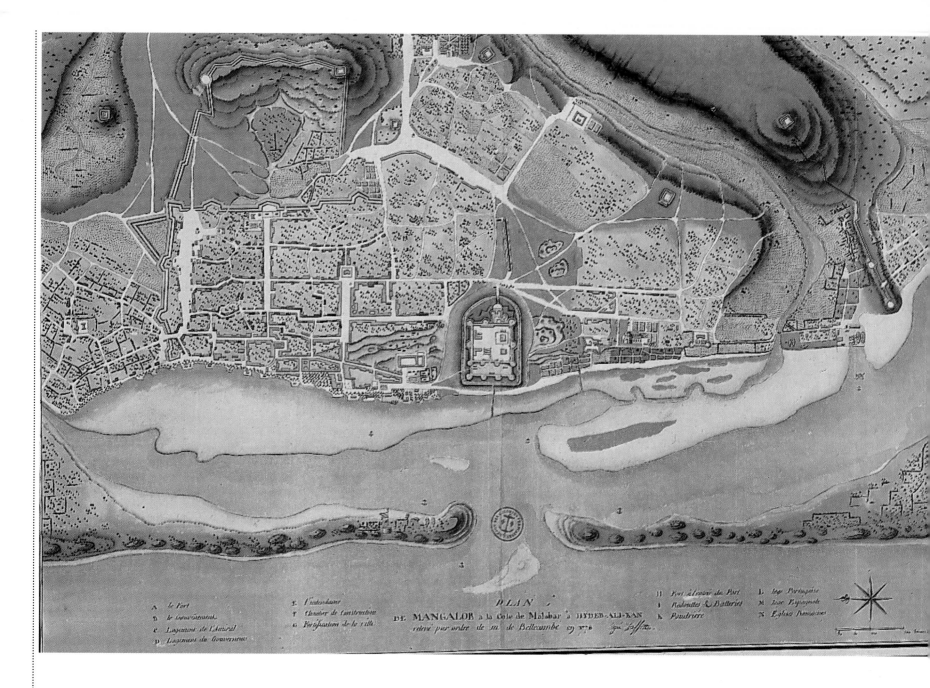

PLAN
DE MANGALOR à la Côte de Malabar à HYDER-ALI-KAN
relevé par ordre de M. de Bellecombe en 1776

A   le Fort
B   le Gouvernement
C   Logement de l'Amiral
D   Logement du Gouverneur

E   l'Intendance
F   Chantier de Construction
G   Fortification de la ville

H   Fort à l'entrée du Port
I   Redoutes & Batteries
K   Poudrière

L   Loge Portugaise
M   Loge Espagnole
N   Eglises Paroissiales

43

PLATE 8

Plan de la Ville de Cochain à la Côte Malabar, appartenant aux Hollandais

Plan of the City of Cochin, Malabar Coast, belonging to the Dutch

By Lafitte de Brassier
1778
Collection: CAOM, DFC 30 B 197
Scale [1/3990]
730 mm x 525 mm

Cochin's excellent deep-water harbour, perhaps the best on the Malabar coast, was the only port south of Bombay till 1858 where large ships could be built. Cochin has a long trading history. The Greeks and the Romans came there to load their vessels with South Indian goods. A Jewish community came and settled there 2000 years ago. In the sixteenth century there was a new wave of Jewish settlers from several European countries, and it was they who built the synagogue that still stands there today. Cochin was always an international trading centre visited by travellers, merchants, mission-aries of every creed, sailors, pilots and sea-captains.

In 1503, Albuquerque obtained permission to build a fortress at Cochin, and the Portuguese quickly settled in that city. François Xavier, one of the founders of the Society of Jesus at Paris in 1534 (Societas Jesu, the Jesuit Order, which was approved by the Pope in 1540), turned it into a great intellectual centre. The first book printed in India was printed here by the Jesuit Fathers, in 1577.

In 1663 the Dutch occupied Cochin and stayed there until they were overthrown by the English in 1795. According to Thornton, the city was inhabited by Jews, Hindus and Mahomedans who developed extensive commerce. Trade relations with Arabia were very good, and many Arab ships made two voyages annually. Also, Venetian sequins brought from Egypt were in common circulation. A plan and several views of Cochin engraved in Baldaeus's book, published in 1672, show the town just after it was captured by the Dutch. The Dutch archives at Cochin, consisting of 1643 big leather-bound volumes (of which about 1400 survive), were transferred to Madras in 1891. Judging from what has been published of these archives, the collection is particularly rich in material on the political, economic and social history of that part of India.

The Rajas of Cochin maintained their independence much longer than other Hindu princes. They were initially compelled to pay tribute to Tipu Sultan; in 1791 the Cochin Raja managed to throw off the Mysore allegiance and transferred it to the British. But Cochin 'always entertained a decided partiality to the French nation and commenced an un-provoked and preposterous war against the British which was extinguished with little trouble and his tribute augmented to 2,76,037 rupees' (Thornton).

In 1776, when the French started looking for a place to land the expedition-ary corps they planned to send to India, Admiral Tronjoly made a port of call at Cochin and Lafitte de Brassier spent sixteen days preparing a map of the city, at a cost of Rs 16 (43 livres, 4 sols). Conspicuous in the map are the long avenues bordered by trees that lead from the main city to Villejuif, the Jewish quarter of Cochin called Mattancherry, about a mile from the city. It was, in 1820, 'wholly tenanted by Israelites' (Hamilton).

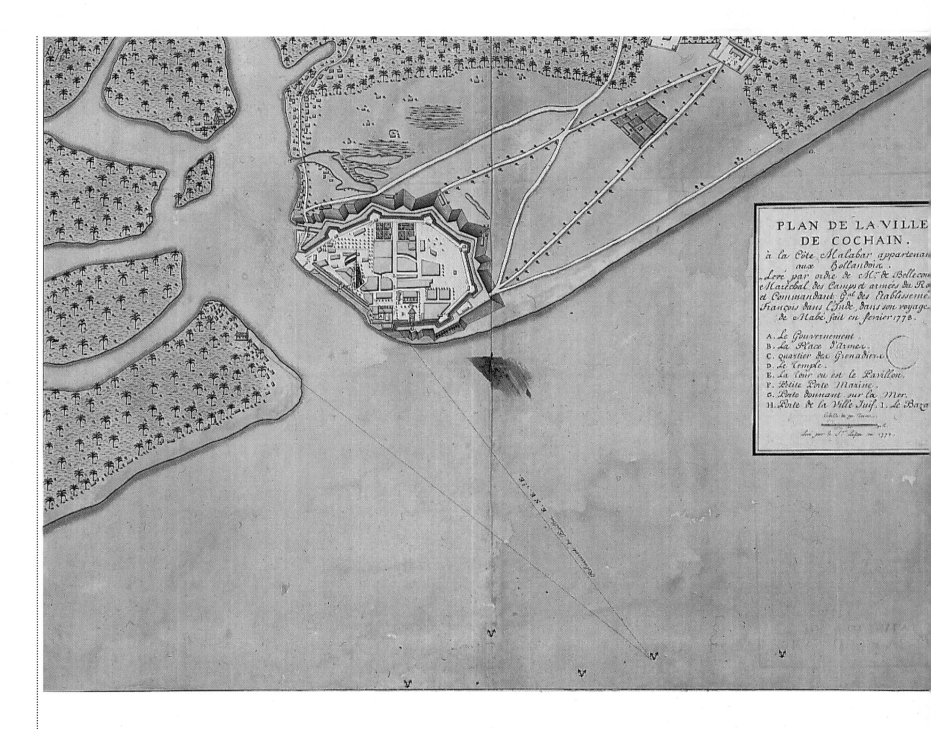

PLAN DE LA VILLE
DE COCHAIN.

à la Côte Malabar appartenan
aux Hollandois.
Levé par ordre de Mr. de Bellecon
Maréchal des Camps et armées du Ro
et Commandant Gnl. des Etablisseme
François dans l'Inde, dans son voyage
de Mahé fait en fevrier 1778.

A. Le Gouvernement.
B. La Place d'Armes.
C. Quartier des Grenadiers.
D. Le Temple.
E. La Tour ou est le Pavillon.
F. Petite Porte Marine.
G. Porte donnant sur la Mer.
H. Porte de la Ville Juif. I. Le Baza

Echelle de 90 toises

Levé par le Sr. Lafitte en 1778.

PLATE 9

Plan et Coupe du Fort de Mahé, de la Batterie des Roches et de la Redoute de la Montagne Verte. Par Ranger, 17 janvier 1770

Plan and Cross-section of the Fort of Mahé, of the Battery des Roches and of the Redoubt of the Green Mountain. By Ranger, 17 January 1770

By Ranger
17 January 1770
Collection: CAOM, DFC 35 A 39
Scale of the fort [1/430] (plan) and [1/210] (cross-section)
Scale of the battery [1/280]
Scale of the redoubt [1/200] (plan and cross-section)
965 mm x 600 mm

Mahé, a minuscule territory on the Malabar coast, was acquired by the French on 2 April 1721 through an agreement with the *bayanor*, the local sovereign. The Mahé river was navigable by boat for a considerable distance, and in fair weather small crafts could safely cross the sandbar at its entrance. Mahé's main export was pepper, and it made the fortunes of some French and Indian families in Pondicherry. Being the only French settlement on the Malabar coast, and situated as it was opposite the British factory of Tellichery, Mahé developed a political importance from the 1750s, which is largely forgotten today.

From the early days of Hyder Ali it was through Mahé that men, arms and ammunitions passed on their way to Mysore. In E. Thornton's analysis it was a 'long and serious and vexatious source of annoyance to the British by affording the French a footing in the Malabar, and a ready communication with Mysore and its ruler'. It was for this reason that it was stormed and dismantled by an English force from Bombay in 1779. That in turn was the cause cited by Hyder Ali for his devastating invasion of the Carnatic in 1780. Proof, if it be needed, of the importance of Mahé for Mysore in the 1770s.

Hyder Ali had given standing orders to the commandants of his fortresses near Mahé to give aid to any French officer or soldier coming from Mahé to join him at Srirangapatnam. This was a dangerous journey. Maistre de la Tour narrates the story of five French soldiers, three of them with Indian wives, who were killed on their way from Mahé to Mysore. The Bibliothèque Nationale has 123 volumes of correspondence, reports, etc., by Picot de la Motte, who was for a long time the Administrator of Mahé. These include his correspondence with South Indian sovereigns between 1760 and 1780: with Hyder Ali himself; with Hyder Ali's admiral, Ali Raja, who commanded the naval expedition to the Maldives; and with petty local sovereigns commanding small kingdoms and principalities in the mountainous *ghats*, most of whom were little known to the Europeans.

Mahé also played a role in intellectual and cultural exchanges between India and France. Engineer Deydier, who had worked at Pondicherry for several years, was sent to Mahé in 1726–28 to draw up plans and build several works. The CAOM houses several of these maps and plans of the city and its monuments—along with memoirs bearing his signature. Deydier was a man of great curiosity who took a keen interest in the Syrian Christian communities of the Malabar coast. He purchased their sacred books, copies of which he intended to offer to the King's Library in Paris. When he left India in 1729, he took with him to France 'a great deal of curious items from these areas [Mahé, Malabar] which he knew so well'. He is specifically mentioned by the Jesuits of Pondicherry as being a great collector of Indian books.

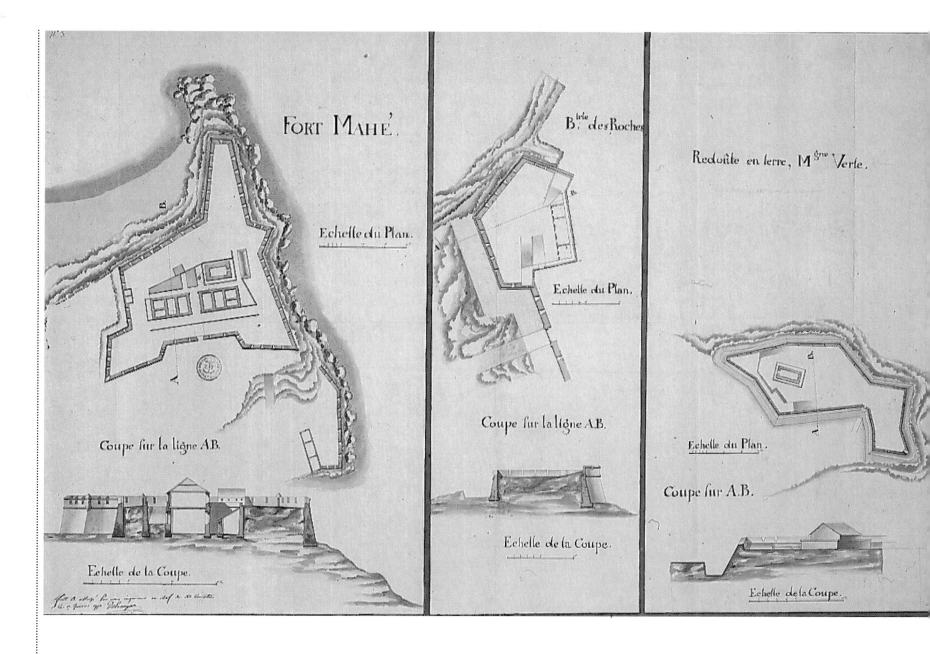

FORT MAHÉ.

Echelle du Plan.

Coupe sur la ligne A.B.

Echelle de la Coupe.

B.[rie] des Roches

Echelle du Plan.

Coupe sur la ligne A.B.

Echelle de la Coupe.

Redoûte en terre, M[gne] Verte.

Echelle du Plan.

Coupe sur A.B.

Echelle de la Coupe.

PLATE 10

Magasin au Comptoir de Mahé

Magazine in the Settlement of Mahé

By Bellanger
1770
Collection: CAOM, DFC 35 B 43
Scale not given
675 mm x 495 mm

Mahé at its greatest expansion comprised an area of only 2600 hectares. This was in 1776, after Hyder Ali contributed several *aldées* during his second invasion of the Malabar coast. However, though small, Mahé had a political and strategic importance. In 1785 it was considered as the possible location of the headquarters of French settlements in India, replacing Pondicherry, which had twice been occupied by armies of the East India Company. The *raison d'être* of Mahé was its economic significance. It was the centre for the pepper, cardamom and sapan wood trade. Alfred Martineau has compiled an interesting survey of the trade and finances of Mahé from 1725 to *c.* 1740, which includes a list of the ships that arrived with gold and silver for the purchase of pepper. The local trade (*commerce d'Inde en Inde*) was conducted by private ships, often from the fleet of Ali Raja of Cannanore, and there was never any trouble from the so-called 'piratical enterprises' of the Angrias or the Sidis. The commercial exchanges at Mahé in the late 1760s averaged 800,000 to 900,000 French livres per annum. Law de Lauriston, appointed Governor General of Pondicherry in 1765, wrote in a *Mémoire* dated 1767 that the proceeds from trade were not sufficient considering the military expenses incurred to protect Mahé during those particularly troubled times.

The Centre des Archives d'Outre-Mer, DFC, has numerous plans and maps of Mahé and its territory, including drawings of the surrounding hills with their elevation. There are also plans, views and cross-sections of buildings such as Fort Mahé and its military supports, including the Batterie des Roches, the *redoubt* of the Montagne Verte (Green Mountain), the ramparts and their advanced positions, and the powder magazines. Other views show the administrator's residence which had formerly been the residence of the local sovereign or *bayanor*, the tribunal or *chaudrie*, the place for storage of arms, and the magazine.

Ranger made a cross-section of the magazine from the river to the *place d'armes* (CAOM, DFC 35 C 44) dated 22 February 1770. Section A (black) of this plan was completed in 1768, section B (red) in 1769, and the third section (yellow), including the forge, was left unfinished.

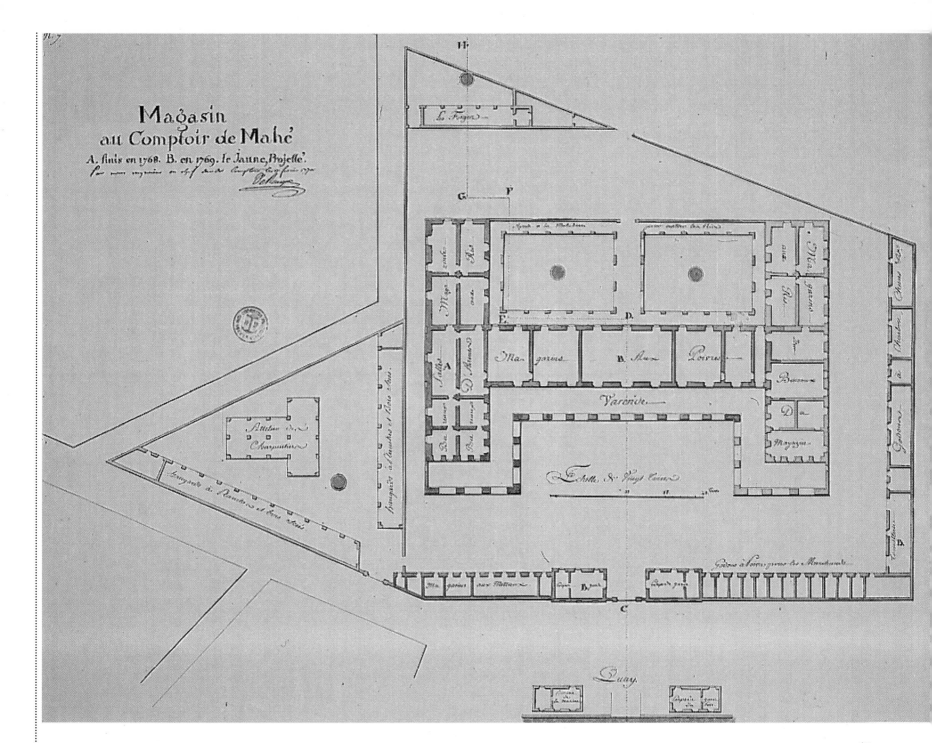

Magasin
au Comptoir de Mahé

A. finis en 1768. B. en 1769. le Jaune, Projetté.

49

PLATE 11

Plan de la Ville de Trisir-a-pally, levé en 1755

Plan of the City of Trichinopoly, drawn in 1755

Artist unknown
1755
Collection: CAOM, DFC 30 A 233
Scale [1/3440]
1155 mm x 460 mm

Tiruchirapally, also called Trichino-poly, is a city famous for its rock fort. It is also famous for its temples in the town and on Srirangam island. The early history of the city goes back to when it was the capital of the Nayaks of Madurai. In 1616 it was occupied by a scion of the Maratha family. Chanda Sahib laid siege to it in 1736 on behalf of the Nawab of Arcot and lost it to the Marathas in 1741.

Nizam ul-Mulk occupied it in 1743 and entrusted it to Anwar ud-Din, his deputy in the Carnatic. After Anwar ud-Din died in 1749, the French decided to support Chanda Sahib as the new Nawab of Arcot, while Mehemet Ali was the British candidate. In 1750, Mehemet Ali fortified himself within the walls of Trichinopoly, and in 1751, the British from Madras decided to reinforce his position with two strong contingents. The second of these, 1600-strong with eight field guns, which marched from Fort Saint-David (Cuddalore), was commanded by Captain Gingins, a Swiss officer of Pays de Vaud. Gingins's commissariat officer was Hon. Lieutenant Robert Clive.

The long counter-siege on Trichinopoly was conducted by different Indian armies (Chanda Sahib first, then the Marathas, with or without the help of Mysore) who were assisted by French contingents. They proved unsuccessful against the Indian and British forces who defended the city, and who were assisted by elite Swiss units recruited in Switzerland by the East India Company.

The story of these Swiss units deserves to be narrated. In 1751, the East India Company raised a full regiment in Switzerland, the Suisse–Anglais, and sent it to Madras in 1752. The regiment had four companies of foot soldiers and one company of artillery with heavy guns and siege guns. Under the command of Stringer Lawrence first and then Clive, these French-speaking Swiss, all of them Huguenots (Protestants), played an important role in tilting the balance in favour of England. Assisted by Indian 'commandants' of great valour like Yusuf Khan, Captains Frischmann, Gingins, Polier (Paul-Philippe, uncle of Antoine-Louis Polier of Awadh fame), Caillaud, Paschoud, Zeigler, Gaupp and their corps of grenadiers, were remarkably efficient against the elite French troops whom they confronted in the Carnatic. These Swiss units defended Trichinopoly with obduracy. They then helped the East India Company to gain control of the countryside in 1756–57. Daniel Frischmann was entrusted with important commands in South India and Madras before he retired to Switzerland in 1770. Some other Swiss officers (Caillaud, Gaupp, Paschoud) followed Clive to Bengal. Jean-Claude Paschoud commanded the English artillery which played havoc with the Indian army at the Battle of Plassey in 1757. He returned to Switzerland with a superb collection of Indian artefacts which he exhibited in his '*cabinet de curiosités*' at Dalliens.

The East India Company used Trichinopoly as a powerful base during the Mysore wars against Hyder Ali and Tipu Sultan, especially in 1780–84, when the Mysore armies threatened Madras. It came under the direct control of the East India Company in 1801. On the bridge which later joined the island of Srirangam to the mainland on the north, an inscription commemorated the defence of Trichinopoly by Stringer Lawrence, 'which mainly contributed to lay the foundations of the British empire in India'.

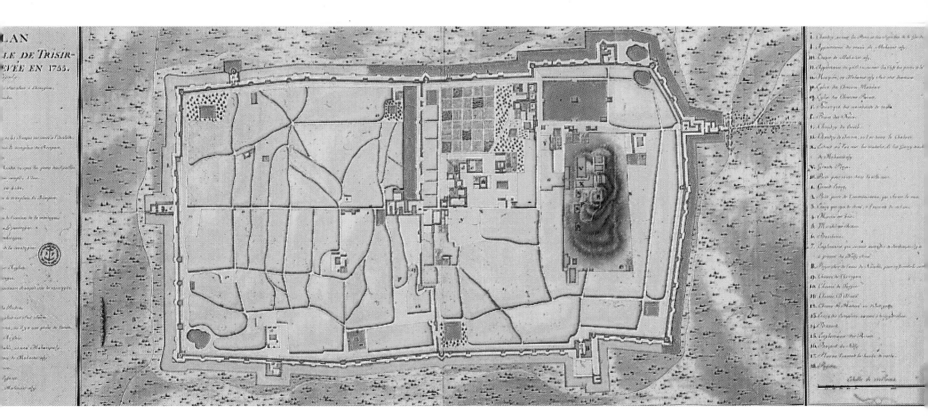

51

PLATE 12

Vue de Trisir-a-pally
View of Trichinopoly

Artist unknown
c. 1742
Collection: CAOM, DFC 30 C 234
544 mm x 355 mm

Trichinopoly is the city that rocked Dupleix's ambition. Held by the English in the name of Mehemet Ali, who had been set up by the British East India Company against Chanda Sahib, backed by the French as the Nawab of Arcot, Trichinopoly became a symbolic place where the French and the British fought each other with the help of their respective Indian allies.

Hamilton (1828) and Thornton (1858) have described the old city, called 'The Fort', with its massive walls fortified by strong masonry. It bore the appearance of having been regularly built. The walls, in some parts doubly reinforced, were 20 to 30 feet high, of considerable thickness and 2 miles in circumference. The houses and the huts were arranged along 'tolerably' straight, wide and regular streets usually crowded with multitudes of pedestrians, bullock-carts and cattle (Thornton). The city's fortifications were razed to the ground in the late nineteenth century. The Rock Fort, which contains a temple dedicated to Ganesha, dominates the city and its surroundings.

This view of Trichinopoly shows the old city with its ramparts, close to the Rock Fort. The wall (no. 9) is 'the rampart dividing the old city from the new one'. The artist says that 'he did not try to meticulously draw each and every building. He only drew the most important.' Among them are the palace of the Raja (no. 1) and the palace of the Queens (no. 2), the 'large Madhman' or the One Thousand Pillars Hall (no. 3, which was turned into a powder magazine and destroyed by an accidental explosion in 1772), the four square columns 44 feet high (no. 4), the 'very old Pagoda' (no. 5, at the top of the Rock), the great powder magazine (no. 7) and the 'Pagoda at the foot of the Rock which is one of the most beautifully and tastefully decorated (*du meilleur goût*) buildings in India' (no. 8). The artist's appreciation of Indian architecture, painting and sculpture echoes Jacques Maissin's sympathetic curiosity towards Hinduism, its myths and monuments in the 1750s (see Plate 13).

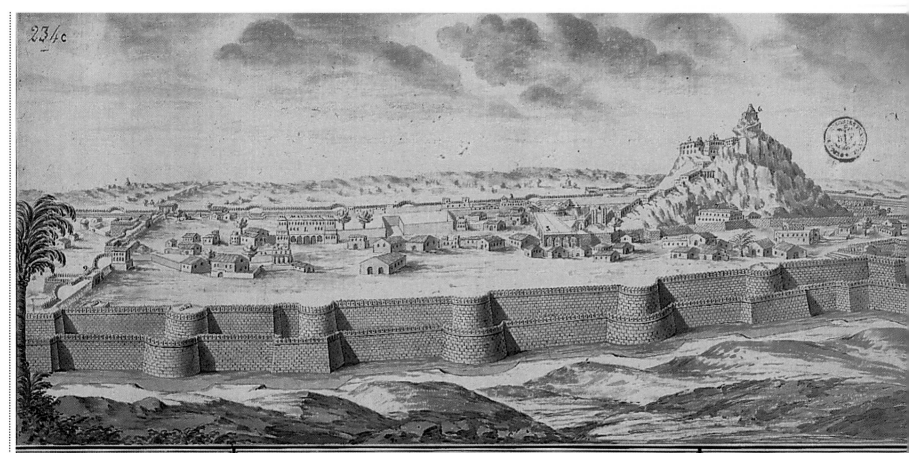

VUE DE TRISIR-À-PALLY

Ville des Indes Orientales dans la presqu'isle en deçà du Gange, située dans les terres par 10. deg. 24'. 20". de lat.e N.e et par 96. deg. 21. 23". de long.e Merid.e de l'isle de Fer à 44. lieuës dans le S.t O.t 1. deg.e S.t de Pondichery. Elle fut prise en 1738. par le Nabab Sabder-Aly-Kan apres un siége de 2. ans. et reprise par l'armée des Marâttes le 26. mars 1742. en 3. mois de siége.

RENVOY DES CHIFRES.

1. Palais des Rajas.
2. Palais des Reines, ou la derniere mourut priesmaide au mois d'Aoust 1740.
3. Madham spacieux. C'est un bastiment ou les Brahmes s'assemblent les jours de leurs fêtes, sa couverture platte en est soutenuë par mille colonne de 12 pieds de haut. Chacune dias seule pierre.
4. Ce sont quatre colonnes quarrées, chacune d'un seul bloc de pierre de 42 pieds de haut sur 3 pieds de chaque espace qui doit peser 77. milliers.
5. Pagode tres ancienne, ou l'on parvient au moyen d'un escalier à plusieurs repos.

SUITE DU RENVOY.

6. Petite Pagode au sommet du rocher d'environ 450. pieds d'élévation, d'ou l'on découvre distinctement les tours des Pagodes de la Ville de Tangaour distante de 24. lieuës droit dans l'Est, qui est la capitale du Royaume de ce nom.
7. Grand magazin à poudre avec étage soutenu par colonnes.
8. Pagode au pied du rocher qui est un des bastimens des Indiens le mieux décoré extérieurement et du meilleur goust.
9. Mur de cloture qui sepáre l'ancienne ville de la nouvelle. On ne s'est point attaché à representer scrupuleusement toutes les maisons et cahutes qui sont dans cette ville. On a seulement dessiné les plus apparentes.

PLATE 13

Plan du Grand Chiringam

Plan of Great Srirangam

By Gérard
c. 1755
Collection: CAOM, DFC 30 A 229
Scale [1/2300]
475 mm x 480 mm

The island of Srirangam is in the middle of the Cauvery river, 10 kilometres north of Trichinopoly (Tiruchirapalli). It has two temples that are among the holiest shrines of the Hindus: one is dedicated to Ranganatha Swami (Vishnu) and is called Great Srirangam, and the other to Jambukeshwara (Shiva), called Small Srirangam. Great Srirangam is renowned for some of its priests such as Nathamuni in the tenth century; Yamunacharya, the founder of the Sri Vaishnava movement, in the eleventh century; and Ramanuja in the eleventh/twelfth centuries.

One of the most famous of Indian diamonds, the Orlov, which is now in the Kremlin in Moscow, was reputed to be the eye of one of the statues of the Srirangam temples. Legend has it that a French deserter disguised as a Hindu (and a brahmin!) stole it, but this story, 'a feat that necessitated years rather than months of planning', according to Ian Balfour, 'cannot be relied upon as authoritative'. In the 1750s conversion to Hinduism was not possible, and moreover, we know of Maissin's strict orders banning any profanation of the sanctuaries of Srirangam during the siege of Trichinopoly. Other versions of the 'Orlov' travels in Europe are even more lurid and can be found in Balfour's chapter 'Orlov', which talks about the two diamonds of Srirangam. Anquetil Duperron, in his autobiography, refers to a similar robbery of a ruby which was the eye of the main statue at Jagannath.

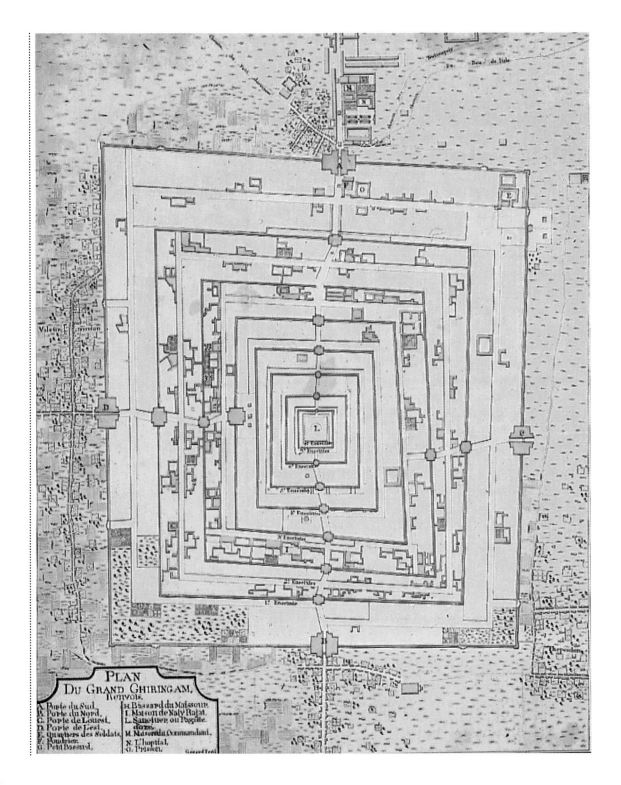

PLAN
Du Grand Ghiringam.
Renvois.

A. Porte du Sud.
B. Porte du Nord.
C. Porte de l'Ouest.
D. Porte de l'Est.
E. Quartiers des Soldats.
F. Poudrier.
G. Petit Bassard.

H. Bassard du Maïssour.
I. Maison de Naly Rajat.
L. Sanctuer, ou Pagode dorée.
M. Maison du Commandant.
N. L'hopital.
O. Prison.

PLATE 14

Plan du Petit Chiringam

Plan of Small Srirangam

By Gérard
c. 1755
Collection: CAOM, DFC 30 A 229
Scale [1/2300]
300 mm x 425 mm

Between 1750 and 1760, Trichinopoly was a hotbed of rivalry between different local powers, Hindu and Muslim, competing to dominate South India, some backed by the English, and others by the French. The besieged held the city and the fort, while those laying siege usually occupied the island of Srirangam, the areas around the two temples which were not forbidden to non-Hindus.

From August 1754 to April 1755, the French troops in Srirangam were commanded by Jacques Maissin, an assistant to the Maratha General, Nandi Raja. Maissin was deeply impressed by what he discovered about Hinduism and religious life around the temples. He drew up plans of the temples and initiated investigations into the holy areas of the sanctuaries where he could not enter. He befriended priests from whom he obtained rich information on Hinduism and its texts and legends. Many years later, when he had retired to Ile de France, he reworked his notes and compiled his observations under the title, '*Recherche de la vérité sur l'état civil, politique et religieux des Hindus [...] avec les figures nécessaires, le plan de trois temples fameux de la cote de Coromandel*' (Research on the truth concerning the social, political and religious condition of the Hindus ... with the necessary illustrations, plans of three famous temples on the Coromandel coast).

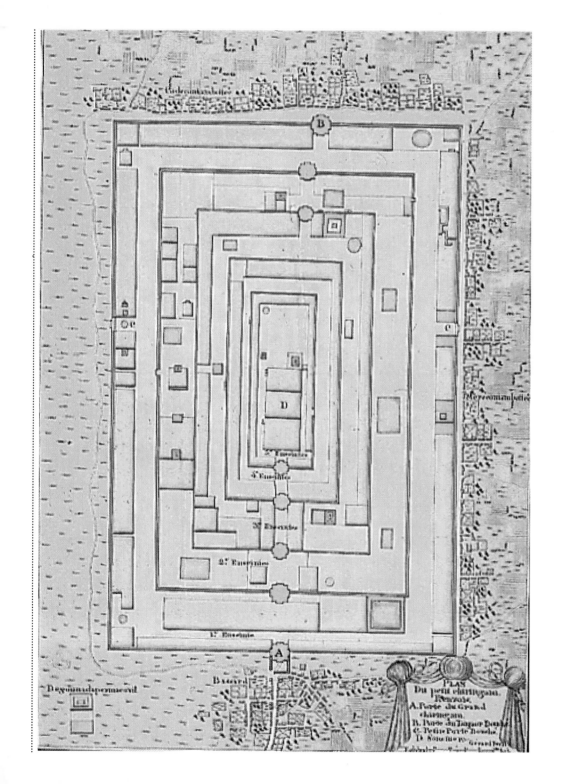

PLATE 15

Plan de Tanjore, Ville dans la Presqu'île de l'Inde, Côte de Coromandel

Plan of Tanjore, a Town in the Indian Peninsula, Coast of Coromandel

Artist unknown
No date
Collection: CAOM, DFC 30 C 237
Scale [1/14620]
500 mm x 305 mm

Tanjore was one of the most important political and cultural centres in South India, with territory that extended up to the Coromandel coast. The Dutch settlement at Negapatnam, the Danish settlement at Tranquebar and the French settlement at Karikal, all originally belonged to the kings of Tanjore, who granted the various European East India Companies permission to settle there because of the economic and political boost they gave to the local power base.

In 1674, a Maratha dynasty was established at Tanjore, and from 1740 onwards they were engaged in resisting Muslim expansion (Nawab of Arcot) by complying alternatively with the French and the British. In 1760, Partab Singh, Raja of Tanjore, decided to modernize his army and requested French officers—Flamicourt, Dumont, and then Marchant—to raise and train a regiment of French and Topas soldiers. In 1762, that troop entered the service of Yusuf Khan at Madurai. Tanjore thereafter became a satellite power of the British East India Company which used it as a military base during the Mysore wars against Hyder Ali and Tipu Sultan. In 1781, the Raja of Tanjore opened secret negotiations with General Duchemin, who commanded the first instalment of troops sent to India under the command of Bussy, but to no apparent effect. Reverend Schwartz of the Danish mission of Tranquebar settled down in Tanjore, from where he tried to negotiate peace among the various belligerents. In 1773 Tanjore had been given by Madras to Muhammad Ali, the Nawab of Arcot, but the decision was cancelled in 1776 on special instructions from London and the city reverted to its legitimate ruler. The dynasty of Tanjore lasted till 1853, when the state became British territory and a pension was granted to the former ruling family.

An 1820 description of Tanjore is to be found in Hamilton's *Gazetteer*: 'This place consists of two parts, the fortified city, and the fort or citadel, built on the same level as the city and connected to it by a curtain and narrow passage. The walls are lofty and built of large stones, and on the corners of the ramparts are *cavaliers*. The ditch, which is broad and deep, is cut out of the solid rock and has a well-formed *glacis*. The city itself is more regularly built and contains a larger proportion of solid and ornamental edifices. The principal streets intersect each other at right angles.'

The artistic riches of Tanjore and the splendour of its school of paintings, which can still be seen in its temples, palaces and manuscripts, drew the attention of Europeans. In 1758, Porcher Desoulches, 'Commandant of the Town, Fort and Dependencies of Karikalle, Kingdom of Tanjore', commissioned an extraordinary *Histoire et figures des Dieux des Indiens, ou théogonie des Malabariquais* ('History and Images of the Gods of the Hindus, or Theogony of the People of Malabar') in four volumes, illustrated with 581 paintings (Cabinet des Estampes, Bibliothèque Nationale, Paris, Od 39, 39a, 39b and 39c). These paintings, executed on full pages or double-page spreads, were the work of local artists in the highly-coloured Tanjore style. There are detailed inscriptions in Tamil with French translations on the pictures. The selection of the texts and their French translation may be tentatively attributed to the learned Tamil interpreter, Maridas Pillai. The volumes were given high praise by Anquetil Duperron.

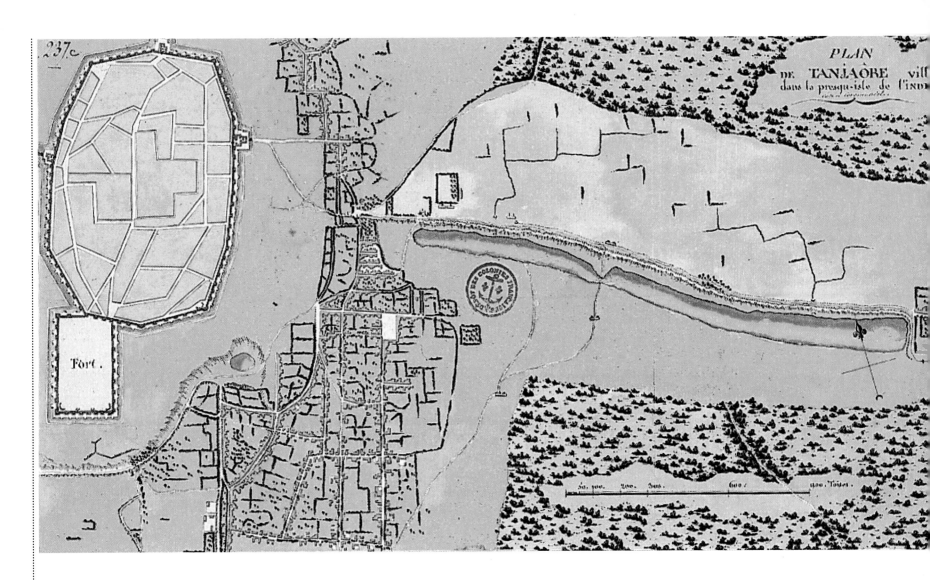

PLATE 16

Carte Marine,
Côte de Coromandel

Maritime Map,
Coast of Coromandel

Artist unknown
c. 1756
Collection: Private
Courtesy: Colonel Chinailh
480 mm x 645 mm

The Coromandel coast on the east of India stretches from Pointe de Godvarin to the Pagoda of Canimère. It is a long, flat plain broken by the hills of Ginji, to the west of Cuddalore and Pondicherry. The *gopurams*, pyramidal gateways, of temples served as the only landmark for sailors. From the north to the south they were: the seven pagodas north of Sadras, the temple of Chalembarang (Chidambaram), the Pagoda of China, and the Pagoda of Canimère. The Coromandel coast, according to the map, was considered safe for ships except for the sandbanks off Pettapoli and near Armegon.

There were a number of European settlements along that coast, and the letters on the map identify their nationality: A (English), D (Danish), F (French), H (Dutch), P (Portuguese).

The settlements were, from north to south: Masulipatnam (Dutch, English, French); Paliacat (Dutch); Madras (English); Pondicherry (French); Fort Saint-David and Cuddalore (English); Tranquebar (Danish); Karikal (French); Negapatnam (Dutch).

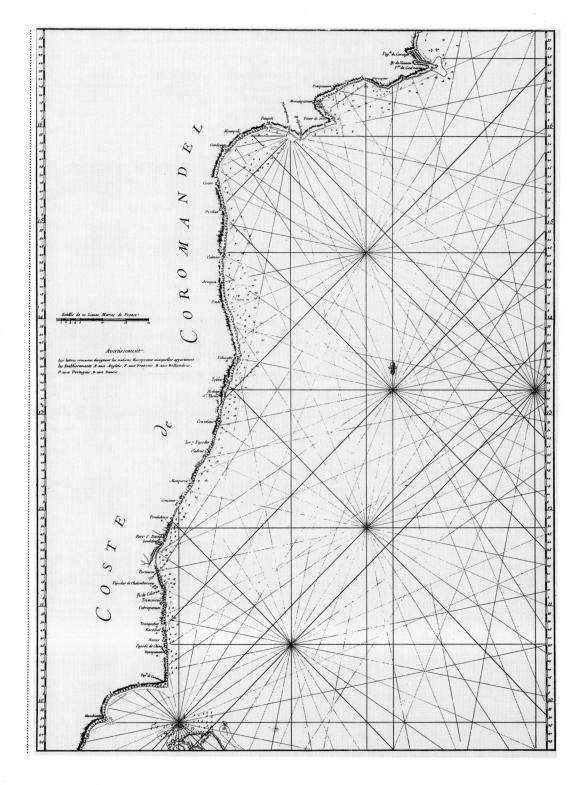

61

PLATE 17

Plan de la Ville de Trinquebar, aux Danois, en 1778

Plan of the City of Tranquebar, belonging to the Dutch, in 1778

By Lafitte de Brassier
1778
Collection: CAOM, DFC 30 A 251
Scale [1/2400]
960 mm x 660 mm

In 1616, a Danish vessel anchored at Tranquebar (Turangaburi) and received permission from the Raja of Tanjore to occupy a small territory of 5 miles by 3 miles, for which they had to pay an annual rent of Rs 4000. In 1620, the Raja of Tanjore gave the Danes the entire town and they built a fort (Dansborg) there with a garrison of about twenty men. The settlement became royal property in 1624 and continued its peaceful existence. Unofficially, it took sides with the French more often than with the British during the wars of the eighteenth century. Families evacuated from French settlements took refuge there in 1761 and again in 1778. The present fort was restored and modified in 1792. The town was built with remarkable neatness and regularity. The fort as well as most of the houses being white, the place was conspicuously visible when viewed from the sea.

Since it was 'neutral' territory, Tranquebar was also a place through which French, English and Indian intelligence agents travelled, and where different squadron leaders had agents who provided them with information on enemy forces. According to Louis Garneray, in 1800 Robert Surcouf, a French *corsaire*, signed a contract with two Danish officials of Tranquebar, a consul and a sea captain, who prepared for him an album of paintings representing the enemy's ships in the Bay of Bengal, from Moluccas and Batavia to Ceylon. The album was given to him at a rendezvous at sea, and the drawings came in very useful during the cruise of his ship *La Confiance*.

In the spiritual sphere of activities, the King of Denmark decided in the early 1700s to set up a Protestant mission in Tranquebar—the first in India—and he contacted German missionaries from Halle for that purpose. Bartholomeus Ziegenbalg, who arrived there in 1705, started remarkable work on the linguistics of the Dravidian languages; this subject later became the speciality of several other missionaries, like Benjamin Schulze. The Protestant mission at Tranquebar had a printing press long before the Catholic mission of Pondicherry, and the French Jesuits protested vehemently about their precarious spiritual situation to the King of France. Reverend Schwartz, a Prussian missionary who arrived there in 1750, was a distinguished linguist who enjoyed considerable standing among the Indian political elite of the region, such as Yusuf Khan at Madurai, the Raja of Tanjore and the Sultan of Mysore. Even the English at Madras used his services to negotiate peace with the local sovereigns.

In 1845 King Christian VIII sold Tranquebar and Serampore (the latter in Bengal had been in Danish hands since 1755) to the British East India Company for a sum of Rs 1,250,000. Among all the old European settlements in India, these two cities are especially known for their charm.

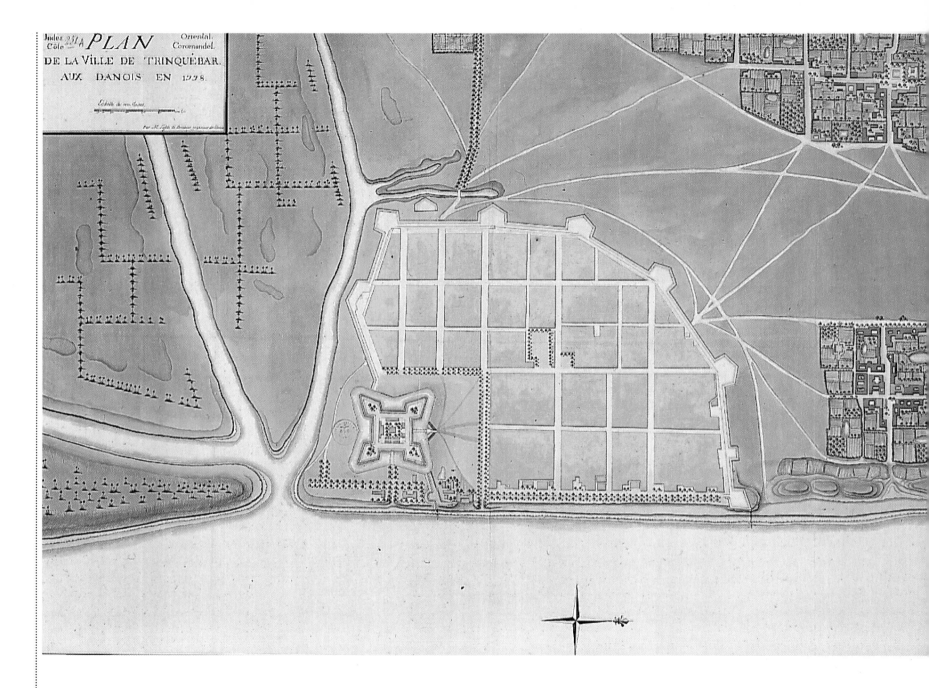

PLATE 18

De Stadt Negapatnam op de Kust van Cormandel

The City of Negapatnam on the Coast of Coromandel

Artist unknown
post-1656
Collection: CAOM, DFC B 239
725 mm x 515 mm
Drawing, fragment

Negapatnam is an ancient city on the mouth of the Cauvery river whose commercial relations with the Graeco–Roman world were attested from the first century BC. A Portuguese trading post existed there in the early seventeenth century. The Dutch occupied it in 1658 and, after the foundation of Pondicherry by the French in 1674, Negapatnam became its rival city.

Franco–Dutch rivalry in Europe had its origins in an earlier political connection when the Spanish dominated the Netherlands, as well as in religious developments after the Reformation. The expansion of Protestantism in Holland, the upsurge of Catholic fundamentalism in France after the Edict of Nantes which granted the status of religious minority to the Huguenot section of the French population in 1598, and the revocation of that Edict by Louis XIV in 1685, fuelled this enmity. The revocation was preceded and followed by extensive persecutions and a massive exodus of Huguenots who took refuge mainly in Switzerland, Germany (Prussia), Holland and England. Some of them also went to India: François Martin, the founder of Pondicherry, often refers in his *Mémoires* to the French Huguenots who entered the service of the 'Dutch United East India Company'.

The Dutch East India Company, or 'De Verenigde Oost-Indische Compagnie' (VOC) was a source of both fascination and worry for the French in India. The riches of the VOC, the volume and diversity of its trade, its naval and military power, and the extensive land area it covered attracted French attention. The peculiar system of indirect government that the Dutch were able to implement in some of the territories they controlled was carefully studied and discussed by Frenchmen such as François Martin, Robert Challe and Joseph Dupleix. Caron, the first Director of the French East India Company factory at Surat in 1668, was a former employee of

the VOC. Their hidden admiration was marred by the fact that a large number of French Huguenots held important civil and military positions in the VOC and they were particularly active—and offensive—during the Franco–Dutch wars in India at the end of the seventeenth century. A number of 'Dutch' soldiers and officers involved in besieging the French army of Blanquet de la Haye at San Thomé, in 1672–74, were actually French and they were often successful in inciting French soldiers to desert. François Martin's *Mémoires* contain significant references to the effect.

After Blanquet de la Haye surrendered at San Thomé in 1674, François Martin founded Pondicherry. A powerful citadel was then erected in Negapatnam, which became the headquarters of the VOC on the Coromandel coast in 1690. In 1693, the Dutch besieged and captured Pondicherry, and they officially purchased it from Ram Raja, the ruler of Ginji. Pondicherry was occupied by the VOC from 1693 to 1697, and the Dutch modernized it by building a new rampart with several bastions. When the Treaty of Ryswick obliged them to give back Pondicherry to the French, the latter had to pay 16,000 gold pagodas to the VOC as reimbursement of their expenses in purchasing and fortifying Pondicherry.

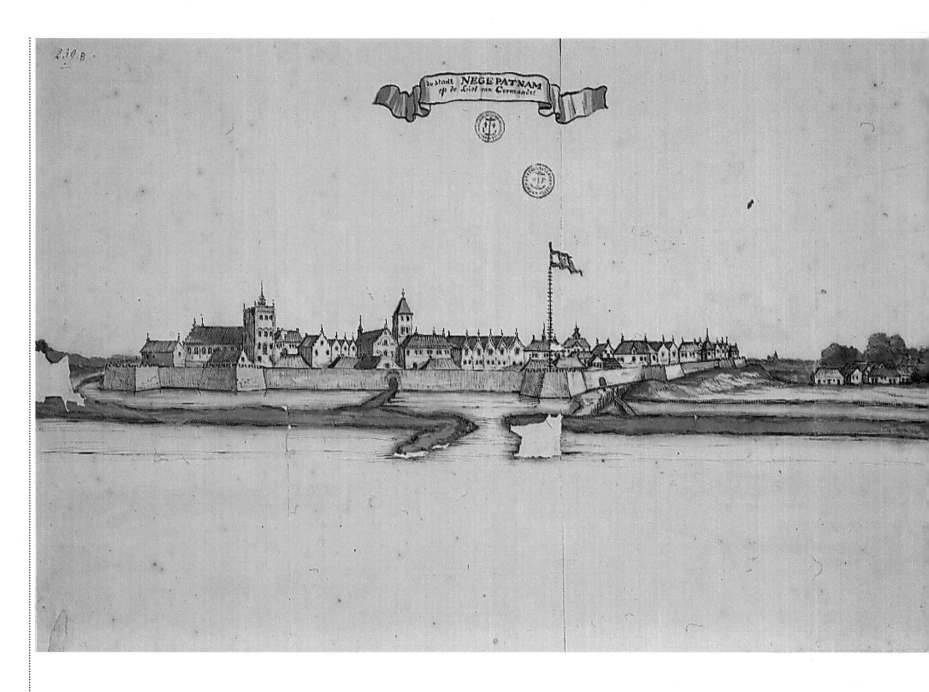

de stadt NEGEPATNAM
op de Cust van Cormandel

65

PLATE 19

Plan du Fort et Ville de Negapatnam, aux Hollandais

Plan of the Fort and City of Negapatnam, belonging to the Dutch

By Lafitte de Brassier
1778
Collection: CAOM, DFC 30 A 244
Scale [1/2700]
1020 mm x 600 mm

The Dutch East India Company (VOC) had two major settlements on the Coromandel coast: Paliacat (established in 1612, where they immediately built a fort) and Negapatnam. In Bengal, their main settlement was Chinsura, on the Hoogly river. These three trading posts and a cluster of sub-stations and *loges* on the coast and in the countryside, allowed them access to the commercial networks of the Mughal empire, the kingdom of Golconda and the local dynasties of Coromandel. Their vast commercial empire in the east in the seventeenth century gave them an eminent position as a trading power. S. Arasaratnam has calculated that Dutch annual investments in the Coromandel, which was about Rs 1.5 million in the 1660s, rose to Rs 2 million in the 1670s and culminated at Rs 2.8 million in 1687. The influx of bullion from America, Europe and Japan into India via the European East India Companies was an important factor that contributed to India's prosperity in the seventeenth century and, as Arasaratnam observes, 'it is not surprising that rulers of the Coromandel states always sought to entice European trade to their dominions with concessions'.

Competition between the European East India Companies was often exacerbated by conflicts in Europe; on more than one occasion these extended into India and the Indian Ocean. During the seventeenth century there were major conflicts between the French and the Dutch, with dire consequences for Pondicherry in India. The continual conflicts between France and England from 1740 onwards reached a peak in 1778 with the American War of Independence, in which the French played a decisive role by taking sides with the future 'Americans'. A similar French intervention in India was contemplated but it materialized only partly and did not yield positive results because the Preliminary Peace Treaty of Versailles, signed in January 1783, did not allow General de Bussy and Admiral de Suffren time to achieve their military objectives.

As mentioned in the introduction, Laffite de Brassier's missions on the eastern and western coasts of India were directly connected to preparations for a French intervention in India similar to the one contemplated for North America. The ports on both coasts had to be surveyed for landing troops and artillery, and harbouring fleet. During the American War of Independence, the French considered disembarking their expeditionary corps in the harbour at Negapatnam, which was much better than the anchorage at Pondicherry. Lafitte de Brassier spent ten days surveying it at a cost of Rs 15 (36 French livres), but in 1781 the English occupied Negapatnam as a preventive measure, forcing Suffren to land his men and material at Porto Novo. In 1785, the East India Company decided to keep Negapatnam as compensation for the cession of Trinquemale (Ceylon) by the French to the Dutch.

In 1820, as Hamilton wrote, 'two rows of old-fashioned Dutch houses, forming two sides of a square, having the ruins of a fort in the centre, with some straggling houses along the beach and the river, were all that remained of this once-flourishing settlement. Many of the houses had been pulled down to procure the glass sash windows which were sent to Madras and sold. The native portion of the town is more extensive, and appears to have been laid out originally with considerable regularity. A church of tolerable appearance has its place on the north side of the quadrangle, and the whole spot is luxuriant with trees.'

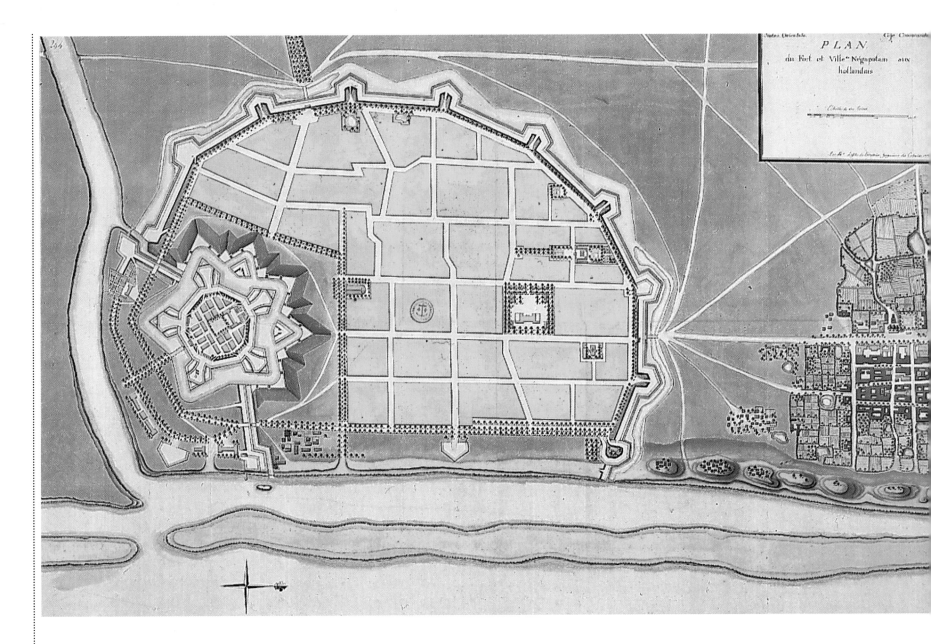

PLATE 20

Plan du Fort Saint-David et de la Ville de Goudelour [tels qu'ils étaient en 1754]

Plan of Fort Saint-David and of the City of Cuddalore [as they stood in 1754]

Artist unknown
1754
Collection: CAOM, DFC 31 A 276
Scale [1/11500]
815 mm x 560 mm
Caption: Coming from the Saint Priest collection

In 1689–90 the East India Company purchased Cuddalore from Sambhaji, son of Shivaji, and built a powerful fort (Fort Saint-David) there. After the French captured Madras in 1746, Cuddalore became the centre of British resistance to French influence in the Carnatic: Robert Clive escaped from Madras and started his impressive career at Cuddalore. Dupleix laid siege to Fort Saint-David several times, but without success. In 1748, a British army was constituted at Cuddalore which attacked Pondicherry but failed to take it. From 1749, the English officers directed their military operations in the Carnatic from Cuddalore.

In 1758, on the same evening that Count Lally landed in Pondicherry with his army, some of his best French regiments marched against Cuddalore. The town capitulated immediately. The citadel, partly defended by Swiss troops under Paul-Philippe Polier, resisted for twenty-seven days. After it capitulated on 2 June 1758, Lally, disregarding Polier's request, dismantled Fort Saint-David in retaliation for the destruction of Chandernagor by Watson and Clive in March–April 1757.

Twenty-five years later, the situation was reversed. Pondicherry was occupied by the English in 1778, and in 1781 General Duchemin and his troops—the first instalment of the army of Bussy—took Cuddalore. It was the French headquarters until 1785. Because the town was unhealthy, the French camp was established at Mangicoupam, a beautiful *aldée* in the countryside with lots of trees, fresh air and good water. Admiral Suffren, commanding the French squadron in the Indian Ocean, had a friendly meeting with Hyder Ali near Cuddalore in July 1782, and on 20 June 1783 he defeated the fleet of Admiral Hughes off Cuddalore. Bussy had just repulsed a major offensive by General Stuart against the French positions at Cuddalore on 13 June, and on the 24th he led an attack against the British lines with limited success. The two commanders were considering their next move towards Madras when a British frigate brought news of the signing of the Preliminary Peace Treaty of Versailles in January. Suffren and Bussy had no option but to stop their military operations in India, leaving Tipu Sultan to fight his war alone against the East India Company. The Treaty of Versailles of 1783 ratified the birth of the United States of America, but it left out the second proclaimed aim of the war for the French, the liberation of Indian territories captured by the East India Company that were to be returned to their legitimate rulers. According to the Treaty, Pondicherry was to be restored to the French and Cuddalore to the English. The exchange took place officially in 1785, after the complicated return of Trinquemale (Ceylon) to the Dutch.

The Dépôt des Fortifications des Colonies has many drawings on the work planned or executed in the fortifications and city of Cuddalore between 1781 and 1785. There are also several large maps showing the English and French positions during the 1783 military campaign, including three different plans of the battle of 13 June 1783.

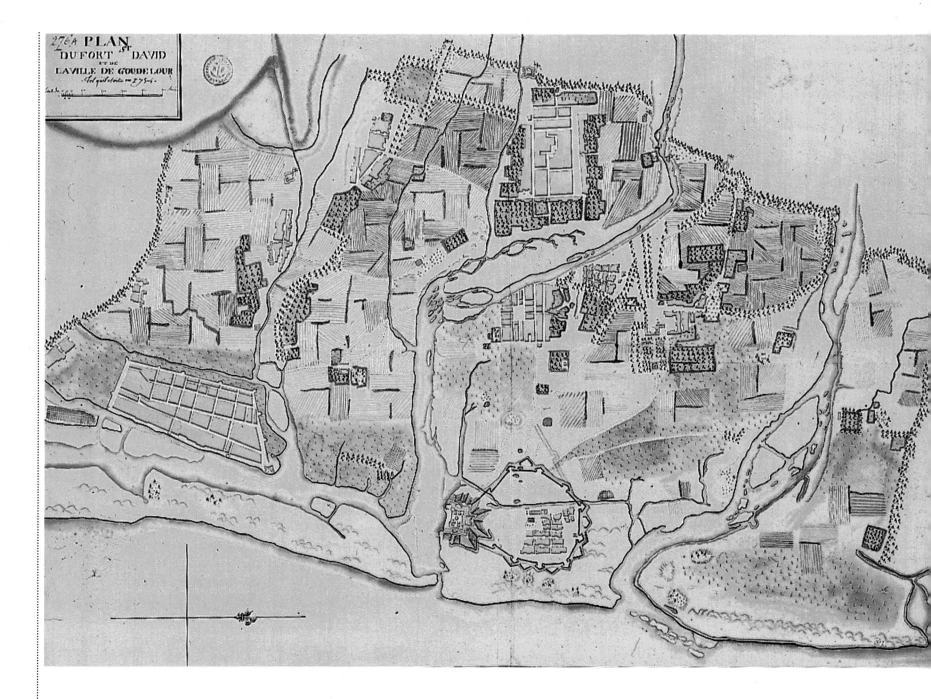

PLAN
DU FORT St DAVID
ET DE
LA VILLE DE GOUDELOUR
Tel qu'il étoit en 1756

69

PLATE 21

Plan des Ville et Forteresse de Gengy, dans le Carnate, Côte de Coromandel

Map of the City and Fort of Ginji, in the Carnatic, Coast of Coromandel

Artist unknown

No date

Collection: CAOM, DFC 31 C 268

370 mm x 280 mm

Ginji was considered to be one of the strongest fortresses in the Carnatic. Situated 35 miles north-west of Pondicherry, it was founded in *c.* AD 600 (Pallava period) and repaired in 1442 by the son of Vijaya Ranga Naik, Governor of Tanjore, for the sovereign of Vijayanagar. In 1638 it was captured by the Muslim ruler of Bijapur. The Marathas took it in 1677 and kept it till 1698, when it was captured for Aurangzeb by his general, Zulfikar Khan. The Mughals, however, found the site so unhealthy that they stationed their main army on the plains of Arcot, and in 1712 Sadat-Ullah Khan shifted the Mughal headquarters for the Carnatic there. François Martin's *Mémoires* give precise and detailed information on Ginji between the years 1674 and 1699: that the French entertained a brahmin as a permanent envoy at Ginji; that a French surgeon practised his skills there; and that Martin occasionally sent one of his assistants named Germain and the interpreter Cattel to Ginji.

Each of these occupations left its trace on the military architecture of the fortress. Three detached rocky mountains of very difficult ascent, connected by rows of fortifications, enclose an extensive triangle of land. This plain is divided by another fortified barrier into an outer and an inner lower fort. The ramparts, 20 feet high and 15 feet wide at some places, were 6 kilometres long with well-defended gates.

Ginji was stormed by Bussy on 11 September 1750. It remained under French occupation till 1761. During these years the defensive structure of the fortress was modified. A French bastion still exists from that period, along with sentry posts, the remains of ramparts with holes for musketry and a modernized defence system for the fort gates. Maps kept at Aix-en-Provence show the location of the French camp, the cantonments for European soldiers and sepoys, the residences of the commandant and chief surgeon. Ruins of the French period are to be found even today near the Pondicherry Gate.

The map also shows a new city east of the fortress, with smaller defences. There are numerous descriptions of Ginji in various travelogues. They mention the Kalyana Mahal and the seven-storeyed tower of the palace in the inner fort, the elephant pool, the impressive granaries, and the main temple with its remarkable *gopuram*. These well-known monuments exist to this day.

One interesting aspect of life at Ginji in the 1750s, that is largely overlooked today, was the reason why Anquetil Duperron travelled from Pondicherry to Ginji in 1756. According to the autobiographical introduction to his *Zend Avesta*, one could go to three places in South India to learn excellent Sanskrit: Chidambaram, Srirangam (near Trichinopoly) and Ginji. Being short of money, Anquetil chose Ginji, where he was given hospitality by Legris, the French Commandant of the fortress.

In 1780 Hyder Ali captured Ginji and the fortress remained in Mysorean hands till the fall of Tipu Sultan in 1799. In his *Mémoires* Piveron de Morlat describes Hyder Ali's and Tipu Sultan's activities in the region from 1780 till 1783. They contain particularly detailed information on Hyder Ali's disease, the surgery that was performed on him and his death in December 1782. Piveron stresses the measures taken by him and Count d'Hoffelize, Commander of the French army at Cuddalore, to cooperate with Hyder Ali's three *'gouverneurs'* of Mysore state and to ensure Tipu Sultan's smooth accession to the *gaddi* of Mysore. The elite units of that small army, the first instalment of Bussy's expedition, swiftly moved from Cuddalore to Ginji and encamped in battle array under its walls in order to prevent any uprising that challenged Tipu's legitimacy. As soon as he arrived at Ginji, Tipu Sultan expressed his thanks to Piveron and d'Hoffelize for having acted so judiciously in cooperation with his three governors.

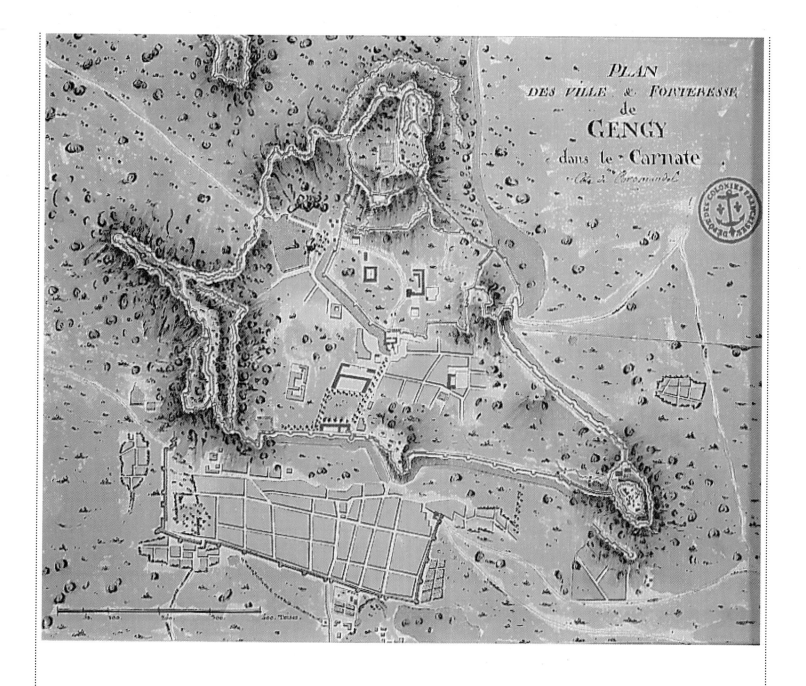

PLAN
DES VILLE & FORTERESSE
de
GENGY
dans le Carnate
Côte de Coromandel

71

PLATE 22

Vüe de la Montagne de Chandraine

View of the Chandraine Rock

Artist unknown
No date
Collection: CAOM, DFC 31 C 272
335 mm x 180 mm

Ginji was defended by six forts, with the most important one strategically placed at the top of a rock, 240 metres high. This was Rajagiri, with the most powerful defences, lying west of the city. The two other fortified rocks were Krishnagiri to the north-east and Shakkilidurgam to the south. One enters Krishnagiri, which is about 120 metres above the plain, through a series of fortified gates. At the top is a small palace with a granary and two temples, one dedicated to Sri Ranganatha and the other to Krishna; the latter gave the rock its name. Shakkilidurgam, or Chandra Dourgam, or Chandraine, as the French called it in the 1750s, is also 120 metres high.

Ginji was thought to be impregnable, yet it was repeatedly attacked and captured during the seventeenth and eighteenth centuries. François Martin's *Mémoires* give details about the capture of Ginji by Shivaji in 1677–78, and the initial details of the siege of Ginji by the Mughal army from 1690 to 1693. The latter is a first-class account of a major war between two Indian superpowers fighting for the supremacy of South India with minimal use of European artillery or of European systems of warfare in spite of the numerous Europeans already serving in the Mughal army. François Martin says that the sound of gunfire at Ginji was audible at Pondicherry, but the Mughal artillery could not penetrate the Maratha defences. There was no interference from the European powers who were watching the wars from their settlements at Negapatnam, Caveripatnam, Tranquebar, Pondicherry and Madras. Particularly interesting are Martin's observations about the effects of the war on the local population. The Mughal army's destruction and misuse of Hindu temples precipitated a migration *en masse* towards the European settlements and the last remaining Hindu kingdoms of the south. The descriptions of the disastrous conditions of the countryside, the financial stress faced by the belligerents, their way of waging war and their unending efforts to enrol on their side the tiny military contingents of the European settlements, are of great interest to historians, especially to specialists in military history. Also of interest is the question Martin asked himself: could the remaining Hindu powers, the Marathas and others, unite to resist Mughal expansion in the south? The story of relations of cooperation among the European settlements in order to protect themselves and gain information on what was going on in the region makes interesting reading. Last but not the least, we get an idea of the relations between the European settlements and local rulers at a time when nobody was sure who would be the next local authority: the Mughals or the Marathas. It is surprising to learn that such a tiny settlement as Pondicherry was capable of resisting the pressure mounted on it by both the Marathas and the Mughals to join their respective camps, and that, despite this it continued to receive, within its walls, Mughal and Maratha soldiers and officers wounded during the fights—who were treated by Jesuit physicians and surgeons in the Jesuit hospital.

Vüe de la Montagne de Chandraine.

272

PLATE 23

Vüe de la Montagne de Rasegadou

View of the Rajagiri Rock

Artist unknown
No date
Collection: CAOM, DFC 31 C 273
255 mm x 230 mm

Rajagiri, or the 'Mountain of the Raja', called Rasegadou by the French, was situated at a height of 240 metres above the plains and was the highest of the fortresses that defended Ginji. Martineau describes it as follows: 'The Rock is almost vertical, 245 metres above the plain. It was reached through a small gate that pierced the thickness of the rampart. After the gate, an extremely narrow path only 2 to 3 metres wide leads to the top. It leads to the east, then the north side of the rock, overlooking the precipice. At one place there was a wooden bridge 8 metres long above the precipice. At the top, there was one temple, one tank collecting the rains, one granary, and guns.' Anquetil Duperron visited it in 1756, and said that the bridge was in fact two huge beams attached with iron chains. The fort was manned by one sergeant, four French soldiers and, probably, an unspecified number of sepoys.

Reports dated 12 September 1750 show that the fortresses of Ginji had a lot of artillery. The great gun, still *in situ*, bears the number 7560. When Bussy took Rajagiri, the garrison took refuge in the other fortresses which kept up their resistance for another twenty-four hours. Eleven years later, the French were besieged in Ginji during the siege of Pondicherry by the English. The French cavalry, which was of no use in a besieged city, had left Pondicherry. Hussards commanded by Hugel and *'Volontaires des Grenadiers à Cheval'* in which René Madec was then serving, were in Ginji. Pondicherry capitulated on 14 January 1761, and the English army moved towards Ginji and Thiagar, the last two places held by the French. It was then decided to send the cavalry to Bangalore, to Hyder Ali, rather than to Madurai held by Yusuf Khan, and later Hugel helped Hyder Ali during his *coup d'état* at Mysore. Madec, who was sick and stayed back at Ginji, has left us this description of the fall of Ginji: 'The troops were divided between the three fortresses defending that place, and so distributed we resisted for three months against their [British] whole army. After that time we had to surrender, having no more food and no hope of relief.' Madec became a prisoner of war, and soon afterwards started his extraordinary career in North India.

At the top of the Rajagiri rock, besides the Sri Ranga temple, there was a *darbar* room, a treasury, barracks and magazines.

Vüe de la Montagne de Rasegadou.

PLATE 24

Plan général des Dépendances de Pondichéry, aux Indes Orientales, sur la Côte de Coromandel, avec les ouvrages proposés et faits en 1702 et 1703. Par Nyon, 9 février 1704

General plan of Pondicherry Territory in the East Indies, on the Coast of Coromandel, showing the works done and to be done in 1702 and 1703. By Nyon, 9 February 1704

By Nyon (de Nyon or Denyon)
1704
Collection: CAOM, DFC 32 A 7 bis
Scale [1/5700]
1690 mm x 625 mm

François Martin founded Pondicherry in 1674, and the first fort—Fort-Louis, called Fort Barlong—was constructed soon after. There is an early description of this written by Robert Challe when the squadron of Admiral du Quesne made a port of call at Pondicherry in 1690. The Dutch occupied the city in 1793. They did not make any notable modifications to the fort, but they did build the first rampart with bastions around the town and laid out the city on a regular grid. According to S.J. Stephen, the Dutch plan of 1794 shows that 'many streets of the weavers, washers, painters, silversmiths, coppersmiths, carpenters, hookers, trumpeters, shepherds, oil mongers, rope makers and barbers came into existence in the inner structure of the town. The grid was so designed as to keep each section of the inhabitants in their separate places.' All these workers were certainly there before 1694 since they could not have been new settlers in a city that had just suffered a severe siege. We specifically know of François Martin's earlier efforts to attract workers to the French settlement. Robert Challe mentions *'une infinité de gens'* (the large number of people) who took shelter at Pondicherry during the war between the Marathas and the Mughals in the Carnatic (the siege of Ginji by the Mughal army). He specifically mentions one of the refugees, a rich *bania*, who offered him and other officers of the fleet a sumptuous lunch at his residence, served in beautiful porcelain dishes. The civilian population of Pondicherry left the city before the siege and they probably returned after the capitulation of the French garrison. In 1698, when the Dutch gave back Pondicherry to the French, the XVII Herren, Directors of the VOC, ordered the weavers to evacuate Pondicherry and to move to other Dutch settlements on the Coromandel coast.

In 1699 François Martin reoccupied Pondicherry after paying the Dutch 16,000 gold pagodas, the same price they had paid Ram Raja, the Maratha ruler of Ginji, from whom they had purchased Pondicherry. But the Mughals had just

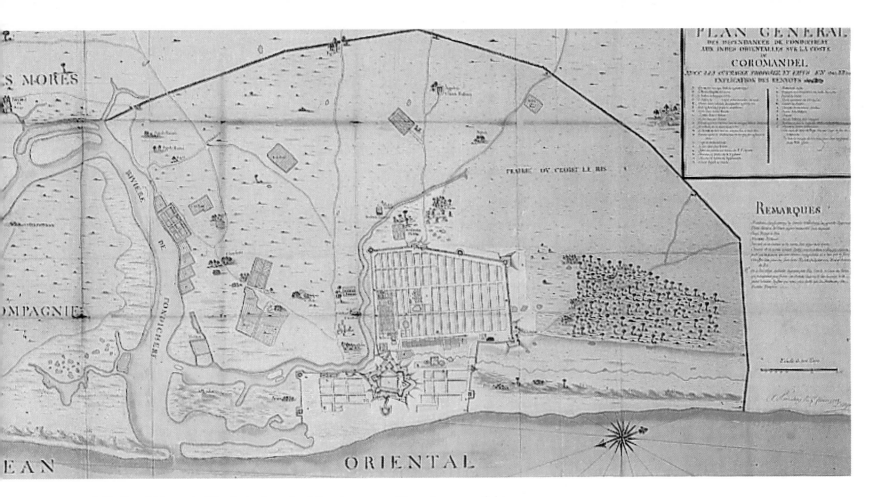

conquered Ginji and François Martin had to pay the Nawab of Carnatic Rs 10,000 and his subordinate officers Rs 2000 to get permission to build better fortifications. The permission was granted but there were neither plans nor engineers to start building the new fort of Pondicherry.

In 1701 Louis XIV created a 'Conseil Souverain' at Pondicherry, and in 1702 commandant de Boissieu and engineer de Nyon arrived there. They immediately set to work. In 1704 de Nyon levied this general map of Pondicherry, on which he showed the work done in 1702–03 and in the following years. Many features of this map already existed on Dutch maps and might even precede the Dutch occupation of the city; for example, the fountain of the Gentils (the Hindus), the garden of the Brahmins, the church of the Malabars for Indian Christians. One *blanchisserie* is shown *intra muros*, south of the Madras Gate. The fishermen's villages are situated to the north and south of Fort-Louis.

The '*Terres des Mores*' at the top of the map shows the land which had come under the authority of the Mughals only in the recent past.

77

PLATE 25

Plan particulier du Fort-Louis de Pondichéry, fait à la hauteur du rez-de-chaussée. Par Nyon, 15 février 1709

Particular plan of Fort-Louis at Pondicherry, ground-floor section. By Nyon, 15 February 1709

By Nyon
1709
Collection: CAOM, DFC 32 A 10
Scale [1/720]
555 mm x 820 mm

The Dutch were not sure they would keep Pondicherry after they captured it in 1793. They, therefore, only added a *fausse-braye* around Fort Barlong which had been built by François Martin a few years before. Pondicherry was returned to the French in 1699, and in 1702 engineer de Nyon started building the new Fort-Louis.

The plans he used were plans of the model fortress of Tournay, a French city that is now in Belgium, that was built by Vauban from 1668 onwards. As at the fortresses of Tournay, Arras and Lille (the fortress of Lille is excellently preserved till today), the basic design was a regular pentagon with two levels of fire. These fortresses, which were provided with barracks, magazines, powder magazines and arsenals, were designed to control the political life of the territory they protected and serve as bases for operating on the frontiers.

The five bastions of the new Fort-Louis were erected around Fort Barlong, which de Nyon preserved for reasons of security. Bastion Dauphin is on the west and bastion de Bourgogne, built in 1703, is on the south; bastion du Berry, built in 1704, is protected by a half-moon to the north; bastion de Bretagne, built in 1705, and bastion of the Compagnie [des Indes] built in 1706, are on the seaside. The ditches were filled with 6 feet of water. The escarp and counterscarp were in baked brick, and the counterscarp had a covered way *palissaded* with care. The *glacis* permitted the *courtines*, the bastions and the covered way, to fire indiscrimi-nately on an incoming enemy; grape fire was employed for the guns and fire-at-will for the muskets. The construction of the fort cost 275,000 French livres. An *'ouvrage à corne'* (also called *'à bonnet de prêtre'*) was built in front of the *Porte Marine* (Sea Gate) in order to cover the beach with fire and prevent the landing of troops. Lighter than the other fortification works, it cost only Rs 3880.

Inside the fort the old Saint-Louis church was used till the building of the new church was completed. Many other imposing buildings were erected, including barracks for the garrison, powder magazines where 130,000 pounds of powder were stored, and an arsenal where 20,000 cannon balls of every calibre of the 240 guns mounted on the ramparts and bastions were kept. The governor's palace was also situated inside the fort, and it remained there until 1732, at which time Governor General Dumas decided to renovate Pondicherry and build a new *Palais du Gouvernement*.

The plan of de Nyon bears close comparison with the model of the Fort of Tournai, kept in the Musée des Beaux-Arts, Lille, and the citadel of Lille, which is still intact.

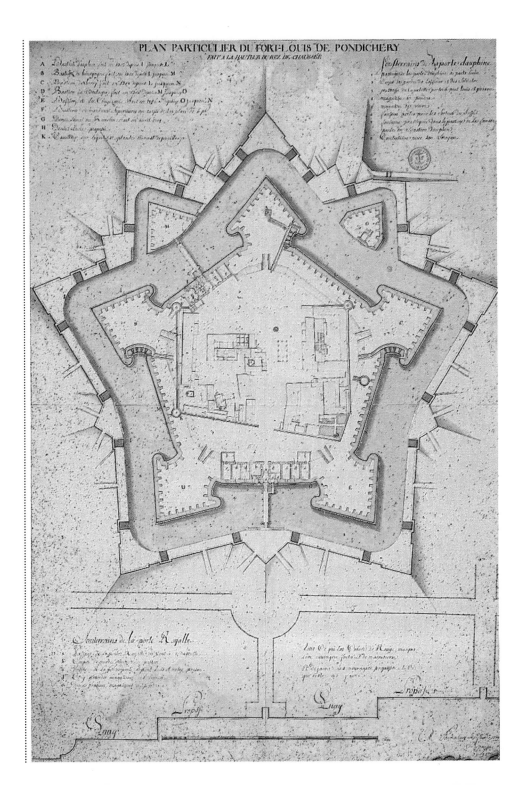

PLAN PARTICULIER DU FORT-LOUIS DE PONDICHÉRY
FAIT A LA HAUTEUR DU REZ-DE-CHAUSSÉE

PLATE 26

Plan et élévation du Gouvernement de Pondichéry

Front view of the Governor's Palace at Pondicherry

By Champie de Fontbrun
1755
Collection: CAOM, DFC 33 A 81
Scale [1/120]
935 mm x 595 mm

A governor's palace already existed in Fort Barlong, the earlier fort which was retained inside the new Fort-Louis erected by de Nyon between 1702 and 1706. But it did not match the image the French wanted to give of themselves in India and, besides, by the 1720s it was in a dilapidated condition. Since the reign of Louis XIV—if not before—urban and palatial architecture in France had been linked to the symbolic grandeur of the king and the nation. In 1722 the *Loge* at Chandernagor, erected inside Fort d'Orléans, had been built in monumental proportions that were not necessarily appropriate to the commercial importance of the settlement at that time. In 1738 Governor General Dumas started building the new Governor's Palace at Pondicherry on a similar grand scale.

The plans were prepared by architect Gerbault. Building activities commenced in 1738, were discontinued in 1741, taken up again in 1742, and finally completed in 1752. Dupleix and his wife Jeanne looked after the construction and were actively involved in the interior decoration. The front facade, which opened onto a courtyard planted with trees, was 'decorated with twenty-four Ionic columns "white as snow, whiter than alabaster". They were duplicated on the upper storey and supported three pediments. The central pediment was rectangular, the ones on the sides had curved profiles. A balustrade with small columns and ornamented vases ran along the roof of the terrace. Two wings flanked the central building. The decoration was sober and regular, with thirteen glass doors downstairs and thirteen entrances upstairs. Each of the pediments bore a different coat of arms: that of the Compagnie des Indes, the city of Pondicherry and Dupleix's own' (M. Labernardie, *Le vieux Pondichéry*).

The magnificent palace, a symbol of the French *aura* in India, was systematically plundered before being blown up in 1761. In 1762 John McLean made a drawing of the 'Ruins of the Citadel of Pondicherry', with himself sketching in the foreground. The sketch was dedicated to the Honourable George Pigot, Esq., President of the Council and Governor of Fort Saint-George (Madras). A melancholic engraving made by Le Gentil, an astronomer who fixed his telescope on the ruins of the Tour du Pavillon, is titled 'View of Part of the Ruins of Pondicherry in 1769'. The letters HH correspond to the 'Ruins of the Governor's Palace' in Le Gentil's engraving.

Echelle de 10 Toises

PLAN
ET
ELEVATION
DU
GOUVERNEMENT DE
PONDICHERY.

81

PLATE 27

Coupe et arrière-façade du Gouvernement de Pondichéry

Cross-section and back view of the Governor's Palace at Pondicherry

By Dumont
1755
Collection: CAOM, DFC 33 A 85
Scale [1/120]
940 mm x 580 mm

The interior of the Governor's Palace at Pondicherry was extremely elegant in plan and decoration. On the ground floor, protected from the sun by a large veranda, the central hall was cooled by a fountain playing in a marble basin. Five marble statues imported from Europe decorated it. On one side of the hall was the council chamber and on the other, a reception room and several offices for high-ranking Company servants.

An impressive staircase led to the first floor, called '*le bel étage*' ('the beautiful storey') because of its splendid reception halls. The main hall was used for official receptions of foreign dignitaries. It was also used as a ballroom and was richly decorated. Ananda Ranga Pillai gives a vivid description of its silvered panels, huge mirrors imported from Europe and long green velvet curtains with golden fringes. West of the main hall was another reception room, the '*salon de parade*', and a second council chamber. To the east, facing the sea, were the private apartments of the governor, consisting of his cabinet room, a retiring room and a '*salle d'armes*' (arms room). A gallery outside the suite provided a *promenade*, most welcome when the cool breeze came in from the sea. On the top of the palace was a big terrace with a balustrade decorated with ornate vases.

The interiors were tastefully decorated with precious fabric and carpets, crystal chandeliers, mirrors, console tables, elegant furniture imported from France as well as local furniture in the Indo–French style. Collections of rare and precious artefacts, gifts from the Royal Court—some of them from Madame de Pompadour to Madame Dupleix—beautiful arms and a wide range of *curiosités* were exhibited in showcases. Dupleix had a rich personal library with magnificent books and prints from Europe and an Oriental section with Indian (Persian) manuscripts and albums of paintings. It is possible that one of his albums of South Indian miniatures came into Lally's collection in 1758. We know that Dupleix loved to show his books and prints to his guests.

Ananda Ranga Pillai records that every visitor to the city wanted to see the magnificent residence and take a stroll in its gardens. An engraving by Huguier, done in Paris, offers us a glimpse of the famous *berceau* (arbor). The Dupleixs received guests in their sumptuous apartments and the lovely gardens. Dupleix received his Indian guests, princes and ambassadors, in the Indian way. He would wear his Mughal insignia and review a parade, accompanied by the traditional music of the land. For French evenings, there were great dinners—some of the menus have been preserved—and balls with European music played by the governor's personal orchestra. We are told that Dupleix sometimes joined in on his violin.

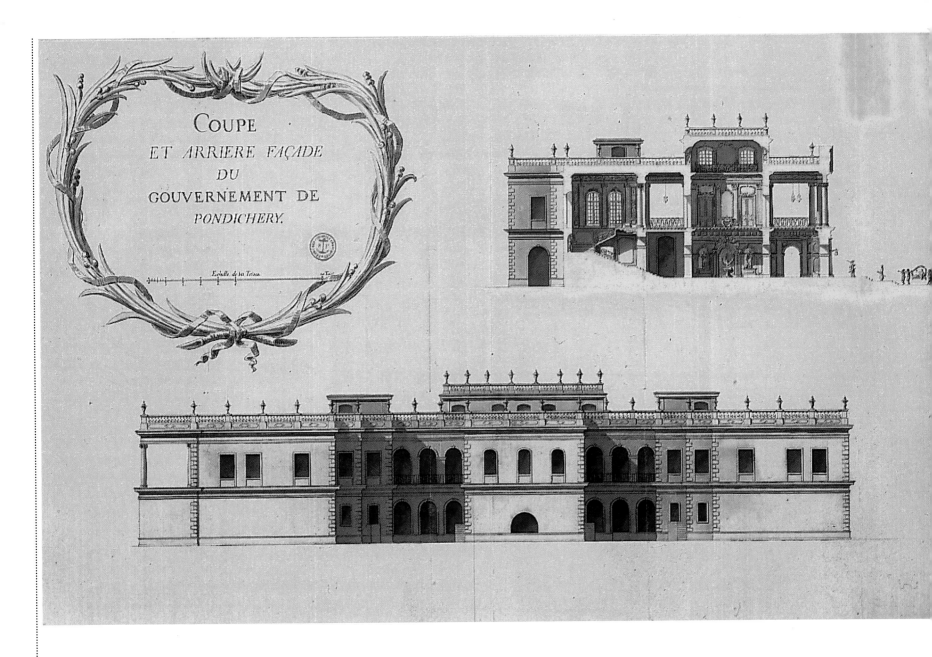

COUPE
ET ARRIERE FAÇADE
DU
GOUVERNEMENT DE
PONDICHERY.

Echelle de la Toise.

83

PLATE 28

Plan et profil de la Blanchisserie, Pondichéry. Par Bourcet, 28 février 1768

Plan and cross-section of the 'Blanchisserie', Pondicherry. By Bourcet, 28 February 1768

By Bourcet
1768
Collection: CAOM, DFC 33 B 217
Scale of plan [1/600]
Scale of profile of cross-section [1/275]
600 mm x 485 mm

One of the reasons for the French presence in Pondicherry was the manufacture of fine cloth, as both cotton and indigo grew easily in the countryside. Lime from the soil was used to whiten the cloth. Water from the swamps, and soon cleaner water from Ginji conducted to Pondicherry, permitted the washing of the manufactured products.

A small village of weavers may have already existed in Pondicherry at the time the Danes built the first house there. A weavers' village did exist north of White Town in the late 1690s. François Martin invited weavers and painters to the city in 1674 and they built forty houses that year on a plot of land he had given them. The weavers' sector of Pondicherry quickly developed into one of the picturesque spots of the town, with craftsmen working under trees planted along the avenues. Several Frenchmen—Captain Beaulieu, Pierre Poivre, Father Coeurdoux S.J., and later Le Goux de Flaix and many others—did their best to understand the secrets of manufacturing and fixing colours employed by Indian dyers. Beaulieu's manuscript, *Manière de fabriquer les toiles peintes dans l'Inde* ('How to manufacture painted cloth in India'), kept in the Museum d'Histoire Naturelle, Paris, is illustrated with original cloth samples.

The old *Blanchisserie*, or place for bleaching cloth, was a special building constructed a few hundred metres north of the residences inside the rampart, close to the Gate of Madras. Dupleix built a new *Blanchisserie* that was so long and so wide that it had to be constructed outside the fortifications, on the road to Madras. From the Gate of Madras a broad avenue specially laid and planted with trees led to the Place de l'Etoile, from where the Madras road started along the eastern facade of that great building. The plans, cross-section and views of the new *Blanchisserie* that are kept in the CAOM show the special rooms and the equipment used to prepare the cloth.

This impressive, though purely functional, building is a clear reminder of the aim of the Compagnie des Indes Orientales: trade. Philippe Haudrère, in 1993, gave the following estimate of the bullion brought by the French into India. 'During the eighteenth century only, approximately 350 million livres tournois, making 3 to 4 thousand tons in gold and silver (3 to 4 million kilograms), equivalent to one fourth of the metallic stock in France on the eve of the Revolution. Before 1730, the French sent per year around 4 million livres, equivalent to 20 tons of bullion. From 1730 to 1740, 8 million livres per annum (40 tons of bullion). Between 1750–55, annual trade reached 10 million livres (50 tons of precious metal). After 1765, the average imports reached 6 million livres (30 tons).' Besides trade, war sometimes brought in riches. Bussy and some of his officers in the Deccan amassed huge fortunes which they partly transferred to France in pouches of diamonds. In 1749, Pondicherry received approximately one million rupees after Auteuil and Bussy's victory at Ambur over Anwar ud-Din, Nawab of the Carnatic, but such booty did not come every year. War finally absorbed the benefits of trade, leading to the recall of Dupleix by the shareholders of the Compagnie in 1754. Gold and silver for diamonds, cloth and saltpetre: such was the general pattern of exchange, private and official, between France and India during the eighteenth century. The gold and silver remained in India, thus increasing the wealth of that country.

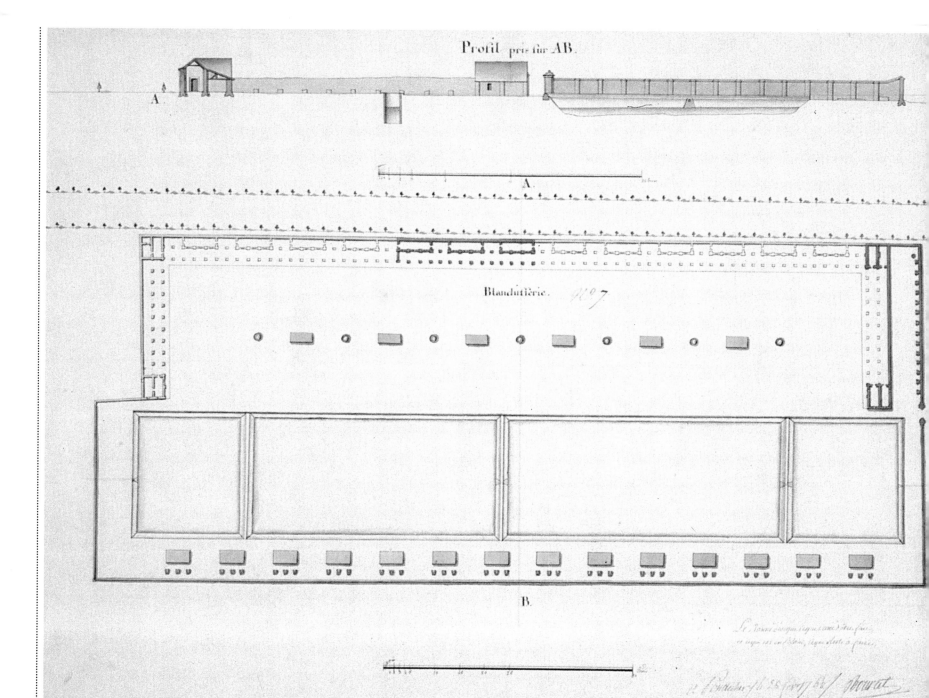

Profil pris sur AB.

A

A

Blanchisserie.   N°7

B.

PLATE 29

Elévation intérieure et extérieure de la Porte Villenour, Pondichéry

Internal and external elevation of the Gate of Villenour, Pondicherry

Artist unknown
1788
Scale [1/70] and [1/60]
Collection: CAOM, DFC 34 B 616
670 mm x 530 mm

Villenour was a small city west of Pondicherry. Famous for its temple with two monumental entrance towers, it was a place of sightseeing for the people of Pondicherry. Challe visited it in 1690, and the astronomer Le Gentil, in 1760. Le Gentil reproduced the main tower in a plate of his *Voyage dans les mers de l'Inde*, published in 1780.

Work on the new ramparts of Pondicherry was started by Governor Lenoir in 1724. The walls were 5 metres high, with three main gates flanked by protecting towers with *corps de garde*. The bastions were 7 metres high. Deydier, of Mahé fame, was then *ingénieur du roi* in the city and he personally worked on the northern ramparts and the *corps de garde*. The Gate of Villenour, and the Gates of Madras and Valdaour, were the most strongly fortified gates of the city of Pondicherry. A plan of 1741 shows that the Villenour Gate as well as the towers were protected by a bastion overlooking the ditch.

The ramparts of Pondicherry were blown up in 1761–63. Law de Lauriston, Governor in 1765, was accused of procrastination in rebuilding them. At this time, Bourcet and Desclaisons were vying with each other at Versailles to get permission to conduct the work. Pondicherry was again occupied from 1778 to 1783. From 1783 to 1785, Bussy was allowed to reside there but he did not have any authority in the city because of his refusal to turn Trinquemale over to the British East India Company. That was settled in 1785, a few weeks after Bussy's demise. Souillac, the new Governor General, ordered a survey of the fortifications and started rebuilding the ramparts. Today nothing remains of the fortifications of Pondicherry.

Élévation extérieure de la Porte Villenour

Élévation de la Porte du passage de la Demi-lune Villenour

Élévation Intérieure de la Porte Villenour

PLATE 30

Nouvelle méthode de fortifier les places. Bourcet Cadet, 1 février 1776

New methods of fortification. Bourcet Junior, 1 February 1776

By Bourcet Junior
1776
Collection: CAOM, DFC 34 C 514
Scale [1/900]
465 mm x 250 mm
Mémoire 101 bis (513): 'Lettre d'envoi d'un profil des fortifications de Pondichéry, by Bourcet, 1 February 1776', 1 folio

In 1765 Pondicherry was restored to the French; they had thirteen years, till September 1778, to rebuild the fortifications of the city. In 1766 Bourcet Senior, the engineer working on the restoration of Pondicherry, submitted a plan for reconstruction of the ramparts. The plan was sent to Versailles for approval of the costs of reconstruction. In his proposal Bourcet Senior suggested that the former line of the ramparts be reconstructed starting from the north, which was the most vulnerable spot. His main idea was to make the fortifications *rasantes* (a little raised, above the level of the surrounding country), similar to the new Fort William of Calcutta. He also suggested that a high and wide wall of earth covered with *revêtements* be made to absorb artillery shots. The rampart was to have bastions at regular intervals on the north, west and south. His plans, which would take three years to implement and cost 3 million French livres, were approved by the Council of Pondicherry in 1769, and work commenced immediately.

Bourcet had almost finished constructing the ramparts with the four bastions in the north and one in the south, when he was recalled to France in 1770. He was replaced by engineer Desclaisons, who was a protégé of the Duke of Praslin. Desclaisons preferred the old technique of building with brick and lime, which he thought to be more solid, but which was certainly more difficult and more expensive. He started working on the south side of the fortifications, and in 1771 put forth the suggestion to Versailles that Bourcet's earthen rampart of the north be destroyed. He was recalled and in 1774, Bourcet was sent back to Pondicherry. M. Labernadie observed that 'from 1769 to 1775 the work was interrupted six times, and in six years there were only twenty-five months of work'. It was Bourcet who criticized Fourcroy de Ramecourt's idea to build a new citadel on Coconut Tree Island, south of Pondicherry, on the grounds that the island was from time to time entirely submerged in water. Bourcet had his residence at Virapatnam in Pondicherry, and thus knew that area well.

Bourcet had to resume work basing himself on Desclaisons' modifications of his plan; by 1775 he had completed three bastions on the west side, one bastion on the south side, and installed a battery to protect the eastern walls. Unfortunately, Bourcet died at the end of 1776, leaving the instructions and plans for completing the work to his younger brother, Bourcet Junior, who forwarded them to Bellecombe, the new Governor General. Bourcet's old opponents demanded that the work be stopped and new plans for rebuilding the ramparts were sent to Versailles. Bourcet Junior also submitted a *mémoire* to Versailles that defended the work already done, and the text of this *mémoire* provides an important description of what had been achieved up to then. Practically nothing more was done to the fortifications until July 1778, when the English army started moving towards Pondicherry. At that time Bellecombe asked engineer Dulac to fill up, as best as he could, the gaps in the ramparts. S.P. Sen has justly observed that 'the fall of Pondicherry after a short siege may be attributed largely to the dilatory policy of the Paris authorities and their indecision and change of plan, although the French had sufficient time after 1765 to put their principal settlement in India in a proper state of defence'.

The '*nouvelle méthode de fortifier les places*', as it is illustrated on the plate, is similar to the remains of the fort built by de Boigne for Sindhia at Aligarh in the late 1780s.

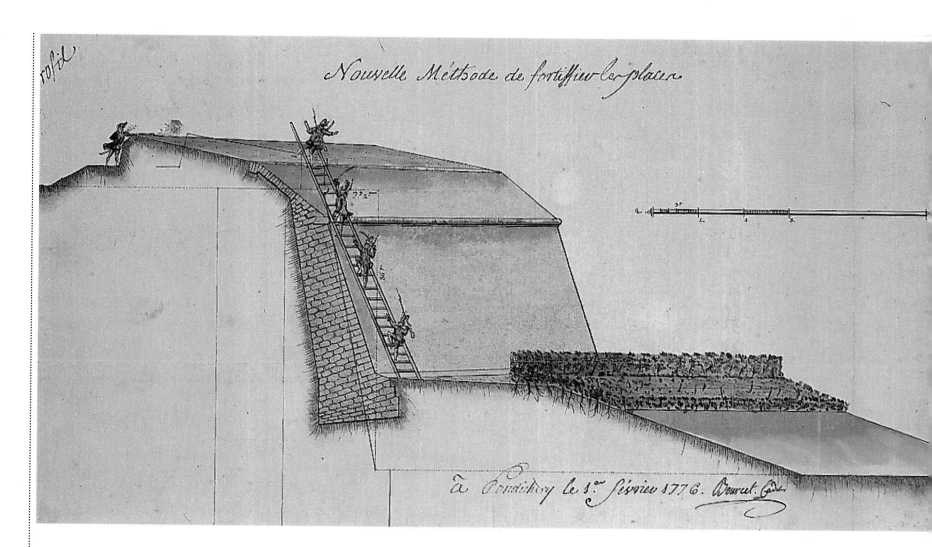

Nouvelle Méthode de fortifier les places

à Pondichéry le 1er février 1776. Bourcet Cadet

89

PLATE 31

Pondichéry, 1771. Fortifications. Projet relatif aux moyens de mettre le front du sud en état de défense

Pondicherry, 1771. Fortifications. Project for protecting the southern sector

Artist unknown
1771
Collection: CAOM, DFC 33 C 366 bis
Scale [1/70]
420 mm x 270 mm

French military architecture from 1670 to 1720 was largely inspired by Vauban's twenty-six fortresses on the country's northern borders. During the eighteenth century 'not many fortifications were built, but there was a proliferation of the theoretical systems as a result of scientific and erudite reflections' (Philippe Prost). In 1761, Marquis de Montalembert advertised the publication of the first volume of his *La fortification perpendiculaire...*, but the Minister of War requested him not to publish it because of the damage incurred by France after the publication of Vauban's *Traité de l'attaque des places* in 1737. Montalembert complied. The book was later published in ten volumes over several years, from 1776 to 1795. In 1761, the same year that Montalembert had advertised his book, the English captured Ile d'Aix on the Atlantic coast of France and Montalembert was sent to fortify Ile d'Oléron, opposite Ile d'Aix. The fortifications he constructed there were excellent. Nevertheless, he was greatly criticized by his main opponent Fourcroy de Ramecourt, who authored his own *Mémoires des fortifications*.

Fort-Louis and the ramparts of Pondicherry had been razed to the ground by the English in 1761. The two engineers alternately in charge of the reconstruction, Bourcet and Desclaisons, had totally different concepts of the fortifications, and their acute rivalry paralysed the progression of the work. In 1771 Fourcroy de Ramecourt proposed a project for restructuring the defences of Pondicherry: he offered to build a new, huge and impressive citadel in the Ile des Cocotiers (Coconut Tree Island, on the Aryancoupan river, south of Pondicherry). However, Paris and Versailles were informed that under certain conditions of tide and winds, Coconut Tree Island went under water.

In 1773, Montalembert was requested to prepare plans for fortifying Pondicherry and Port Louis in Ile de France — Mauritius. He proposed a series of four detached forts from south to west on the main roads leading to Pondicherry, and a long fortress *en aile de pigeon* (in a pigeon-wing shape) covering Pondicherry on the north, towards Madras. A commission was formed in January 1776, whose members went to Montalembert's residence to see the model plans of the two projects. But Fourcroy de Ramecourt, who was appointed *Directeur Général du Génie*, put a stop to the project.

When, on 8 August 1778, the English army besieged Pondicherry, it was an open city, since Bourcet and Desclaisons had been fighting with each other over the fortifications. Bellecombe hurriedly raised earth embankments wherever the ramparts had not been built, but he had to surrender on 17 October 1778.

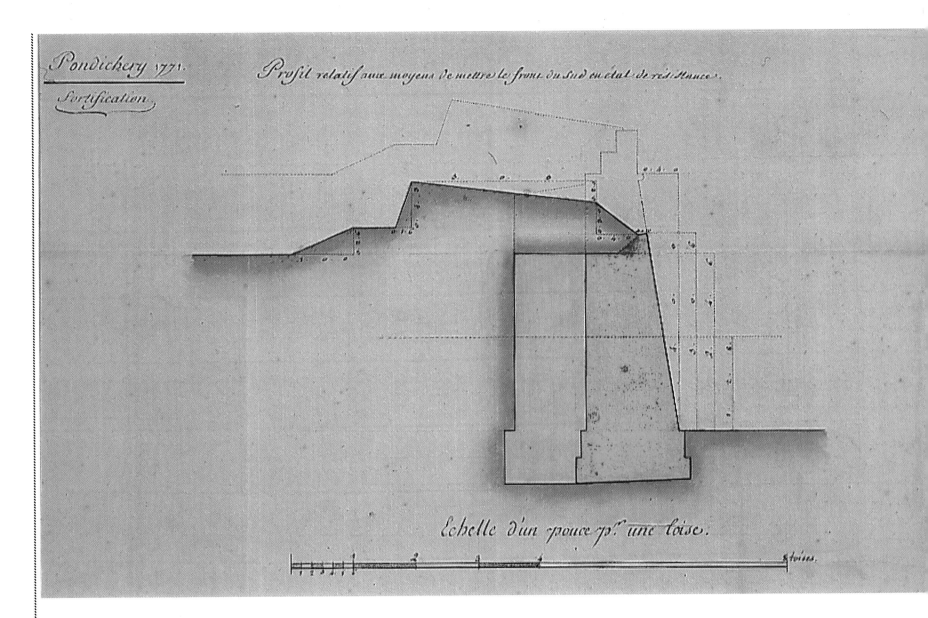

Pondichery 1771.

Fortification.

Profil relatif aux moyens de mettre le front du Sud en état de résistance.

Echelle d'un pouce p.r une toise.

Stoises.

91

PLATE 32

Plans des ouvrages exécutés à Pondichéry pendant les années 1785 et 1786

Plans of the buildings constructed at Pondicherry during the years 1785 and 1786

By La Lustière
c. 1786
Collection: CAOM, DFC 34 A 596
Scale [1/1200]
1355 mm x 455 mm
Mémoire 102 (595): 'Lettre de La Lustière au ministre de la Marine, rendant compte de l'emploi d'une somme de 100,000 livres employée au relèvement du front ouest des fortifications de Pondichéry, 1er juillet 1786', 1 folio

On the surmise that peace established between England and France by the Treaty of Versailles would be shortlived, Bussy began to prepare for the next round of political and military hostilities in 1783. It took him two years of remarkable negotiations to give back Trinquemale in Ceylon, the best harbour in the Indian Ocean, to the Dutch. Meanwhile, the English were pressing him to give it back to them 'provisionally'. In 1785, Trinquemale was returned by the French to the English, who had to transfer it to the Dutch immediately. This great feat of diplomacy was to be the last, almost unnoticed, success of Bussy in his brilliant career in India. Bussy did not live to see it, for he died in Pondicherry on 7 January 1785, a few weeks before the restitution. That is why he could not build new fortifications for Pondicherry.

Pondicherry remained a permanent threat to British power in India. The independence of the United States, which was recognized only in 1783, haunted English diplomacy in London and in Calcutta until 1815. This was a secret fear, not one that was revealed in public discourse or displayed in front of the numerous French officers heading various *partis* and serving some of the most powerful independent states in the Indian peninsula.

From 1793 onwards Pondicherry was occupied again, but this time with a difference, since some of the occupying forces were French-speaking Swiss officers and soldiers belonging to the Régiment de Meuron, in the service of the English.

In 1802, contrary to the stipulations of the Treaty of Amiens, Calcutta gained time in giving back Pondicherry to the French. Wellesley was right in doing so: General Decaen was bringing with him 1200 young French officers and soldiers who were to train regiments of sepoys, and he hoped to work in coordination with Sindhia and Perron, who then commanded some 45,000 regulars belonging to the 'French' brigades of Hindustan. Decaen was unable to land at Pondicherry and returned to Ile de France. In 1810 the Royal Navy landed an army in Ile de France which proceeded to capture it, as also Ile Bourbon (La Réunion).

Facing page, below:
Plan of the City of Pondicherry dedicated to the memory of Monsieur Dupleix (detail of the western section)

Collection: IGN, Paris

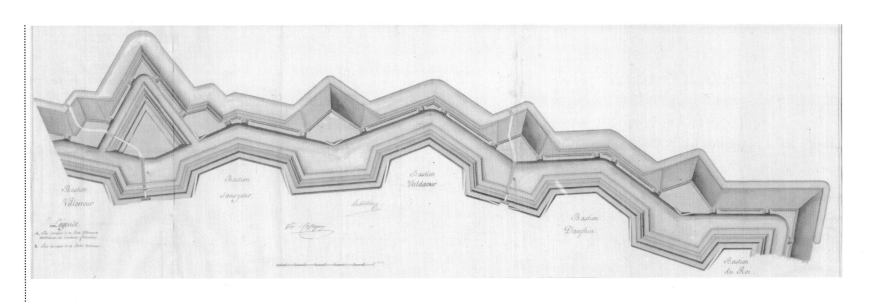

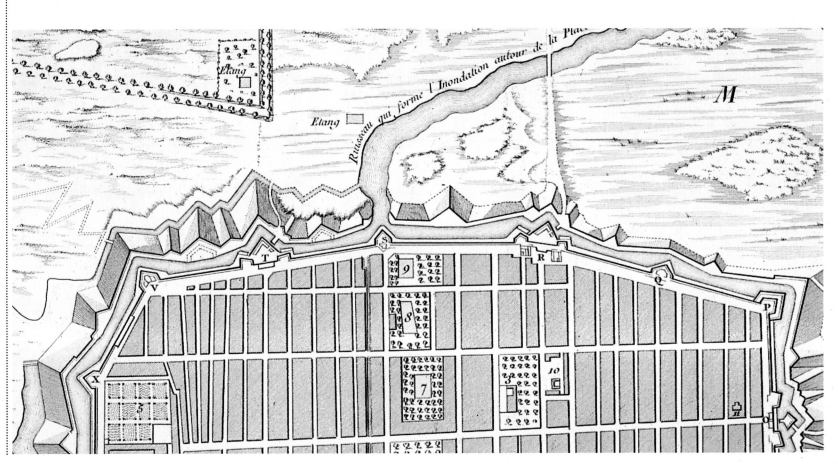

PLATE 33

Plans des ouvrages exécutés pendant les années 1785 et 1786 en conséquence des ordres de M. le Vicomte de Souillac

Plans of the buildings constructed in 1785 and 1786 by orders of M. the Viscount de Souillac

Artist unknown

c. 1786

Collection: CAOM, DFC 34 A 597

Scale of the plans [1/1800]

Scale of the profiles [1/181]

1380 mm x 465 mm

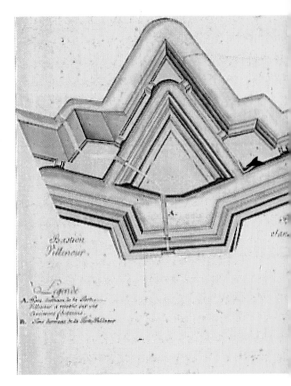

Viscount de Souillac, an officer in the French navy, was appointed Governor of Ile de France (Mauritius today) in 1779. An energetic and active man, he was informed of the French government's decision to follow a policy in India similar to their policy of intervention in North America, and he actively prepared for Suffren and Bussy's expeditions to India. He persuaded Piveron de Morlat, who was on his way back from Pondicherry to France, to join Hyder Ali's court in Mysore as French Agent. In early 1782, when the first part of Bussy's army arrived with Suffren's squadron in Ile de France, he sent all the 2800 men to the Coromandel coast. Bussy, expected from France, was supposed to follow immediately with the main army and another squadron. De Souillac constantly backed Admiral Suffren against his senior captains who did not comply with his orders and refused to fight the Royal Navy during his campaigns in the Indian Ocean. When Bussy actually arrived and took overall command of the expedition, de Souillac helped him efficiently, although he personally did not approve of Bussy's policy towards the Indian states.

In 1785 de Souillac was appointed in place of Bussy at Pondicherry, and he arrived there in May that year. However, Versailles—and Paris—had been discussing the question of whether Pondicherry would remain the headquarters of the French settlements in the east, or whether that seat should be transferred to Mahé on the Malabar coast or Trinquemale in Ceylon or elsewhere in the Indian Ocean. In May 1785, it was decided to base it at Port Louis, Ile de France, and in October 1785 de Souillac left India to sail back to the Mascarenas Islands.

During the five months he spent on the Coromandel coast, de Souillac started repairing the defensive system of Pondicherry: an earthen rampart was quickly constructed, new barracks were completed in 1786, and a powder magazine in 1787. De Souillac also tried to explain to the Indian rulers, especially Tipu Sultan, what the French had achieved in North America—the French contributions to the victory of Yorktown, the Treaty of Versailles and the birth of

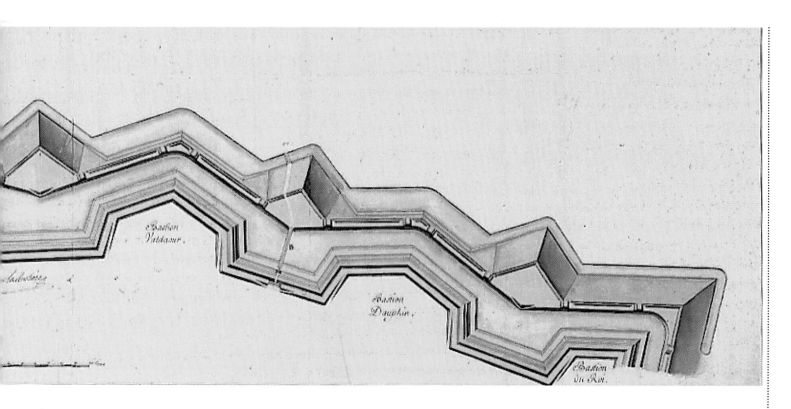

the United States. It was perhaps the brevity of his stay in India and the transfer of authority from Pondicherry to Port Louis that kept these Indian rulers from understanding why the same French policy which had succeeded in America, had failed in the subcontinent.

When de Souillac left India in 1785, Tipu Sultan officially expressed the high regard he had for a man who neither lied to him nor betrayed him; this was a clear criticism of Bussy's policy towards Mysore. When he retired to France, de Souillac kept his archives with him. He was one of the high-ranking officials who was accused of keeping maps and plans which should have been returned to the concerned offices of the government.

PLATE 34

Fort d'Arcate, au Nabab

Fort of Arcot, belonging to the Nawab

By Valory
[1777–78]
Collection: CAOM, DFC 30 B 253
Scale not given
570 mm x 470 mm

Aurangzeb conquered the kingdom of Golconda in 1687, and one of his generals captured the Fort of Ginji, west of Pondicherry, in 1698. In 1712, when the Mughal imperial structure started disintegrating and new 'regional' powers emerged, Sadat-Ullah took the title of Nawab of the Carnatic, making Arcate (Arcot), 66 miles west of Madras, his capital. Madras and Pondicherry became dependent on this new political centre.

French bullion brought to India by the Company's ships was carried from Pondicherry to Arcot and struck there as 'Arcati rupees' against payment of 6 per cent of the value to the Nawab.

In 1736 Emperor Muhammad Shah gave permission to the French to strike coins in Pondicherry. However, relations remained extremely cordial between Arcot and the French settlement, so cordial indeed that when the Nawab of Arcot was killed by the Marathas in May 1740, his wives and children sought protection from Governor Dumas. He received them in Pondicherry and gave them *intra muros* a beautiful residence with gardens. Raghoji Bhonsle, the Maratha general, ordered Dumas to deliver some of these women to him but Dumas refused. Later Raghoji Bhonsle congratulated Dumas for his courageous stand. The new Nawab of Arcot was himself most grateful to Dumas and conferred upon him a *saropa*, the title of Nawab with a *mansabdari* of 4500 horses. Dumas left India just after the Maratha invasion of the Carnatic, and Dupleix, the new Governor General, inherited Dumas' honorific title and position.

The plan reproduced here shows the elaborate defence system of the Fort of Arcot, a formidable citadel with huge bastions and one half-moon protecting the most exposed side of the rampart. Arcot was an extremely embattled place during the Anglo–French rivalry in the Carnatic, and Robert Clive's courageous defence of the fort against Chanda Sahib and his French auxiliaries in 1750–51 is justly

famous. Nawab Muhammad Ali, whom the British installed on the *gaddi* of Arcot against the French, was a *de facto* prisoner of the East India Company at Madras until his death in 1795. The Arcot diamonds, which included the five brilliant ones (three of them are now mounted on the Westminster tiara in London) given to Queen Charlotte by the Nawab in 1777, are an interesting testimony of that intricate story. Lord Pigot, Governor of Madras during the Seven Year War, possessed 'a diamond of very considerable value', the 'Pigot diamond', which also had some political connections with Arcot.

Hyder Ali occupied the Fort of Arcot after his *blitzkrieg* in the Carnatic in 1780, but Tipu Sultan evacuated it in 1783, when he had to return to the western coast in order to recapture Bednore and Mangalore after their occupation by English troops. In 1801 the Carnatic passed into the hands of the East India Company. The principal defences of the Fort of Arcot were blown up by the British in 1808–10, and practically nothing remains today of the palaces, residences and gardens which occupied the empty spaces inside the ramparts. What remains inside the walls of the Arcot Fort are some Muslim tombs, a few mosques and a tank in front of what was apparently a former palace, or a great *baradari*. The town was also enclosed by walls. In the 1820s it still contained 'the former palace of the Arcot Nawabs, of which the principal gateway is still entire, but all the rest is a heap of ruins' (Hamilton).

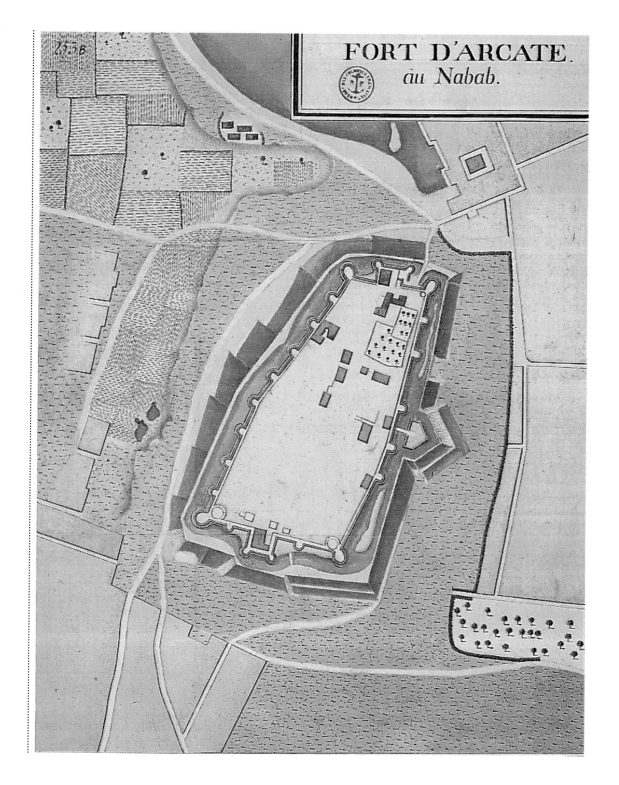

FORT D'ARCATE.
au Nabab.

97

PLATE 35

Plan de Madras-patan

Plan of the Town of Madras

Artist unknown
post-1688
Collection: CAOM, DFC 31 A 287
950 mm x 560 mm
Caption on the back: 'Plan of
Madraspatnam. Second Voyage to Siam,
1687 and 1688'
Notice. Legend. Cut irregularly

Founded in 1639 by the East India Company and protected by Fort Saint-George after 1644, the town of Madras was, till 1653, under the authority of the British settlement of Bantam (Java), founded in 1602. It was then raised to the status of a presidency. During the Franco–Dutch conflicts of the seventeenth century, and particularly during the siege of San Thomé in 1672–74, the attitude of the British government at Madras remained neutral, with intermittent though concealed sympathy for the French. Dutch expansion, which by that time had targeted both Ceylon and South India, was considered a common threat by the French and English East India Companies. Some Frenchmen had settled in Madras and served the East India Company, and the French, including Catholic missionaries, were welcome there from where they could board a ship to Europe or to the Far East.

S. Arasaratnam asserts that by the 1650s, one-third of the British trade in India was centred around Madras. After 1678 the investment was around a million rupees per year, and it rose to Rs 2.5 million in 1684. Since the English exported practically nothing to India at that time, the difference paid in bullion considerably enriched the Indian economy. A declaration by Manucci to Daud Khan, Governor of the Carnatic, in 1702, confirms this largesse: 'From what entered and left Madras alone [Emperor Aurangzeb] collected more than one hundred thousand *patacas*. Many subjects of the king of this realm and others knew very well that every year there were earned in Madras 5 lakhs of gold pagodas (equal to one million of *patacas*, more or less) and over 10 lakhs of silver rupees (which amounts to 500 thousand *patacas*). The whole of this money remained in the country, and in exchange for all this the English carried off to Europe no more than some cotton cloth.'

In the 1690s Madras had a mixed population of Hindus (whose chief merchant Beri Timmana, who died in 1669, built the 'magnificent pagoda or Hindu church called Virena's pagoda' {Abbé Carré}), Muslims, Armenians, Topasses, English, Portuguese and a small minority of other European settlers—French, Italian, Dutch, Danish and German. There were petty merchants, skilled workers, weavers and cloth printers, as well as rich bankers and traders. Madras had practically no defensive structures except Fort Saint-George until 1675, when a low wall was erected on the seaside mounted with about fifty 6- and 8-pounder guns. The first rampart of the city, including the Black Town, was built later, in 1690–92, by Governor Yale, who founded Yale University in North America in 1701.

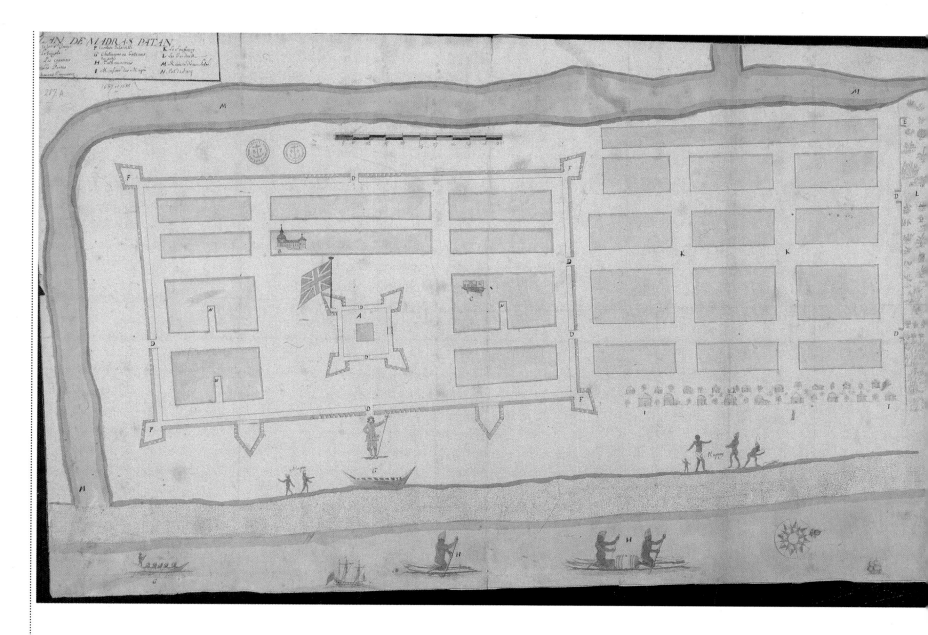

99

PLATE 36

Plan du Fort Saint-George de Madras et la Ville Noir [*sic*] avec ses environs en 1780

Plan of Fort Saint-George of Madras and the Black Town with its surroundings in 1780

By Lafitte de Brassier
1780
Collection: CAOM, DFC 31 A 303
Scale [1/3700]
1300 mm x 1020 mm
Mémoire 97 (300): 'Detail of Fort Saint-George of Madras according to its position', 3 folio

From the beginning of the eighteenth century onwards, relations between Madras and the Mughal authorities at Arcot were tense. English relations with the French in India changed too, due to modifications in the political balance in Europe. Dupleix, Governor General of the French establishments in India since 1741, hoped to maintain peace between the British and French East India Companies even if war was declared between France and England in Europe. Morse, Governor of Madras, seemed to fall in line with this thinking, but Walpole's policy in England and Morse's statement that he had no authority over the Royal Navy in the Indian Ocean took the French by surprise. The years 1744 and 1745 were disastrous for the Compagnie des Indes Orientales as their trade was totally disrupted by the British Royal Navy.

In 1746, a powerful fleet under the command of La Bourdonnais captured Madras. The city was ransomed, and some of its public monuments were dismantled and reused for the beautification of Pondicherry. In 1749 Madras was given back to the British East India Company in exchange for Louisbourg in North America. During the Seven Year War (1757–63), in 1758, Count Lally laid siege to Madras unsuccessfully; he himself was besieged in Pondicherry, which capitulated in 1761. Both Lally and Pigot were products of European intolerance and religious fanaticism: Lally, the French Commander-in-Chief in India, happened to be an Irish (Catholic) refugee commanding an Irish brigade in the service of France, whereas his opponent Pigot, Governor of Madras, was a French Huguenot whose family had taken refuge in England. The English took architectural ornaments from Pondicherry to Madras and then razed Pondicherry to the ground, just as they had done to Chandernagor in 1757.

When the War of Independence in America was officially declared in 1778, Pondicherry was occupied by the Madras army. Lafitte de Brassier became a prisoner of war. Before his deportation to Europe he spent thirty-six days in Madras, where he 'purchased the plan of Fort Saint-George of Madras and the Black Town from an Indian draftsman working for the English'. The map cost him Rs 70 (168 French livres). By that time the East India Company was, for all practical purposes, master of the Carnatic. It dominated South India. The Treaty of Versailles, which recognized the birth and independence of the United States, did not give Bussy and Suffren any time to complete their military campaigns in India. Indian powers like Tipu Sultan in Mysore, the Nizam in Hyderabad, the Sindhias and the Marathas, and later Maharaja Ranjit Singh of Punjab, were left alone to build up 'modern' armies with the help of French officers, to fight the increasing power of the East India Company. Madras, like Bombay and Calcutta, became another capital of British India.

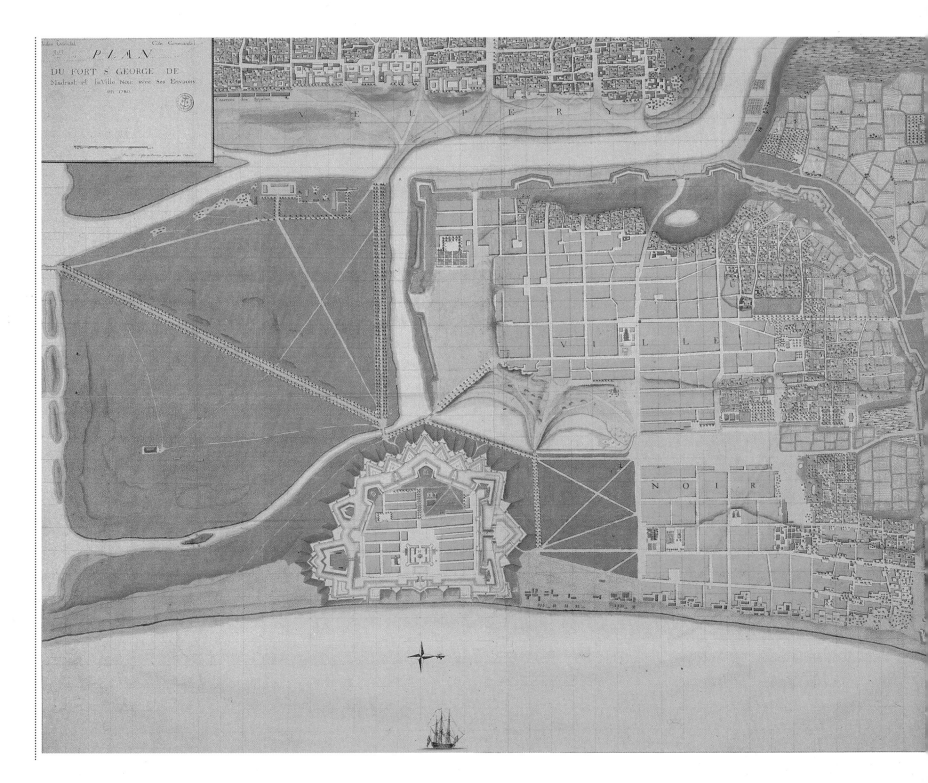

PLAN
DU FORT S.ᵗ GEORGE DE
Madras et la Ville Noire avec Ses Environs
en 1780.

PLATE 37

Plan du Fort de Schinglepet, aux Anglais

Plan of the Fort of Chinglepet, belonging to the English

By Lafitte de Brassier
1780
Collection: CAOM, DFC 31 A 320
Scale [1/3100]
Tracing from CAOM, DFC 31 A 319
980 mm x 670 mm

Chinglepet or 'Singhalla Pette', the City of the Lotus, was a fort built under the Vijayanagar dynasty. It was taken by the army of Golconda in 1646, and by Aurangzeb in 1687. The palace and other buildings inside the fort are Mughal. The French occupied Chinglepet in 1750, Clive occupied it in 1751, and Muhammad Ali, the 'English' Nawab, graciously offered it to the East India Company. The cession was confirmed by Emperor Shah Alam II in 1765.

Situated 35 miles south-south-west of Madras, Chinglepet occupied a strategic position between Madras and Pondicherry. The fort was a massive construction. It enclosed various buildings and was topped by the battlements of an inner fort, considerably elevated, within which the palace stood. An artificial lake provided the water used for the moat and for cultivation (Hamilton, 1820).

In 1752, the Swiss regiment raised by the East India Company disembarked at Madras and some of its units were posted at Chinglepet to keep an eye on the French. In 1755 Paul-Philippe Polier, with a body of Swiss officers and troops, took command of Chinglepet and restored and extended the fortifications. The next year he received a strong reinforcement of sepoys, and in December 1756 he was ordered to select or build and man a line of bastions and small forts covering Madras. He was then appointed Commander of Fort Saint-David at Cuddalore where, after a courageous defence, he capitulated to Lally on 2 June 1758.

Lally's next move was towards Madras, defended by Lawrence, which he besieged in December 1758. In spite of strong advice from his staff Lally did not take Chinglepet, which was immediately reinforced by British troops under Preston and by sepoys under Yusuf Khan. Preston and Yusuf Khan led a most effective guerrilla war against the French, cutting Lally's army arrears and defeating Lally himself at Trimliwash. Then, under the united command of Caillaud, who came with reinforcements from Trichinopoly, Preston and Yusuf Khan decisively defeated the French force at Porto Novo. This defeat forced Lally to raise the siege on Madras on 16 February 1759. The friendship that developed between Preston and Yusuf Khan at Chinglepet during this period had a tragic end at Madurai in 1763, when Preston was mortally wounded while leading a storming party of British troops against the city defended by Yusuf Khan, who by that time had become for the English 'the Rebel Commandant'.

Lafitte de Brassier spent six days executing the plan of Chinglepet, which cost him Rs 10 (24 French livres). The plan clearly shows the residence and gardens of the Mughal governor of the fort. Most of the buildings, the royal suite, armoury and granaries survived until a railway line was built through the middle of the site.

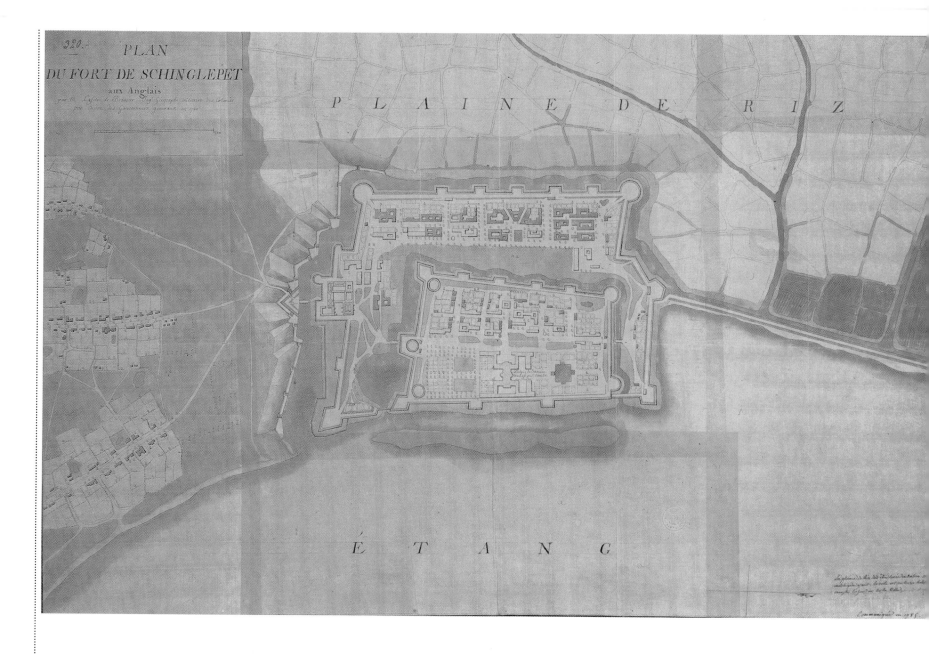

PLAN
DU FORT DE SCHINGLEPET
aux Anglais
par M. Lafitte de Brassier Ing. Géographe interieur des Colonies
pris sous les Gouverneur Général en 1760

PLAINE DE RIZ

ÉTANG

PLATE **38**

Carte Marine Gergelin Orixa Bengal

Maritime Map
Gergelin, Orissa, Bengal

Artist unknown
c. 1756
Collection: Private
Courtesy: Colonel Chinailh
480 mm x 645 mm

This map covers the area north of the Bay of Bengal from the sandbanks of Sabor on the east, to the Yanaon river and Pointe de Godvarin on the west.

It shows the perils of entering the mouth of the Ganga, after Pointe des Palmiers, by way of the two main rivers, the Piply and the Balassore. The sandbanks were especially dangerous for big European vessels carrying heavy cargo and they had access to only a few passages. The figures on the seashore give the depth of the water in *'brasses'* (1 *brasse* = 1.60 metres). Navigators for ships on the rivers usually lived at Balassore and guided the ships from there up to Calcutta (English), Bankibazar (Ostende Company: Austro–Hungarian Empire), Serampore (Danish), Chandernagor (French), Chinsura (Dutch), and Hoogly–Bandel (Portuguese). Very light ships could sail up to Kasimbazar and Murshidabad.

The drawing of the landscape as seen from the sea is carefully done, with creeks and rivers identified. *Gopurams*, or pyramidal gateways, of temples on the seaside which were excellent landmarks for the sailors are also indicated. These are, from east to west, the Pagode Blanche (White Pagoda), Pagode Noire (Black Pagoda), Pagode de Jagrenat (Temple of Jagannath), Karapas (Pagoda of Montercote) and, in the south-west corner, the Pagoda of Corango. Masuli-patnam (English) and the mouth of the river flowing next to Yanaon (a French settlement) are also visible on the map.

Particular drawings show these pagodas, as well as the sea coast, as seen from the sea at a particular angle and from a particular distance; these were used by the navy officers to estimate their position. In 1757 Anquetil Duperron described the Temple of Jagannath as follows: 'That place is famous for the three great pagodas, the top of which can be seen from eight or ten lieues (32 to 40 kilometres) by the ships sailing towards Bengal.'

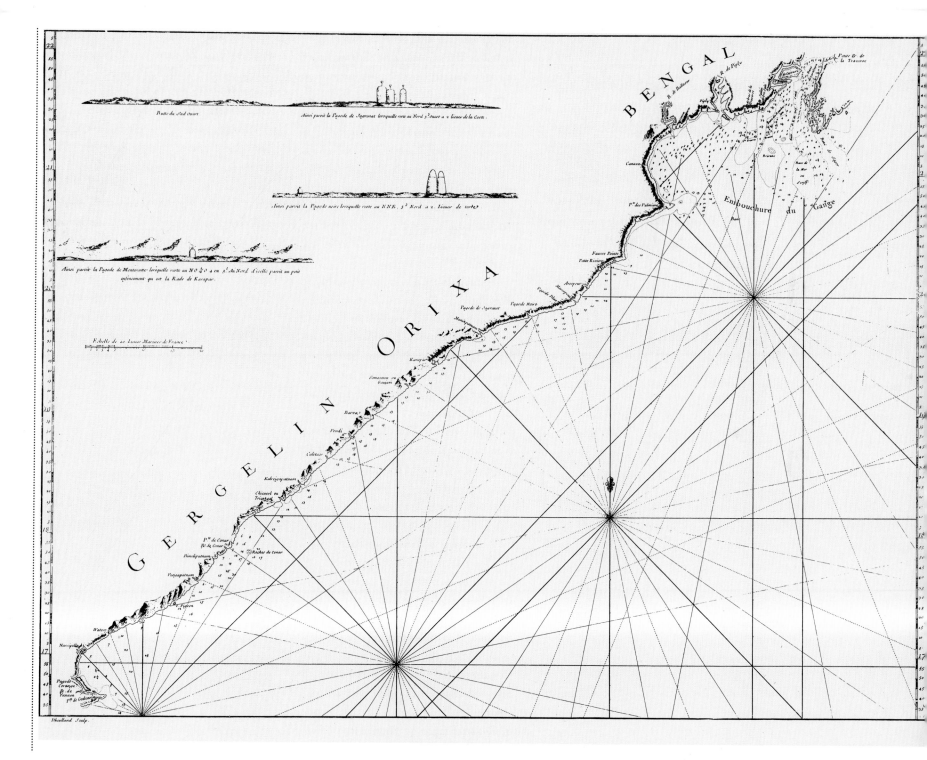

Butte du Sud Ouest

Ainsi paroit la Pagode de Sgarenat lorsquelle reste au Nord 5.º Ouest a 2 Lieuce de la Coste.

Ainsi paroit la Pagode noire lorsquelle reste au NNE. 5.º Nord a 2 Lieuce de terre.

Ainsi paroit la Pagode de Montecotte lorsquelle reste au N.O 4º 3 ou 5.º Au Nord d'icelle paroit un petit enfoncement qui est la Rade de Karapar.

Echelle de 20 Lieuce Marince de France

BENGAL

R. de Piple
R. de Ballasce
Piple
Canaca
P.te des Palmiers
Embouchure du Gange
Banc
Banc de la Mer ou Recciff
Ponte &.c de la Traverce

Fausce Pointe
Petite Riviere
Acopour
Manicpatnam
Pagode Blanc
Pagode Noir
Pagode de Sgarenat
Karapar
Somaroun ou Gaujam
Barva
Pendi
Caletace
Kalvejanpatnam
Chicacol ou Trincapel
I.ste de Conar
R. de Conar
Rache de Conar
Pimelcpatnam
Vepoupatnam
Vepion
Watou
Navopilon
Pagode Coranga
R.e de Yanaon
I.ste de Godowori

GERGELIN ORIXA

Dheulland Sculp.

PLATE 39

Plan de Visagapatnam, établissement de la Compagnie Angloise dans l'Inde, pris par les Français le 26 juin 1757

Plan of Vizagapatnam, settlement of the English East India Company in India, taken by the French on 26 June 1757

Artist unknown
c. 1757–58
Collection: CAOM, DFC 31 A 348
Scale [1/2900]
1190 mm x 570 mm
Caption: Coming from the Saint Priest collection

Masulipatnam, with its two long bridges connecting the harbour to the town and the town to the interior, was the great port of the kingdom of Golconda. It later became one of the sea outlets for the Nizam of Hyderabad. The English, the Dutch and the French had factories and trading facilities with a significant turnover at Masulipatnam, but administrative and fiscal pressure from the Mughal administration obliged the French to move to Yanaon in 1731, and the English to Vizagapatnam.

Vizagapatnam has an excellent harbour dominated by Dolphin's Nose, a 1500-foot-high peak that protects ships from the monsoon winds. The English established a factory there in 1683 but in 1689, when war broke out between Aurangzeb and the East India Company, Vizagapatnam like Masulipatnam was occupied by the Mughal forces. When allowed to return to their former settlements, the English preferred to develop Vizagapatnam as their main base in this area. In 1726 the total expenses of the East India Company was 628 pagodas at Masulipatnam and 6000 pagodas at Vizagapatnam, which enjoyed practically all the profits of English trade on that coast. The large Indiamen ships preferred to use Vizagapatnam as their port of call, and as a result other settlements declined.

In 1753 the area known as the Four Circars was given by the Nizam of Hyderabad to Bussy as *jagir* for his troops. After the capture and destruction of Chandernagor by Watson and Clive in March 1757, Bussy marched to Vizagapatnam, which capitulated within a few hours on 27 June 1757. Jean-Baptiste Gentil participated in that expedition and in his *Mémoires sur l'Indoustan* he has a vivid description of Vizagapatnam including details of its capitulation, the minutiae of the occupation and the extremely courteous correspondence between Marguerite Clive, wife of Robert Clive who was on board the *Malborough* off Vizagapatnam, and Bussy, concerning five sailors of that ship whom Bussy immediately set free. The town was recaptured by the English in 1758, and in 1759 Lally ordered Bussy to retreat to the Carnatic with his troops, thus sealing the fate of French political influence in India.

PLAN
DE.
VISAGAPATAN ETABLISSEMENT DE
LA COMPAGNIE. ANGLOISE, DANS L'INDE pris
PAR LES FRANÇOISE 26 juin 1757.

PLATE 40

Plan du Fort Wilhams et de la Ville Noir [*sic*] et ses environs en 1779, aux Anglais, Calcutta

Plan of Fort William and the Black Town and its surroundings in 1779, belonging to the English, Calcutta

By Lafitte de Brassier
1779
Collection: CAOM, DFC 31 A 361
Scale [1/350]
995 mm x 665 mm

Construction of the first Fort William at Calcutta began in 1694. It was taken and destroyed in 1756 by Siraj ud-Daula, the Nawab of Bengal. Clive and Watson recaptured the city in January 1757 and work on the new Fort William was started in May 1757. From 1762 to 1764, the engineer in charge of the construction was Antoine-Louis Polier, a young Swiss officer, nephew of Paul-Philippe Polier. A few years later the younger Polier was at Faizabad and Lucknow with Colonel Gentil and Claude Martin.

Fort William was one of the most powerful European fortresses in India. Shuja ud-Daula, Nawab of Awadh, and his French allies wanted to acquire the plans of the fort. Modave in his *Mémoires* narrates the story of how Chevalier, Governor of Chandernagor, got hold of a duplicate of the plans at Polier's residence in Calcutta through one of Polier's draftsmen, which recorded the first stage of the construction. Modave also gives a description of the fort as it was just after completion, in 1773–74. He notes its strength, the complexity of the defences and the profile *extrêmement rasant* of the ramparts and the bastions.

The plan reproduced here was made by Lafitte de Brassier in 1779. It took forty days to make, at a cost of Rs 60 (144 French livres). The plan can be read against a technical description of the fort published in 1828:

'Fort William is of an octagon form, five of the sides being regular, while the forms of the other three next to the river are according to circumstances. As no approach by land is to be apprehended on this side, the river coming up to the *glacis*, it was merely necessary to guard against any attack by water by providing a great superiority of fire, which purpose has been attained by giving the citadel towards the water the form of a large salient angle, the faces of which *enfilade* the course of the river. From these faces the guns continue to bear upon the objects until they approach very near to the city, when they would receive the fire of the batteries parallel to the river. This part is likewise defended by adjoining bastions and a counterscarp that covers them.'

'The five regular sides are towards the land; the bastions here have all very salient *orillons*, behind which are retired circular flanks, extremely spacious, and an inverse double flank at the height of the *berme*. This double flank would be an excellent defence and would retard the passage of the ditch, as from its form it cannot be *enfilated*. The *orillon* preserves it from the effects of ricochet shot, and it is not to be seen from any parallel. The *berme* opposite to the curtain serves as a road to it, and contributes to the defence of the ditch like a *fausse-braye*.'

'The ditch is dry with a *cunette* in the middle, which receives the water of the ditch by means of two sluices that are commanded by the fort. The counterscarp and covered ways are excellent; every curtain is covered by a large half-moon without flanks, bonnet or *redoubt*; but the faces of each mount has thirteen pieces of heavy artillery, thus giving to the defence

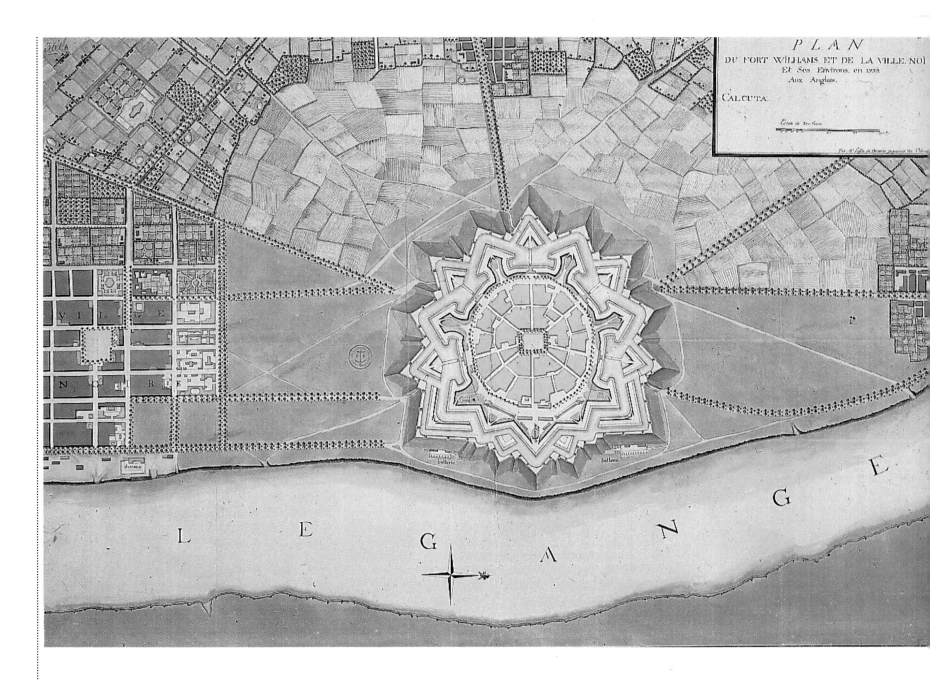

PLAN
DU FORT WILLIAMS ET DE LA VILLE. NO?
Et Ses Environs, en 1728.
Aux Anglais.

CALCUTA.

109

of these *ravelins* a fire of twenty-six guns. The demi-bastions, which terminate the five regular fronts on each side, are covered by a counterguard, of which the faces, like the half-moons, are pierced with thirteen *embrasures*. These counterguards are connected with two *redoubts* constructed in the place of arms of the adjacent re-entering angles; the whole is faced and *palissaded* with care, kept in admirable condition. The advanced works are executed on an extensive scale, and the angles of the half-moons, being extremely acute, project a great way so as to be in view of each of the others beyond the flanked angle of the polygon and capable of taking the trenches in the rear at an early period of the approach.'

Fort William mounted 619 guns and could accommodate 15,000 men. The large *maidan* around was carefully kept clear of any building; earlier, in 1756, some English residences too close to the ramparts of the first Fort William, had prevented the firing of grape shots from the guns of the fort.

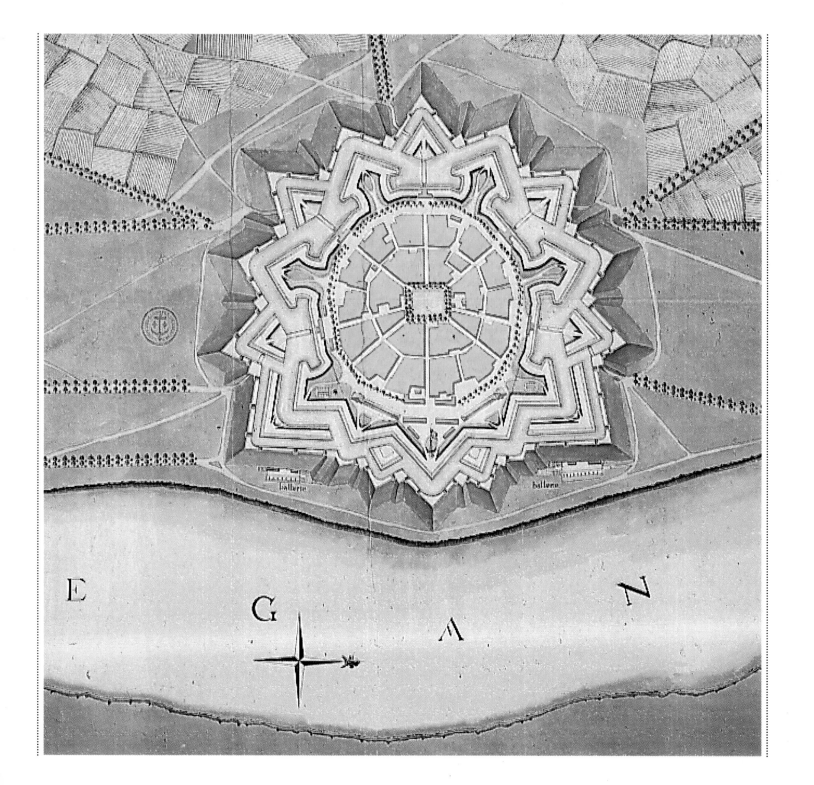

ballerie

balleru

E G A N

111

PLATE 41

Plan de Chandernagor et de ses dépendence [*sic*] appartenant à la Compagnie de France dans le Royaume de Bengal, MDCCXXII

Plan of Chandernagor and its territory, belonging to the French Company in the Kingdom of Bengal, 1722

By Riftierre
1722
Collection: CAOM, DFC 35 A 1
Scale [1/4000]
980 mm x 660 mm

The first French presence in Bengal is known to date back to 1674, when Captain Duplessis got permission from the Mughal authorities there to settle at Chandernagor and conduct commercial operations freely in the province. Chandernagor was occupied in 1690 but officially founded only on 23 January 1693, through a *farman* of Ibrahim Khan, the Mughal Governor of Bengal. It authorized the French to settle there and open *loges* wherever necessary in the kingdoms of Bengal and Orissa and the province of Bihar. That concession was confirmed by the Delhi court in 1698.

Several *loges* were opened in the following years, from Patna to Chittagong. Political disturbances caused by the rebellion of Sobha Singh in 1696–97 obliged the French to seek permission to protect themselves. Permission was granted to build fortifications, and Fort d'Orléans was constructed.

In 1731 Joseph Dupleix was appointed Director of Chandernagor. During his tenure from 1731 to 1741 French trade developed enormously in Bengal. Associated with Armenian and Indian bankers and traders—Indranarayan Chowdhury played a very important role in this field—Dupleix extended commercial relations between Chandernagor and Europe, China and the Middle East. His personal connections with the directors of the other European settlements (Dutch, Danish, English, Portuguese and Austrian with their Ostende Company) allowed him to turn Chandernagor into a kind of European trading centre in Bengal. The city grew rapidly. Because of its prosperity and export facilities, many families of highly skilled workers settled there. The main *loge* of Fort d'Orléans was constructed within its walls. Goods were stored and verified there before being loaded onto ships that anchored in the middle of the Hoogly, protected by the fort. In 1741 Dupleix was appointed Governor General and he left Chandernagor for Pondicherry.

After he left, although trade declined slightly, it has been argued rather convincingly that it was the vigour of the trade that Chandernagor enjoyed that was the real reason behind the English attack on the city in 1757. The French, when requested by Siraj ud-Daula to join him in his attack on Calcutta in June 1756, refused to oblige. But in March 1757 Clive and Watson, who had just destroyed Izdruk in February of the preceding year and recaptured Calcutta in January 1757, decided to destroy Chandernagor. Admiral Watson, with three men-of-war, sailed up the Hoogly and started bombarding the city; it was then stormed by Clive on 23 March 1757. The *loge* and Fort d'Orléans were razed to the ground. Private residences were burnt down. Nothing but desolation reigned in Chandernagor.

The city did not ever recover from that attack although some economic activities survived till India's independence. The charm of the place had always appealed to the Indian and European populations of Calcutta. In the early 1900s, many Bengali freedom fighters—Sarala Devi Ghosal, Aurobindo Ghosh and Birendra Nath Banerji—sought protection at Chandernagor. In 1947 the desire of Bengali freedom fighters to liberate Chandernagor was realized; it became a '*ville libre*' (free city). A referendum was held in 1949, followed by *de facto* independence in 1950. The *Traité de cession* was signed in Paris in 1951, and the '*transfert de jure*' took place on 9 June 1951. Chandernagor thus got its independence earlier than the four other French settlements in India. The territory was merged with West Bengal and consequently does not belong to the Union Territory of Pondicherry.

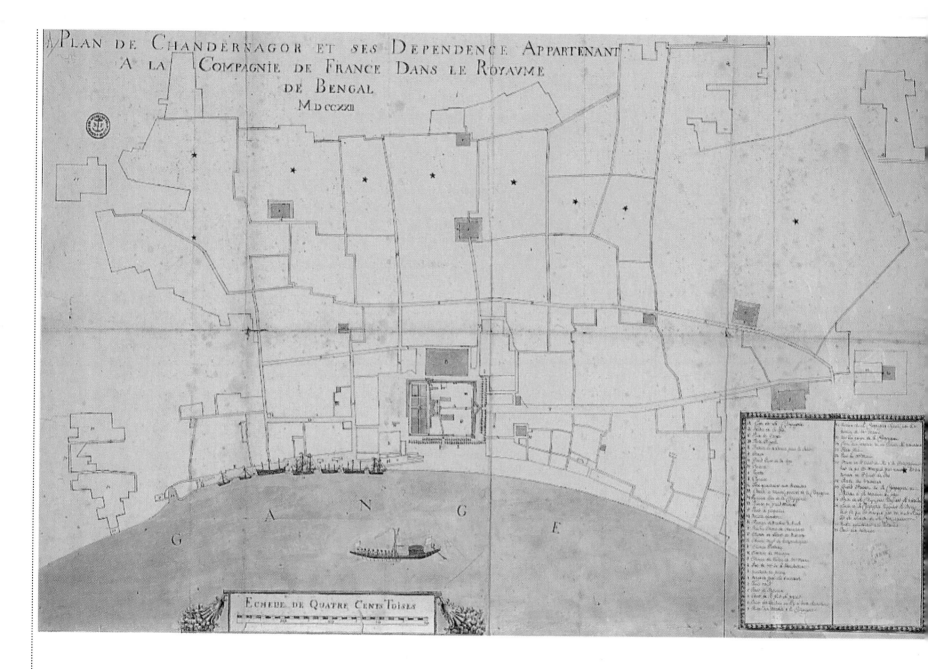

PLAN DE CHANDERNAGOR ET SES DEPENDENCE APPARTENANT A LA COMPAGNIE DE FRANCE DANS LE ROYAVME DE BENGAL MDCCXXII

ECHELLE DE QUATRE CENTS TOISES

PLATE 42

Plan de Chandernagor et du Fort d'Orléans, Etablissement Français sur le bord occidental du Gange

Plan of Chandernagor and Fort d'Orléans, the French settlement on the western side of the Hoogly

By Bourcet
1762
Collection: CAOM, DFC 35 C 7
Scale [1/6800]
585 mm x 275 mm

A small area of 940 hectares or 2321 acres, but 'in every aspect better than Calcutta' (Hamilton, 1828), Chandernagor was turned into a major centre for Bengali exports to Europe, the Middle East and the Far East by Dupleix. A. Martineau calculated that from 1720 to 1723 the volume of commercial transactions was worth one and a half million French livres annually. It grew to 2,250,000 livres in 1730, and in 1732 Dupleix sent to France six ships of the Compagnie des Indes loaded with a cargo worth 6,750,000 French livres. Besides these official transactions, private trading, which had become legal in 1722 and was carried out in association with Indian and European traders and bankers in Bengal, allowed Dupleix to build a large personal fortune: in 1732 he sent out ten small ships, all painted red (he called them his *Rougets*, 'red fish'); most of them were *brigantines* although two carried more than 300 tons. In 1733 he invested money in about fifteen ships, and in 1735 in eleven ships sailing to Jeddah, Mascate, Bandar Abbas, Cochin, Surat, Mahé, Mangalore, the Maldive Islands and Manila. The volume of his personal transactions at Chandernagor is not known, but we can glean some information from what we know of the loss of the ship *L'Aimable*, sent to Jeddah in June 1735. On its return journey to Chandernagor the ship was carrying Rs 500,000 in gold (1,300,000 livres), of which only Rs 24,000 were retrieved from the sinking vessel.

Such cargoes, in spite of the various losses and occasional shipwrecks, brought undisputed prosperity to all the people involved in transactions, from local craftsmen to investors. The city, although never a great example of remarkable private architecture, had numerous two-storeyed houses on the riverside. They can be seen in Dominique Serres' painting, *The Capture of Chandernagor, 1757.*

Dupleix was not a scholar but he did take some interest in Indian culture. It is known that he asked a Frenchman in the service of the Mughal emperor in Delhi to commission for him, from Agra artists, miniatures of Indian sovereigns and grandees in everyday as well as ceremonial dress. He loved engravings, and requested his brother to send him four volumes of prints recently published in France, that cost him 800 livres. Dupleix was also interested in scientific research, and among other publications he purchased Réaumur's books on entomology. For three successive years, he observed and noted the features of precipitation in Bengal and sent his observations to Abbé Pluche, one of the most popular and prolific science writers of the time.

Social life at Chandernagor revolved around meetings, *soirées* and various entertainments organized by the governor, who received guests at his residence—a nice house which he had bought on the riverside. At Goretty, he had a garden and park of 4 hectares or 10 acres, where he set up some of the statues he had previously in his Pondicherry garden. The social elite of the other European settlements, including Sichtermann, the

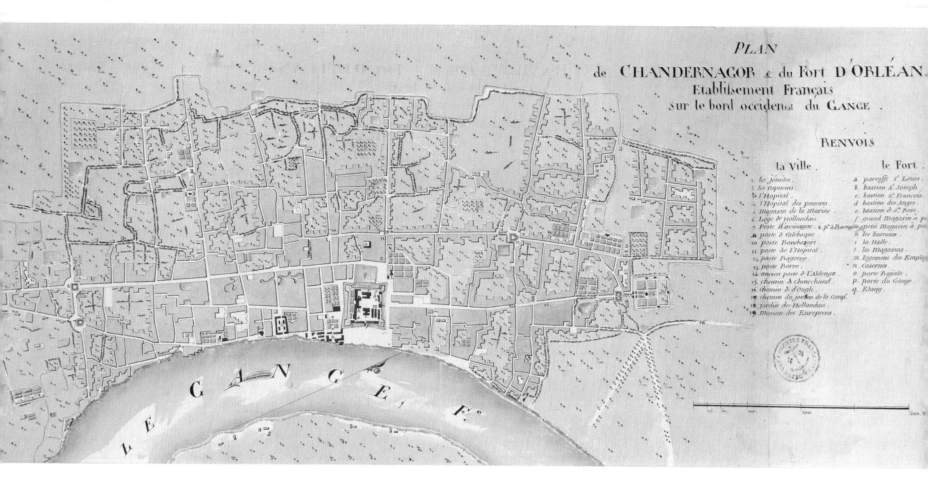

PLAN
de CHANDERNAGOR & du Fort D'ORLÉAN
Etablissement Français
sur le bord occidental du GANGE.

RENVOIS

la Ville.

le Fort.

Dutch Governor at Chinsurah; Braddyth and Stockhouse, Governors of Calcutta; Schonamille, the Austrian Governor of Bankibazar; as well as the captains and staff of the European ships anchored in the Hoogly, attended the musical concerts and the fine dinners served with olives from Provence, champagne and Burgundy wines (*Côte-rôtie*). There is, unfortunately, no record of the Bengali elite who no doubt were also present at these parties. His more intimate circle was a typically eighteenth-century '*confrérie*' (brotherhood) of most agreeable and convivial persons including a number of 'sisters', like sister Jeanne (Mrs Vincent, future Mrs Dupleix) and sister Manon, wife of Mr Aumont.

Such was life at Chandernagor at the peak of its prosperity. Not a big city, not a great capital, but a place where people met each other and lived in comfort. It was still a place with tremendous economic potential in 1757. It is little remembered today that the news of the capture and destruction of Chandernagor in 1757 boosted the East India Company's stock by 12 per cent in London!

115

PLATE 43

Veuë de la Loge de Chandernagor, du costé de la Porte Royale, du costé du Jardin

View of the Loge of Chandernagor, from the King's Gate, from the Garden

By Riftierre
c. 1722
Collection: CAOM, DFC 35 B 5
Scale not given
740 mm x 500 mm

The *Loge* of Chandernagor, with its round baroque *pediment* in early Louis XV style, was probably the first monumental building of the French in India. Its impressive size and decoration reflected the policy in France of using prestigious architecture to reinforce the image of the French king and nation.

The *loge* was used as a huge store for verifying and keeping goods before they were shipped. It was also the residence of the director, although Dupleix preferred his magnificent residence at Goretty, south of Chandernagor. In Goretty, surrounded by beautiful gardens, Dupleix, and his successor Chevalier in 1767–78, held splendid receptions attended by the elite of the European settlements on the Hoogly. Chamber music played by Dupleix's orchestra was a major attraction of these *soirées*, and the governor sometimes joined in on the '*basse de viole*' (violin). Very few drawings of Goretty exist today. It was destroyed in the 1810s because of its dilapidated condition.

Intellectual and cultural contacts developed between the French and the Bengalis. The 'Italian' Capuchin mission to Tibet had a centre there, where a French Capuchin, Father François-Marie de Tours, compiled an interesting dictionary entitled *Dictionnaire de la langue indoustane* (Urdu) in the late 1690s. The manuscript was given to the Propaganda Fide at Rome in 1704, and it was sent to Paris by the Pope, to Anquetil Duperron, who had a copy made of it, a copy that is displayed today in the Bibliothèque Nationale. In the early 1700s, the French Jesuits of the Bengal mission learnt Sanskrit in different schools, 'universities', which flourished in Bengal, at Goptipara for example. In 1757, Father Mozac, the superior of the Jesuit mission at Chandernagor, mentioned to Anquetil Duperron that he had learnt Sanskrit in a place near Kasimbazar where several scholars lived and taught.

This explains how and why the Jesuit fathers at Chandernagor were actively involved in looking for Sanskrit manuscripts for the King's Library in the late 1720s. From 1729 to 1735, they collected originals or copies of 168 major works, including parts of the *Vedas*, the *Puranas*, the *Ramayana*, the *Manusmriti*, and so on. Along with the collections of books made at the same time by their colleagues in Pondicherry, this is one of the oldest and richest European collections of Indian manuscripts, which is still preserved in the Bibliothèque Nationale. The two Jesuit astronomers invited by Raja Jaisingh to visit his newly-constructed *Jantar Mantars* at Benaras, Mathura, Delhi, Ujjain and Jaipur, first met their Indian colleagues in Chandernagor and learnt from them Indian ways of calculating the eclipses and the movements of celestial bodies.

Chandernagor never recovered from its destruction in 1757. In 1812 a new and lovely residence was contructed for the *Administrateur Général*. This imposing, yet gracious building, is today the Institut de Chandernagor and is under the West Bengal government.

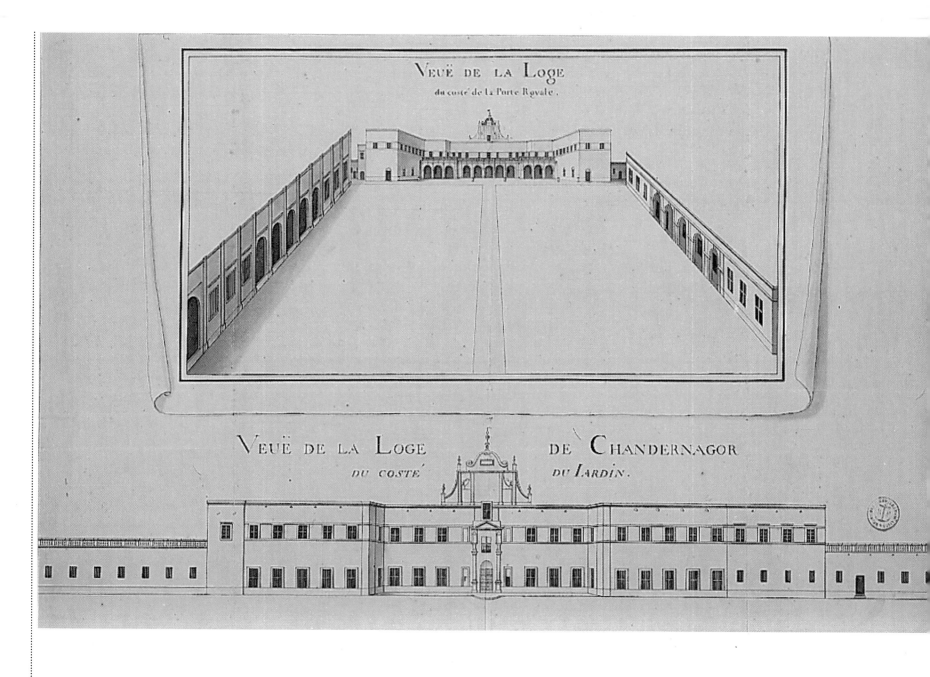

VEUË DE LA LOGE
du costé de la Porte Royale.

VEUË DE LA LOGE DE CHANDERNAGOR
DU COSTÉ DU IARDIN.

117

PLATE 44

Plan de la Loge de Cassimbazard à la Compagnie de France

Plan of the Loge of Kasimbazar, belonging to the French East India Company

Artist unknown

c. 1729

Collection: CAOM, DFC 31 B 369

Scale [1/420] (plan)

Scale [1/488] (cross-section)

730 mm x 490 mm

The development of European settlements along the Hoogly in the seventeenth century was one of the reasons why the capital of the Nawab of Bengal was shifted from Dacca to Murshidabad in 1704. A cluster of European *loges* were quickly established south of that city, the French one being next to the Armenian settlement.

Kasimbazar was one of five important *loges* of Chandernagor, the other four being Patna, Jugdia, Dacca and Balassore. There were also a dozen local stores or buying houses (*aurang*) spread all over Bengal.

The French '*aldée*' (territory) at Kasimbazar was called Saidabad and was 32 hectares (79 acres) in area. It included the *loge* and a village called Bamongatty which had been purchased in 1721: a *Plan de Bamonne Gotha* by Palmas, dated November 1767, is kept at Aix-en-Provence (reference CAOM, DFC 31 B 373, 630 mm x 515 mm). An annual rent of Rs 600 was originally paid to the Nawab of Bengal for the village. The rent was later transferred to a Muslim gentleman who built a mosque beside it.

There are three maps at the CAOM which show the French *loge* at Kasimbazar in 1729: in addition to the one shown here they are *Loge de Cassimbazar à la Compagnie de France* by Lavabre, 3 September 1729 (CAOM, DFC 31 B 367) and *Cassimbazar et l'étendue de l'aldée ...* (anonymous, CAOM, DFC 31 B 366, probably same date). *Plan de Cassimbazar* by Moulut shows the *loge* on 22 January 1753 (CAOM, DFC 31 A 370); a '*retombe*'

(movable paper) makes it possible to see the plan of the ground and first floors as well. These plans also show other European settlements, including an Armenian settlement. The Armenians played a pivotal role in connecting European and Indian commercial networks in Bengal in the seventeenth and eighteenth centuries. Gurgin Khan, a high-ranking civil and military officer of Kasim Ali Khan, the Nawab of Bengal in 1757, was Armenian, and Gentil speaks highly of him in his *Mémoires*. At Chinsurah, the Dutch settlement on the Hoogly, an Armenian church still exists; it has lost its original interior decoration but has most interesting tombstones in its courtyard. The church deserves to be protected as an outstanding historical monument.

The plan of Kasimbazar shows the magnificent two-storeyed *loge* with its magazines and the gardens which extended up to the embankment of the Hoogly river. A document of 1733 quoted by Philippe Haudrère (*La Compagnie française des Indes ...*) describes the factories: 'On the land side, the enclosure is a low thin wall with short foundations. Along half of these walls are the workshops for manufacturing the silk. They can shelter 2000 to 2500 "*vireurs de soye*" (silk-rolling machines). In the same enclosure, next to the residence, there is a big magazine where the silk purchased from the merchants and the silk ready to be sent to Chandernagor are stored. This store is built of bricks. It is a large one, divided in two parts by arcades. The *loge*

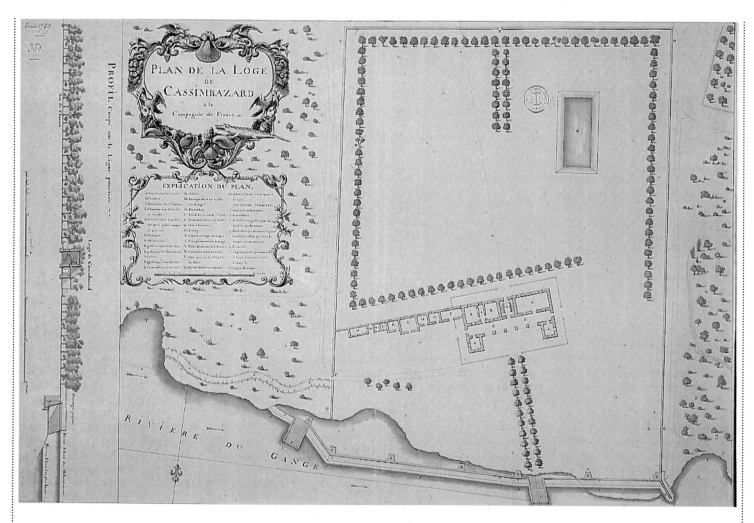

has whatever is necessary for the workers and the soldiers.'

The main staple purchased at Kasimbazar was Bengali silk, the best quality coming from around Murshidabad. The Compagnie des Indes carried on brisk trade there until the *loge* was completely destroyed in 1761. In 1765, when the English East India Company gave it back to the French, only two magazines could be repaired. By 1767 the silk trade of the Compagnie des Indes was down to a mere 200,000 French livres again. Modave, who visited the place in 1774, said that the once beautiful and spacious *loge* had been destroyed by the English in 1761 and that the French Agent now lived in a private house in the village.

368. PROFIL Coupé Sur la ligne ponctuée 7.7.

Rez de Chaussée

PLATE 45

Profil de la Loge de Cassimbazar, par Lavabre, 3 septembre 1729

Cross-section of the Loge of Kasimbazar, by Lavabre, 3 September 1729

By Lavabre
1729
Collection: CAOM, DFC 31 C 368
Scale [1/360]
635 mm x 160 mm

Joseph Cordier observed in the 1820s about Kasimbazar that 'during the rainy season and when the river increases, the level of water is for a while a couple of feet above the level of the former factory and all the country at large'. This cross-section of the French *loge*, two storeys high, shows that in 1729, the '*niveau d'eau des débordements*' (level of overflowing water) reaches the '*rez-de-chaussée*' (ground floor) of the settlement. It was, therefore, necessary to have a strong embankment (*quai*) in order to protect the settlement. A *mémoire* kept at the DFC [97 (374)] speaks of a *Projet de revêtement de fascines*

pour le quai de la loge de Cassimbazar (Project of reinforcing the Kasimbazar embankment with *fascines*) since the embankment was in the process of being wiped out by the river. This three-folio document is anonymous and undated. It has one page of drawings in colour. According to the document of 1733 quoted by Philippe Haudrère, a *quai* was built at that time, that was about 200 metres long.

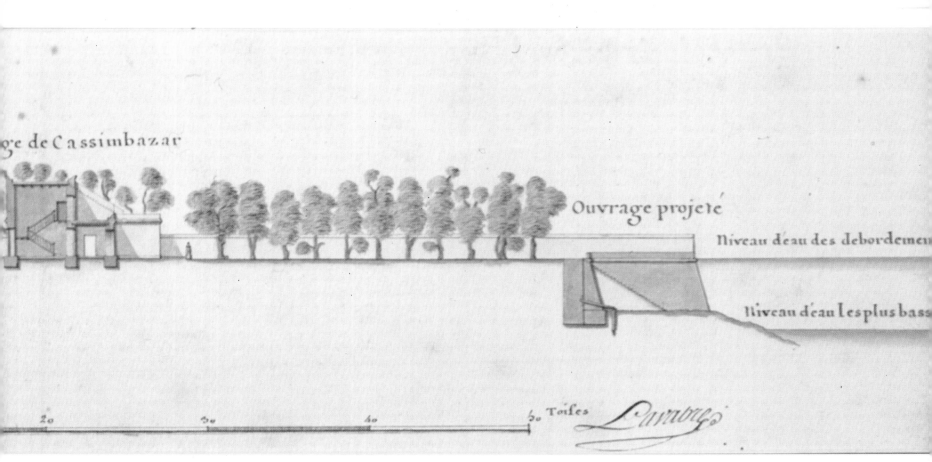

ge de Cassimbazar

Ouvrage projeté

Niveau d'eau des debordemen

Niveau d'eau les plus bass

40 Toises   L'ambre

20   30   40

PLATE 46

Palais de Nisamoulmoulouk à Dély du côté de Gemna, 1774

Palace of Nizam ul-Mulk at Delhi, seen from the bank of the Jamuna, 1774

By an architect working for
Shuja ud-Daula
1774
Collection: BN Od 63/1
Cliché Bibliothèque Nationale de France
1440 mm x 365 mm

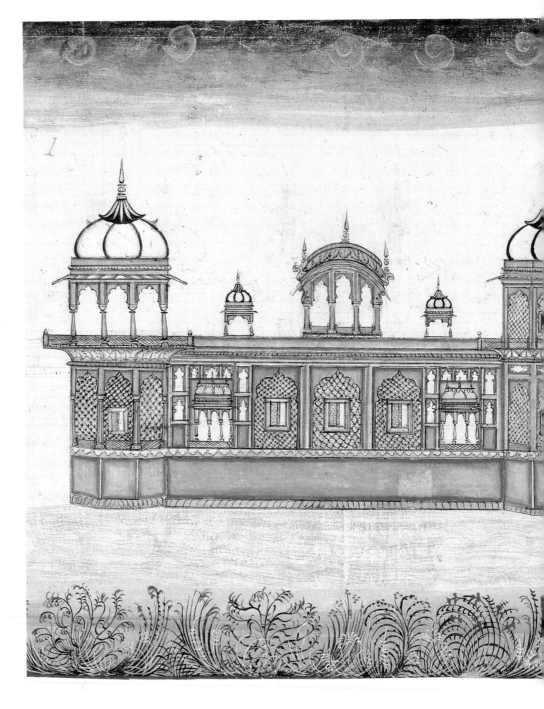

Palais de Nisamoulmoulouk à Dely du côté du Gemna. 1774

123

On the banks of the Jamuna, particularly the branch of the river that once flowed between the Red Fort and the Fort of Salimgarh, many palaces with gardens were built by Mughal princes and the nobility, or by wives and favourites of the Mughal emperors. Dara Shikoh, Nizam ul-Mulk, Safdar Jang and Qudsia Begum, all lived here. These residences were still standing in the late eighteenth century but all that remains today are the Dara Shikoh 'Library', a small mosque in the Qudsia gardens, and a solitary corner-tower of another garden, south of the fort, that was almost demolished in 1997.

Nizam ul-Mulk was one of twenty *mansabdars* who held the highest positions (7000 horses, 7000 troops) in the Mughal empire. He was appointed governor of the Deccan in 1713, and in 1721 Muhammad Shah appointed him prime minister (*wazir*). Nizam ul-Mulk tried to reform the *jagirdari* system of the Mughals and met with a lot of hostility at the court. He left Delhi in 1723, and in 1725 he was at Aurangabad and Hyderabad where Muhammad Shah conferred upon him the title of Asaf Jah. He returned to Delhi in 1737; among his followers was Dargah Quli Khan, the celebrated author of *Muraqqa-i-Delhi*. Several authors, Indian and European, have accused Nizam ul-Mulk of having been instrumental in Nadir Shah's invasion of India. When the massacre at Delhi took place he was one of two high-ranking officers (he was then *Mir Bakhshi*, Commander-in-Chief of the Mughal army) sent by Muhammad Shah to implore Nadir Shah, who was seated in the Golden Mosque at Chandni Chowk, to stop the carnage. Nadir Shah then imposed a fine of Rs 1 crore on the city. Nizam ul-Mulk contributed Rs 50 lakh, the largest amount paid by a Mughal officer. Nadir Shah left Delhi with a load of treasures, including the jewels of the Crown and seventeen thrones, one of them being the Peacock Throne. The booty was estimated to be at least Rs 70 crore by Lockhart, and between 80 and 145 million pounds by Burgess. As Anand Ram remarked, 'the accumulated wealth of 348 years changed hands in a moment'.

In 1741 Nizam ul-Mulk left Delhi for Aurangabad. In 1743 he led an expedition to Arcot, where the English from Madras and the French from Pondicherry sent him presents. In 1744 he appointed Anwar ud-Din *subadar* of the Carnatic at Arcot. He died in 1748 but his family, the Asif Jahi Nizams, ruled Hyderabad until 1948. The descendants of Nizam ul-Mulk and Anwar ud-Din played a major role in the political and military history of South India till the end of the eighteenth century. Salabat Jang, the Nizam from 1751 to 1763, had Bussy and his auxiliary army in his service from 1751 to 1758; his brother Nizam Ali Khan, who succeeded him in 1762, employed General Raymond in 1785. Raymond raised and commanded the Corps de Français de Raymond with a strength of 14,500 for the Nizam in 1798.

Where in Delhi was Nizam ul-Mulk's palace? According to Stephen Blake, Nizam ul-Mulk took over the mansion of Sa'dullah Khan in 1729: 'This palace was the finest in the city. Sa'd-ullah Khan, an

experienced builder, supervised the construction of the Jama Masjid and laid out the square before the Akbarabadi Gate of the [Red] Fort. In 1729, Nizam ul-Mulk had his mansion ransacked and in 1788, Ghulam Qadir alighted at the mansion of Ghazi al-Din Khan near the palace fortress. All of this suggests that the mansion passed from Sa'dullah Khan to Nizam ul-Mulk and on to his son and grandson, Ghazi al-din Khan II and III.'

Besides being an experienced builder—or as a consequence of that—Sa'dullah Khan was also a rich man. When Shah Jahan inaugurated the Red Fort on 19 April 1648, Sa'dullah Khan furnished the Hall of the Private Audience (*Diwan-i-Khas*) with carpets worth Rs 60,000; the same day he received a special *khilat* (robe of honour) from the emperor and a promotion to the rank of 7000 horses and 7000 troops. He selected a fine spot to build his impressive residence, situated as it was immediately south of the Red Fort. Beautifully built, its eastern facade overlooked the Jamuna. The last occupant of the house, Ghulam Qadir, a Rohilla Afghan, blinded Emperor Shah Alam II on 9 August 1788, and plundered the imperial palace of whatever jewellery had been left by the Persians and the Afghans.

The Gentil Album contains several other views and details of Mughal palaces in Delhi: the *Sérail de Mohammed Cha à Dely* (Od 63/6, 1500 mm x 403 mm), the *Maison de Mousafectam* [Muzaffar Khan] (Od 63/10, 1830 mm x 415 mm), the *Sérail de la Maison de Saftadjangui* [Safdar Jang] *à Dely* (Od 63/15, 1920 mm x 518 mm), the *Maison du Raja Bahadour, hors Dely, au bord du Gemna* (Od 63/5, 1790 mm x 480 mm), and *Porte ou Terpolin à Dely* (Od 63/4, 775mm x 575 mm).

PLATE 47

**Palais du Vieux Dély
bâti par Selimcha
qui fit bâtir aussi Selimgar
qui sert de prison aux
princes Mogols. Levé en
1774 par un architecte du
Vizir Sandjan [*sic*] Daula**

*Palace built in Old Delhi
by Salim Shah, who also built
Salimgarh, used as a prison
for the Mughal princes. Drawn in
1774 by an architect of Wazir
Shuja ud-Daula*

By an architect working for
Shuja ud-Daula
1774
Collection: BN Od 63/2
Cliché Bibliothèque Nationale de France
1345 mm x 428 mm

ris du vieux Dely bâti par Selimcha qui fit bâtir aussi Selimgar qui sert de prison aux Princes Mogols.

levé en 1774 par un Architecte du Visir Sandjam daula.

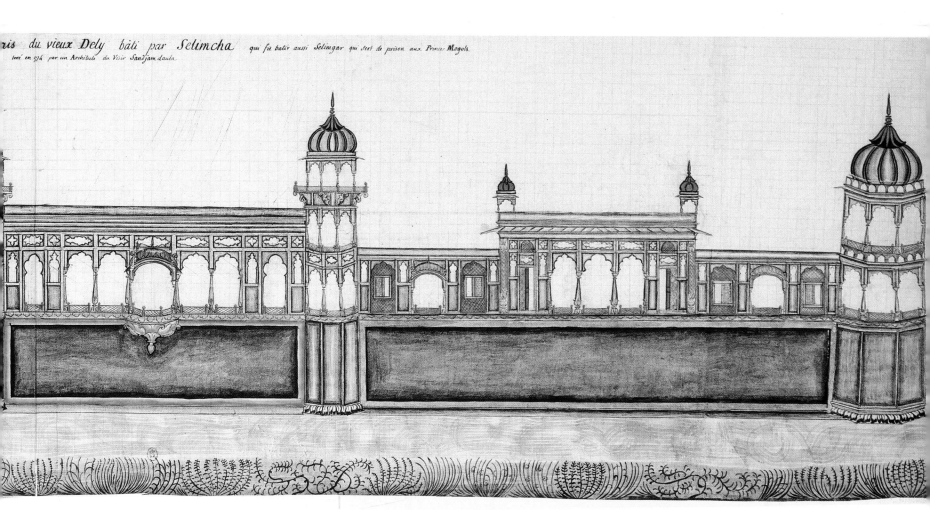

In 1540, Sher Shah Suri almost wiped out the most recent of the invaders from Central Asia, the Mughals, and Humayun, son and heir of Babur, was forced to flee to Persia. Sher Shah Suri built the Purana Qila in Delhi and he built his Shergarh on the ruins of Humayun's city, Din Panah. The remains of Sher Shah Suri's mosques, gates and ramparts can still be seen along Mathura Road in New Delhi.

The construction of the Fort of Salimgarh was started in 1546 by Islam Shah, also called Salim Shah, son and successor of Sher Shah. It still exists but is in such a dilapidated condition that it is almost impossible to visualize its past splendour. Modave left the following description of the fort, as he saw it in 1775: 'Salimguer is an old fort just close to the Palace of Delhi. Some time ago it was used as a State prison. Today it is almost abandoned. This palace, when observed from some neighbouring height, has a striking majestic aspect which moves the imagination. One can see great domes, either in white marble or covered with gold-plated copper. One also sees immense number of trees filling the gardens inside the ramparts, and these trees, mixed with these white or golden domes and the red colours of the high walls make a *coup d'oeil*, the beauty of which it is impossible to exaggerate.'

While the caption of the drawing reproduced here says that the Fort of Salimgarh was used as a prison for Mughal princes, Modave says that a part of the Red Fort had recently been specially arranged in order to accommodate some eighty members of the imperial family. This more modern prison was close enough to the emperor's residence for him to hear the 'poor wretches' clamouring for food in 1775.

The drawing from the Gentil Album shows the facade of the Palace of Salim Shah in Old Delhi; the location of the palace is not clear. Modave writes: 'Old Delhi is a very extensive city. It is separated from the new [Shajahanabad] only by a large avenue [the present Asaf Ali Road]. One can see a great number of old palaces still intact. On the other side of the city opposite the fortress is an old palace still intact which is called the Old Delhi Fort [Purana Qila]. It stands at two *cosses* of the new one [Red Fort].' The drawing from the Gentil Album does not resemble the Purana Qila as built by Sher Shah Suri, and identified by Modave as 'the Old Delhi Fort'. It seems clear that Salim Shah beautified the city built by his father, and when he started building Salimgarh (not Salim Qila, a difference to be noted) he selected the site where Shah Jahan later build Shajahanabad in 1639. The return of Humayun from Persia in 1555 put a stop to fifteen years of Suri rule and restored the Mughal dynasty, which then lasted till 1858.

Where was Salim Shah's palace built? Was it inside the Purana Qila, or in the city at the foot of that citadel, as was the case with the Sultan's residential palace at Tughlaqabad? If that was so, it must have been one of the numerous great palaces noticed by Modave when he travelled to

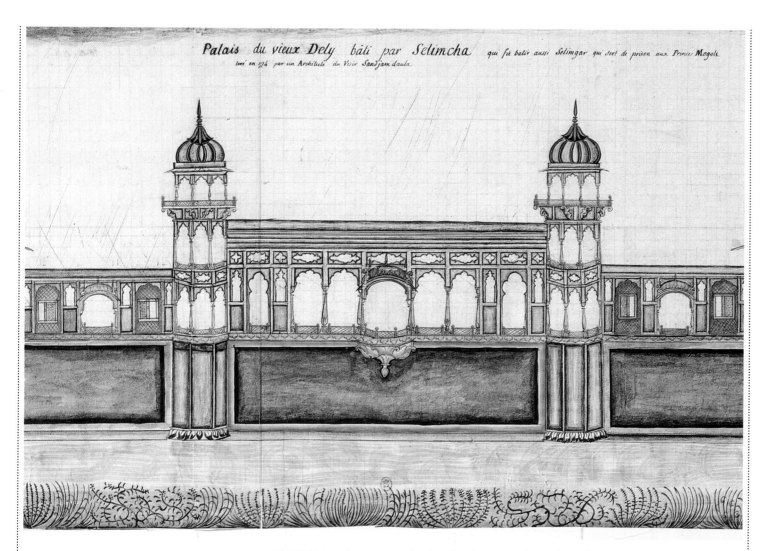

Palais du vieux Dely bâti par Selimcha qui fit bâtir aussi Selimgar qui sert de prison aux Princes Mogols. levé en 1774 par un Architecte du Visir Sandjamdaula.

Old Delhi on his way to the Qutab Minar in 1775. The similar aesthetic tastes of the Suris and the Mughals suggest that Salim Shah's palace lay north of the Purana Qila, on the river front, like so many Mughal palaces and gardens which were later built at Agra and Delhi on the banks of the Jamuna. But these are mere hypotheses.

The Gentil Album, however, has provided us with evidence, in the form of a beautiful coloured picture, of a great monument of mid-sixteenth-century Delhi which still existed in the late eighteenth century, and was celebrated at that time, but which had disappeared when the main monuments of Delhi were painted for Thomas Theophilus Metcalfe, James Skinner and William Fraser by Delhi artists during 1830–35.

PLATE 48

Palais du Grand Mogol, Dely, du côté du Gemna

Palace of the Great Mughal, Delhi, from the bank of the Jamuna

By an architect working
for Shuja ud-Daula
1774
Collection: BN Od 63/3
Cliché Bibliothèque Nationale de France
2240 mm x 465 mm

Shah Jahan began building the Red Fort at Delhi in 1639, at a site that Salim Shah Suri may have previously chosen for his 'Salimgarh'. Its grandiose architecture and splendid decoration have always fascinated European visitors. Bernier described it in 1663, and Modave in 1774.

The Gentil Album has several paintings of the Red Fort: *Aurangzeb's Garden* (Od 63/11, Plate 49), *Apartments of the Palace at Delhi* (Od 63/13, 2380 mm x 514 m), *Gate of the Fort in which is the Palace of the Emperor. Red Stone with White and Black Marble Incrustations. The Domes are in White Marble* (Od 63/14, 890 mm x 590 mm). There are also three paintings of the Jama Masjid. Five paintings close to those in the Gentil Album, one of them dated 1774, and all of

them kept today in the Victoria and Albert Museum, London, probably belonged to the same set. All of them have inscriptions in French, Latin and Persian. Two are views of the Red Fort: *Circumferentia continet 3600 ulnas indicas Fort[e]resse de Delly. Arx Delliensis* [Plan of the Red Fort showing the Walls and Gates] (Reference V&A, AL 1754–1, 820 mm x 750 mm), and *Sérail et jardin du palais du grand mughal à Dély* [Plan of the Emperor's Garden and Seraglio, Delhi] (Reference V&A, AL 1754–5, 2520 mm x 1005 mm). Two other drawings show Chandni Chowk (V&A, AL 1754–3, 1400 mm x 310 mm) and Faiz Bazaar (V&A, AL 1754–3, 1350 mm x 310 mm). The fifth drawing depicts Dara Shikoh's palace at Agra (V&A, AL 1754–3, 664 mm x 2114 mm in

Palais du Grand Mogol à Dely du coté du Gemna

watercolour and gold paint). Another related work is *Bird's eye-view of the Red Fort, Agra, on the Banks of the River Jamuna*, inscribed in Persian only, identifying various parts of the fort. It is not a part of the Gentil set, but as Mildred Archer has aptly observed, the painting is anterior to 1803 and belongs, therefore, to the period when de Boigne and then Perron govern-ed the Doab (and Agra) for the Sindhias and Shah Alam II (V&A, IS 153–1984, 535 mm x 370 mm).

Some paintings in the Gentil series are dated 1774, and the whole collection was probably done at about that time, a year before Colonel Gentil and his family had to leave India for France. Four years later, in 1778, Deshaies de Montigny, a French Agent appointed to the Maratha Confederacy at Pune, travelled to North India and went to Delhi and Agra. His album of maps that are kept at Quimper in French Brittany includes a drawing of the Red Fort in Delhi as seen from the Jamuna, painted by an European artist. The view extends from the Fort of Salimgarh up to the walled city of Shajahanabad. In this collection there is also a plan of the Jama Masjid done by an Indian architect and a painting of the Taj Mahal. Two of these, the Red Fort (detail) and the Taj Mahal, are reproduced in colour in *Reminiscences: The French in India*, (INTACH, New Delhi, 1997).

PLATE 49

Malab [*sic*] Bague. Jardin que fit faire Alemgir dans l'intérieur du palais pour ses femmes à Dely

Mahtab Bagh. Garden made by Aurangzeb for his wives inside the Red Fort at Delhi

By an architect working
for Shuja ud-Daula
1774
Collection: BN Od 63/11
1220 mm x 680 mm

The Mughal gardens are full of poetry. Designed on the pattern of the Persian 'paradise' (*paradeisos*', *pradesh*'), they had a central structure from where the four rivers of paradise flowed, dividing the whole into four gardens (*chahar bagh*). Babur laid out a garden at Kabul and another at Agra. Humayun's brother Kamran Mirza built his gardens and *baradari* at Lahore, on the banks of the Ravi. Akbar laid out the gardens of Wah, one mile from Hassan Abdal and Panja Sahib, now in Pakistan. The Mughal nobility followed the example of their rulers (the gardens of Pinjaur, for instance).

An elaborate system of canals, fountains and waterfalls reminded the Mughals, sons of Central Asia, of the enchanting music of sprinkling water and cascading rivulets in their ancestral land, their '*watan*' dearly cherished by Emperor Shah Jahan. There are illustrations in Mughal manuscripts of the sovereigns establishing paradise-like gardens. Shah Jahan himself baptised the main canal distributing water in the Red Fort, the '*nahr-i-bihisht*' ('paradise canal').

Shah Jahan built the famous Shalimar Gardens at Delhi, Srinagar and Lahore, and many other gardens like the gardens of the Taj Mahal at Agra. In Delhi, between the Red Fort and the city, three large gardens were laid out: the Anguri Bagh (vine garden) in the north-west, the Gulabi Bagh (rose garden) in the west towards Chandni Chowk, and the Buland Bagh (sublime garden) in the south. Within the city itself, an English map of

Delhi made before 1857 shows that practically the whole area north of Chandni Chowk, behind the row of shops and the celebrated Jahanara Sarai, was occupied by gardens. The biggest one (50 acres), called Sahibabad, belonged to Princess Jahanara, the oldest and most beloved daughter of Shah Jahan.

In the eighteenth century the northern part of the imperial residence at the Red Fort was occupied by two gardens. The *Bagh-i Hayat Bakhsh* (life-giving garden) in the east, overlooking the Jamuna river, was planted with beds of flowers, sweet-smelling shrubs and fruit trees. A Persian poem composed by Sa'dullah Khan, Shah Jahan's *wazir*, engraved on the southern and northern arches of the imperial apartments, says: 'The garden of *Hayat Bakhsh* is to these buildings as the soul is to the body and the lamp to an assembly.'

West of Hayat Bagh was Mahtab Bagh (moonlight garden). Mahtab Bagh seems to be a later appellation since the earliest document, Sa'dullah Khan's inscription, gives the name Hayat Bakhsh Bagh only. The later appellation used here might have originated at the time of the modification of the original Hayat Bakhsh which, as the title of this painting suggests, could be linked to Aurangzeb. It is known that Aurangzeb did order some work to be done in the Red Fort—the barbicans of Lahori Gate and the Moti Masjid which lie next to Hayat Bakhsh Bagh are his contributions. Little is known about the garden, said to have been planted with cypresses and white flowers. As S. Blake explained, 'the major structure in this

garden was a *baradari* of red stone called *halal mahal* (the water palace). The *nahr-i-bihisht* flowed through the centre of this building.' It was already totally dilapidated in 1846, when Sayyid Ahmad Khan published his first edition of *Athar al-Sanadid*: 'It seems that [Mahtab Bagh] was originally a beautiful garden, but now there remains only a broad canal. Siraj ud-Din Muhammad Bahadur Shah built a waterfall on its western side' (as translated by R. Nath). Sayyid Ahmad Khan also testifies that the Hayat Bakhsh Bagh was in a very bad condition at that time. After the Great Revolt (Sepoy Mutiny) of 1857, the British built military barracks in that part of the fort. Mahtab Bagh disappeared, so too the western part of Hayat Bakhsh Bagh.

PLATE 50

Maison de Soudjaat Daula [*sic*] à Faisabad

Residence of Shuja ud-Daula at Faizabad

By an architect working
for Shuja ud-Daula
1774
Collection: BN Od 63/24
1800 mm x 445 mm

Shuja ud-Daula, *Wazir* of the Mughal empire and Nawab of Awadh between 1754 and 1775, established his capital at Faizabad on the Ghaghra river, 8 kilometres west of Ayodhya. After the Battle of Buxar in 1764, Shuja had a fort built there, called '*Chhota Kalkatta*' (Little Calcutta) at that time, at a site where a hunting lodge made of thatch previously stood. He built his residence within the fort and established this as his head-quarters. Modave, who visited the place in 1774, described it as follows: 'The Residence of the Nawab, fortified just like the city, is on the side of the river. It is a great building without any particular taste with many courtyards, gardens, workshops of every kind which make it a city by itself.' Modave went on to describe the city of Faizabad with its 'quite agreeable gardens designed and planted with a taste different from ours and which is pleasant enough', its four mosques, *chowk* (marketplace), *topkhana* (artillery store), *karkhana* (arms factory, according to Modave), streets and lively markets.

At Faizabad, and later at Lucknow, Shuja ud-Daula welcomed a large number of Frenchmen who had escaped the destruction of the French settlements in Bengal in 1757. They included Colonel Gentil, 600 soldiers, officers and military specialists, and an unknown number of civilians. These Frenchmen, some of them highly trained and competent in their respective fields, helped Shuja ud-Daula modernize his armies. They imparted disciplined military training, information on arms and guns manufacturing, and

drew up plans for fortifying his two capitals at Faizabad and Lucknow, and other sites and cities on the borders of his territory. Canaple was one among these Frenchmen, at whose residence Modave stayed, although he does not tell us anything about him.

Canaple was one of the military engineers sent by the French government to help the Indian states modernize their military structures and build up their resistance to thwart British expansionism in India. In 1772, Shuja ud-Daula decided to build a new, powerful fort north of Faizabad—almost certainly as a response to Fort William of Calcutta. He entrusted Canaple with the design of the fort and the management of the work. Gentil, in one of his unpublished letters, says that 30,000 workers were busy day

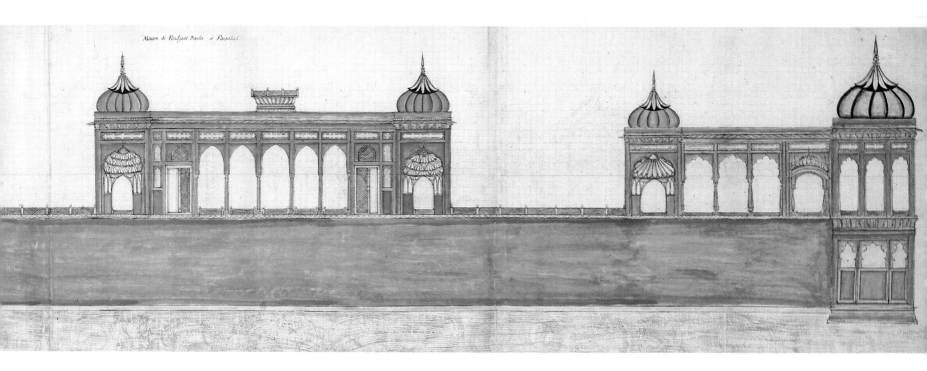

Maison de Badjast Daula à Faizabad

and night, building the ramparts and
bastions under Canaple's direction. The
construction annoyed the East India
Company considerably. Modave testified
that 'the fort, built by a Frenchman
[Modave does not give the name] on the
north of the city, on the side of the river, is
a regular hexagon: completed to its
perfection it would undoubtedly be the
strongest fortress in Hindustan'. Shuja ud-
Daula died before the work could be
completed. Hamilton mentioned 'the
remains of a fortress, and of Shuja ud-
Daula's palace' in 1828, but no trace of the
fort remains today.

In 1773 Major Antoine-Louis Polier, a
Swiss officer serving the East India
Company, was sent to Faizabad to serve
as architect–engineer to the Nawab.
Coming from an old French Huguenot
family who had migrated to Switzerland,
he befriended Gentil and the French in
Awadh. Like Gentil, Polier built a beautiful residence for himself, and he was
involved in many civil and military
activities in the city and in the state.

Another residence of Shuja ud-Daula
still exists in the Fort of Faizabad. It is
undoubtedly modelled on a European
design but the name of the architect is not
known.

Glossary

Academy From the Garden of Akademos at Athens, Greece, where Plato taught. Society for cultivating art and literature in Europe from the fifteenth century. There were academies in most French cities and towns in the late fifteenth to early sixteenth centuries. They were particularly active in the eighteenth century.

Afghans People from Afghanistan. There was in India an old distinction between an Afghan i-Hindustan (from a tribe settled in northern India) as opposed to an Afghan i-Wilayat, an Afghan from Afghanistan.

Aldea/Aldée From the Arabic, through Portuguese: 'An estate consisting of land or a land and a house ... , land yielding revenue'. Widely used in Spain and Portugal because of the Arabic occupation there, it came to India through Portuguese occupation in the early sixteenth century.

Bailli A title in the Order of Malta, a military order created in 1113. Admiral de Suffren, who was a Commander of the Order of Malta, is also known as Bailli de Suffren.

Bania/Banya From the Sanskrit. A trader, a Hindu trader.

Baradari Lit. 'twelve doors'. Building in a garden with three doors on each face: e.g., the *Zafar-Mahal baradari* of Bahadur Shah Zafar II in the Red Fort at Delhi.

Bastion Projecting part of a fortification, round or polygonal, with its base on the line of the rampart. Bastions were normally provided with artillery to protect the *curtains*.

Blanchisserie A place for bleaching cloth.

Brigades of Hindustan Regular corps raised, trained and commanded from 1784 onwards by Benoît de Boigne for Madhoji Sindhia in the Doab. They were 30,000 strong in 1796 when de Boigne returned to Europe, and 45,000 strong when the British launched their attack on the Doab in 1803. Their headquarters was in Aligarh. They were the last units to resist Lake's and Arthur Wellesley's advances in the Doab and into Maratha territories. Also called the 'French' brigades of Hindustan by the British.

The explanations for the terms that have been glossed here have been taken from *Hobson-Jobson*, 1979; *Oxford English Dictionary*; and Robert, *Dictionnaire alphabétique et analogique de la langue française*, Paris, 1979.

Capuchin A section—in 1528—of the Franciscan order. The Mission of Thibet was, in the eighteenth century, entrusted to the Italian Capuchins and was based in Chandernagor. Father François-Marie of Tours prepared, at Chandernagor, one of the first existing Urdu–Latin dictionaries (1704).

Cartaz system A system of permission or passports delivered against payment by the Portuguese to ships sailing in the Indian Ocean and the eastern seas, including ships belonging to 'native' powers like the Mughals, the Marathas, etc.

Cavalier A protruding fortified place inside the ramparts, mounted with heavy artillery in order to fire on enemy positions far away.

Château In French it means both castle (including fortified castles of the Middle Ages) and palace (Château de Versailles, for example).

Corps (de) Français de Raymond A regular corps raised, trained and commanded by J.-M. Raymond for the Nizam of Hyderabad. From 800 men in 1785, the corps increased to 14,500 men in 1798, when it was disarmed by the British; the best units were incorporated into the East India Company troops who moved from Hyderabad to capture Srirangapatnam in 1799.

Corps de garde Guard house.

Corsaire A French ship that had received from the King the *'lettre de course'* (commission) allowing the captain to attack and capture any enemy ship. In the Indian Ocean they were mostly based in Ile de France (Mauritius). The English called them Privateers.

Counterscarp Outer wall or slope of ditch in fortification.

Courbe de niveau Contour line, an ingenious way to mark the altitude on a two-dimensional map.

Covered way Line of defence at the top of the *glacis*.

Croix de Saint Louis The highest military decoration in France of the *ancien régime*. Created by Louis XIV in 1693, the Ordre Royal et Militaire de Saint Louis was restricted to Catholic soldiers and officers. The Protestants (Huguenots) received the Croix du Mérite Militaire, created in 1759 by Louis XV for his Swiss (Huguenot) regiments.

Cunette Drain at the bottom of a ditch.

Curtain Plain wall of a fortified place connecting two towers.

Daftar/Duftar From the Arabic. Chapter of a book. Collection of texts. Ministries (secretariats) of a government.

Darbar/Durbar From the Persian. Government (Shah Jahan's *darbar*). Place where the government meets (Shah Jahan in the *darbar*)

Détroit A strait, a narrow passage of water between two seas (the Straits of Sunda in Indonesia) or between two lakes (the city of Detroit in the USA).

Diwan From the Arabic or Persian. Originally the same meaning as *daftar*: a collection of written leaves or documents. Hence the literary meaning of the word, e.g., the *diwan* of Hafez. It also meant the register of dues to the state, hence the meaning of Finance Minister (in French, *douane*—the custom house—comes from the Arabic and Turkish *diwan*). In every *suba* there was a *subadar* and a *diwan*, the latter being in charge of the revenue administration of the *suba*.

Diwanat The right to collect the revenues of the state. In 1765 Emperor Shah Alam II gave the East India Company, represented by Robert Clive, the *diwanat* of Bengal, and it was under this garb that the British conquered or annexed the whole of what was British India in 1857. One, therefore, understands the legal position of Emperor Bahadur Shah Zafar when, after the 'Mutiny', he was tried for high treason by the East India Company.

Doab The land between the Ganges and the Jamuna rivers. The territory was entrusted to de Boigne by Sindhia, with the gift of 52 *parganas* in *jagir*.

Dominicans A religious order founded by Dominique in 1216 to fight the Albigenses, a heretic sect in the south of France. Most of them being learned theologians, they were given charge of the Inquisition in 1233. They also developed a network of colleges all over the world. They came to India as missionaries before the Portuguese settled in Goa, but developed their activities in Portuguese territories after 1510.

Ducats See Venetian sequins.

Dutch See VOC.

Ecluse A canal lock with sluice gates.

Escarp Inner wall or slope of the ditch in fortification.

Estampe Print, engraving.

Farenghi/Feringhi The Franks, or the French, meaning westerners or Europeans. The military connotation was widespread in the *Dar ul-Islam*, since Babur, in his *Memoirs* (written in Chaghatai Turk) called the artillery he used at Panipat (1526) '*Farangiha*'. The name was attached to the Portuguese right from the early sixteenth century. When the East India Company established its sway in the subcontinent, 'Ferenghi' was more or less replaced by 'Angrezi'.

Farenghi art The name given in Persian to what is now restrictively, and in some aspects wrongly, known as Company art.

Fascine Long faggot used for lining trenches, filling ditches, etc.

Fausse-braye Embankment built at the foot of the rampart to protect it from artillery fire.

Farman/Firman From the Persian *farmadan*, meaning to order. An imperial order, a letter of credentials (also meaning the equivalent of today's passport).

Franciscans A religious order founded by Franciscus of Assisi in 1223. The Capuchins belong to the Franciscan order.

Gallivat 'Large boats [which] carry about six carvel [caravel]-guns and sixty men at small arms, and oars. They sail with a Peak sail like the Mizen of a Man-of-war, and row

with 30 or 40 oars. ... They are principally used for landing troops for a descent'
(1756) (*Hobson-Jobson*).

Great Seignor The Sultan of Constantinople.

Half-moon Fortified outer work, originally circular, then triangular, part of the close
defence of a place.

Hussards European light cavalry of Hungarian origin, with a particularly flamboyant
uniform all over Europe. French hussards served Hyder Ali and Tipu Sultan in
Mysore from 1761 to 1785.

Glacis Bank sloping down from a fort, outside the ditch, on which attackers are exposed
to defenders' fire.

Grenadier A soldier who threw grenades. In the eighteenth and early nineteenth centuries
they formed the elite infantry troops. In France, each regiment of ten companies had
one company of grenadiers.

Jaghir/Jagir A 'place-holding', an assignment of land and of its rent in exchange for
serving the state. Military officers used the revenue for the maintenance of a fixed
number of troops (salary, equipment) and for their own remuneration as well. The
jagirs were not supposed to be hereditary.

Jesuits Societas Jesu, a religious order founded by Ignace de Loyolla in 1534. They were
deeply involved in scientific research (astronomy, mathematics) and teaching. They
developed a network of excellent colleges all over the world right from the 1540s.
French Jesuits settled in Pondicherry in the 1680s, and they were instrumental in
getting 287 Indian manuscripts copied or purchased for the King's Library between
1727 and 1740. The Societas Jesu was banned in Portugal in 1759, in France in
1764, and Pope Clement XIV abolished it in 1773. The present-day Jesuits belong
to the 'new Company' founded in 1814.

Juliana Donna Juliana Diaz da Costa (*c.* 1657–1734)—a Portuguese lady who reached a
prominent position in the courts of Aurangzeb, Shah Alam I and Muhammad Shah.
'Under [Muhammad Shah] she was confirmed in the name "Juliana" as a hereditary
title of honour, and it was her duty, we are told, as the bearer of that title, to place the
crown on the head of the new King' (E. Maclagan). 'Juliana serai' was built by her
in south Delhi. Juliana apparently did not have any daughter. Her title went to her
niece (her sister Angelina's daughter) and remained in the family. In 1761, the
incumbent 'Juliana' was Lucia, whose daughter Thérèse married Colonel Gentil at
Faizabad in 1772 and died in France in 1778. Lucia, who also went to France with
the Gentil family, died in Versailles in 1806.

Khalisa revenue '*Khalisa i-Sharifa* [...] the lands and sources of revenue reserved to the
Imperial treasury' (Irfan Habib).

Kumedan From the French 'Commandant'. Highest grade given to Indian officers
commanding native troops attached to the French army right from the 1740s. These

troops were trained and equipped according to the French system of warfare. The English used the same title for their first sepoy units (Yusuf Khan, for example, was 'Commandant of all the Sepoys' in 1760). This prestigious title was used in the 'French' units created by Sindhia, the Nizam, and later Maharaja Ranjit Singh in the Punjab.

Loge The French differentiated between a *comptoir* (settlement) and a *loge*, a mere trading post: Chandernagor was the French *comptoir* in Bengal with twelve *loges* in that area (Kasimbazar, Balassore, Dacca, Jougdia, Chittagong, etc.) under its jurisdiction.

Maidan Meadow, usually used for playing polo. The open space—bigger than the *glacis*—around a fort for giving place to artillery fire, e.g., the *maidan* around Fort William at Calcutta.

Nawab The Arabic plural of nayab/naib, meaning deputy. It was applied in India in a singular sense as Viceroy, e.g., the Nawab of Arcot, the Nawab of Awadh.

Nizam From the Arabic. Asaf Jah, a general and minister of Aurangzeb, was given the title of Nizam ul-Mulk. He became *subadar* of the Deccan (Hyderabad) in 1713. He was the founder of the dynasty whose sovereigns kept the title of Nizam.

Orillon Round projection of a bastion.

Ouvrage en bonnet de prêtre, or Ouvrage à corne A low protruding defensive work of parallel piped form furnished with artillery.

Parallels Trenches dug by an army besieging a place in order to get to the top of the *glacis* without being under the fire of the besieged party.

Pargana From the Sanskrit. A revenue unit, sometimes a district (the 24 Parganas in Bengal) or the subdivision of a district.

Parvana From the Persian. A letter with the imperial seal, a letter of authority given to a subordinate.

Pré carré A more or less rectangular section of French terrritory on the northern frontier of Flanders (present-day Belgium), extensively fortified by Vauban. The first fortress built by the celebrated engineer was Tournay, the plans of which were used by de Nyon for building the new Fort Saint-Louis at Pondicherry.

Raveline Outwork of fortifications, with two faces forming a salient angle.

Redoubt Outwork or field work, usually polygonal, with a powerful artillery to prevent the enemy from approaching the rampart. At Srirangapatnam, the line of *redoubts* north of the Cauvery river covered an area approximately the size of the island.

Revêtement Revetment, retaining-wall, facing.

Salon A literary and/or scientific circle meeting regularly in the reception room (*salon*) of the residence of a great lady in France of the sixteenth to early nineteenth centuries.

Sepoy From the Persian *sipahi*. A native soldier—originally a horseman. In India an infantryman, disciplined and dressed in the European style. The French 'Spahi' (mounted units of the French army in North Africa) comes from the same Persian word (*aspa* means horse) through Turkish, Algeria having been a Turkish dominion before 1830.

Sarkar/Sircar [Circar] From the Persian, meaning 'head of affairs'. It means the State, the government. It was also applied to an extensive administrative division of territory.

Souba/Suba From the Persian. A province of the empire. Sometimes also used to mean the same as *subadar*, the official in charge of the *suba*.

Successor states The states which emerged in India during and after the decline of the Mughal empire. Most of them were former provinces—*subas*—of the empire.

Topass/Topaz From the Turkish (through Persian). *Top-chi* (gunner), analysed later as coming from *topiwala* (hat-men). In the seventeenth and eighteenth centuries, the name designated soldiers of mixed Portuguese–Indian (Christian) descent, usually serving in the artillery and regular infantry units.

Unrequited export Export whose cash payment is not made in the exporting country.

Venetian zequins/sequins From Italian ducats: gold coins struck in Venice, 'long current on the shores of India' (*Hobson-Jobson*). They were still in use in early-nineteenth-century India: E. Pottinger had some of them stitched onto his garments when he set forth on his exploration of Sindh.

VOC Initials of the Verenigde Oost-Indische Compagnie, the Dutch East India Company, founded in 1602.

Wazir From the Arabic. The principal minister, the Prime Minister, of a Muslim state.

Zenana A Persian word from *zan*, 'woman': literally the *gynécée*, or the section of the house reserved for women.

Select Bibliography

Alam, Muzaffar, *The Crisis of Empire in Mughal North India: Awadh and the Punjab, 1707–1748*, Delhi: Oxford University Press, 1986.

Alavi, Seema, *The Sepoys and the Company: Tradition and Transition in Northern India 1770–1830*, Delhi: Oxford University Press, 1995.

âme [L'] et la lumière, *Armes et canons dans la Marine royale fin XVIIe–XVIIIe siècles*, Paris: Centre Historique des Archives Nationales, 1996.

Ananda Ranga Pillai, *The Private Diary of Ananda Ranga Pillai, Dubash to Joseph François Dupleix, Governor of Pondicherry: A Record of Matters Political, Historical, Social and Personal from 1736–1761* (in 12 volumes), translated from the Tamil by order of the Government of Madras, edited by Rev. J. Frederick Price and R. Rangachari, 1904. [Reprinted in Delhi: Asian Educational Services, 12 volumes, 1985.]

Anquetil-Duperron, A.-H., *Voyage en Inde. 1754–1762. Anquetil Duperron. Relation de voyage en préliminaire à la traduction du Zend Avesta*. Présentation, notes et bibliographie par J. Deloche, M Filliozat et P.-S. Filliozat, Paris: Maisonneuve & Larose, 1997.

Arasaratnam, Sinnappah, *Merchants, Companies and Commerce on the Coromandel Coast 1650–1740*, Delhi: Oxford University Press, 1986.

―――― *Maritime India in the Seventeenth Century*, Delhi, 1994.

―――― 'Masulipatnam', in S. Arasaratnam and A. Ray, *Masulipatnam and Cambay: A History of two port-towns 1500–1800*, Delhi: Munshiram Manoharlal Publishers, 1994, pp. 1–116.

Archer, Mildred, *Patna Paintings*, London, 1947.

―――― *Company Drawings in the India Office Library*, London: HMSO, 1972.

―――― *India and British Portraiture, 1770–1825*, London: Sotheby Parke Bernet, 1979.

―――― 'Colonel Gentil's Atlas: An Early Series of Company Drawings', in *India Office Library & Records, Annual Report, 1978*, London: IOLR, 1979, pp. 41–45.

―――― *Between Battles: The Album of Colonel James Skinner (A Portfolio)*, London: Al-Falak and Scorpion Publications, 1982.

―――― *Company Paintings. Indian Paintings of the British Period*, London: V&A, 1992.

Archer, Mildred and William, *Indian Painting for the British. 1770–1880. An Essay*, London: Oxford University Press, 1955.

Balayé, Simone, *La Bibliothèque nationale des origines à 1800*, Genève: Droz (Switzerland), 1988.

Baldaeus, Philippe, *Naauwkeurige Beschryvinge van Malabar en Chromandel*, Amsterdam, 1672. English translation, *Description of Malabar, Coromandel and Ceylon, 1672*, in A. and J. Churchill's *Collection of Voyages and Travels* ... (*non vidi*).

Balfour, Ian, *Famous Diamonds*, London: Collins, 1987.

Benot, Yves, *La Révolution française et la fin des colonies*, Paris: La Découverte, 1989.

—— *La démence coloniale sous Napoléon*, Paris: La Découverte, 1992.

Bérenger, Jean and Meyer, Jean, *La France dans le monde au XVIIIe siècle*, Paris: SEDES, 1993.

Bernier, François, *Voyages dans les états du Grand Mogol*, re-edited by F. Bhattacharya, Paris: Fayard, 1981. [First edition, 1671.]

—— Constable's translation of *Bernier's Travels* ... , Delhi: Oxford University Press, 1934. [Oriental Reprint, 1983.]

Bertrand, Michel, *Suffren. De Saint-Tropez aux Indes*, Paris: Perrin, 1991.

Biès, Jean, *Littérature française et pensée hindoue des origines à 1950*, Paris: Klincksieck, 1974.

Black, Jeremy M., *War for America*, Stroud, UK: Alan Sutton, 1991.

—— *From Louis XIV to Napoleon: The Failure of a Great Power: French Foreign Policy 1661–1815*, London (forthcoming).

—— 'Britain as a Military Power, 1688–1815: Historiographical Essay', in *The Journal of Military History*, 64, London: Society for Military History, January 2000, pp. 159–77.

Blake, Stephen P., *Shahjahanabad: The Sovereign City in Mughal India. 1639–1739*, Cambridge: Cambridge University Press, 1993.

Blochet, E., *Bibliothèque Nationale, Catalogue des Manuscrits persans*, 4 volumes, Paris, 1905 to 1934.

Bouchot, Henri, *Le Cabinet des Estampes de la Bibliothèque nationale. Guide du lecteur et du visiteur. Catalogue général raisonné des collections qui y sont conservées*, Paris, s.d.

Bodinier, Gilbert, 'Les officiers français en Inde de 1750 à 1793', in *Trois siècles de présence française en Inde*, Paris: CHEAM, 1994, pp. 69–89.

Brioist, Pascal, *Espaces maritimes au XVIIIe siècle*, Paris: Atlande, 1997.

Buckland, C.E., *Dictionary of Indian Biography*, London, 1906. [Lahore: Sang-e-Meel Publications, 1985.]

Burgess, James, *The Chronology of Modern India: 1494 to 1894*, Edinburgh, 1913. [Lahore: Al-Biruni, 1975.]

Bussy, Marquis de, *Journal de Bussy, Commandant Général des forces de terre et de mer dans l'Inde. 13 Novembre 1781–31 Mars 1785*, edited by A. Martineau, Paris: Leroux, 1932.

Butel, Paul, *Européens et espaces maritimes (vers 1690–vers 1790)*, Bordeaux: Presses
     Universitaires de Bordeaux, 1997.

Cabaton, A., *Catalogue sommaire des manuscrits indiens ...*, Paris: Bibliothèque Nationale, 1912.

Cardini, Franco, *La culture de la guerre. Xe-XVIIIe siècles*, Paris: NRF–Gallimard, 1992.
     [Italian edition, Florence, 1982.]

Carré, Abbé, *The Travels of the Abbé Carré in India and the Near East — 1672 to 1674*, 3 volumes,
     translated by Lady Fawcett, edited by Sir Charles Fawcett and Sir Richard Burn,
     Indian edition, Delhi: Asian Educational Services, 1990.

Catalogus Codicum Manuscriptorum Bibliothecae Regiae, Tomus primus, Codices Orientales,
     Paris, 1739. The 'Codices Indici' are listed pp. 434–48, n° 1 to 287.

Challe, Robert, *Journal d'un voyage fait aux Indes Orientales (1690–1691)*, Introduction and
     Notes by F. Deloffre and M. Menemencioglu, Paris: Mercure de France, 1979.

Chase, P. (ed.), *The Papers of George Washington*, Charlottesville, USA: University Press of
     Virginia, volume 1, 1993.

Chauhan, R.R.S., 'The Siddis in the Indian Ocean Regions', in K.S. Mathew (ed.), *Indian
     Ocean and Cultural Interaction (AD 1400–1800)*, Pondicherry: Pondicherry University,
     1996, pp. 35–51.

Chaunu, Pierre, 'Les armées et la guerre' and 'Les armées civilisatrices. Bas-officiers et
     vieux soldats au XVIIIe siècle', reprinted in *L'apologie par l'histoire*, Paris: OEIL–
     TEQUI, 1988, pp. 361–67.

CHEAM, *Trois siècles de présence française en Inde*, Paris: CHEAM, 1994.

Colas, G. and Richard, F., 'Le Fonds Polier de la Bibliothèque Nationale', *Bulletin de l'Ecole
     Française d'Extrême-Orient* (BEFEO), 73, Paris: EFEO, 1984, pp. 99–123.

Compagnies et comptoirs. L'Inde des Français. XVII–XXe siècle [sic], in *Revue Française d'Histoire
     d'Outre-Mer*, Paris, edited by Jacques Weber, numbers 290/91, 1991.

Collin de Bar, *Histoire de l'Inde ancienne et moderne, ou l'Indostan*, 2 volumes, Paris: Le Normant,
     1814.

Compton, Herbert, *A Particular Account of the European Military Adventurers of Hindustan from
     1784 to 1803*, London: T. Fisher Unwin, 1892. [Reprinted in Karachi, Oxford
     University Press, 1976.]

Conway, S., *The War of American Independence, 1775–1783*, London: Edward Arnold, 1995.

Cordier, Joseph, *Historique de Karikal de 1739 au 31 Décembre 1824, rédigé en 1825 par le Capitaine
     de Vaisseau Cordier*, text published and presented by François Gros under the title
     Historique et Statistique de Karikal, Pondicherry: Institut Français de Pondichéry, 1971.

———— and Bédier, Achille, *Statistiques de Chandernagor (1823, 1827, 1858)*, edited by J.
     Deloche, Pondicherry: Institut Français de Pondichéry, 1990.

Corvisier, André (dir.), *Histoire militaire de la France, 2. De 1715–1871*, Paris: Presses
     Universitaires de France, 1992.

Crowe, Sylvia *et al.*, *The Gardens of Mughal India*, London: Thames and Hudson, 1972.

Culture et Développement (ed.), *L'extraordinaire aventure de Benoît de Boigne aux Indes*, Paris: C&D, 1996.

Das Gupta, Ashim, *Indian Merchants and the Decline of Surat, c. 1700–1750*, Delhi: Manohar, 1994. [First published by Franz Steined Verlag, Wiesbaden, Germany, 1979.]

David, M.D., *History of Bombay. 1661–1708*, Bombay: University of Bombay, 1973.

Decker, Michel, *Les canons de Valmy. Exposition du 20 juillet au 20 août 1989. Modèles réduits d'étude d'artillerie de la fin du XVIIIème siècle. Système Gribeauval. Hôtel National des Invalides, Musée de l'Armée*, Paris: Hôtel National des Invalides, 1989.

Deleury, Guy, *Les Indes florissantes. Anthologie des voyageurs français. 1750–1820*, Paris: Laffont, 1991.

Dewey, Clive (ed.), *Arrested Development in India*: The Historical Dimension, The Riverdale Company (USA), 1988. [Delhi: Manohar, 1988.]

Dianoux, D.G., 'Les loges françaises dans l'Inde et au Bangladesh et les Iles Spartley', *Mondes et Cultures*, XLIV, 3, Paris, 1984, pp. 537–630.

Dodwell, H.H., *British India*, volume V of the *Cambridge History of India*, Cambridge: Cambridge University Press, 1968.

Doniol, Henri, *La Participation de la France à l'établissement des Etats-Unis d'Amérique*, 6 volumes in folio, Paris: Imprimerie Nationale, 1886–89.

D'Souza, Florence, *Quand la France découvrit l'Inde. Les écrivains-voyageurs français en Inde (1757–1818)*, Paris: L'Harmattan, 1995.

Dubois de Jancigny and Raymond, Xavier, *Inde*, Paris: Firmin Didot, 1845.

Filliozat, Jean, 'Une grammaire sanscrite du XVIIe siècle et les débuts de l'Indianisme en France', in *Journal Asiatique*, Paris, 1937, pp. 275–84.

_____ *Catalogue du fonds sanscrit, Bibliothèque Nationale, Département des manuscrits*, fascicule I, Paris: Adrien-Maisonneuve, 1941.

_____ *Catalogue du fonds sanscrit, Bibliothèque Nationale, Département des manuscrits*, fascicule II, Paris: Bibliothèque Nationale, 1970.

_____ 'La naissance et l'essor de l'Indianisme', in *Bulletin des Etudes Indochinoises*, XXXIX, 4, 1954, pp. 256–96.

Frykenberg, Robert E. (ed.), *Delhi through Ages. Essays in Urban History, Culture and Society*. Delhi: Oxford University Press, 1986.

Gentil, Jean-Baptiste, *Mémoires sur l'Indoustan ou Empire mogol*, Paris: Petit, 1822.

Gille, Bertrand, *Les ingénieurs de la Renaissance*, Paris: Hermann, 1964.

Gole, Susan, *India within the Ganges*, Delhi: Manohar, 1983.

_____ *Maps of Mughal India Drawn by Colonel Jean-Baptiste-Joseph Gentil, Agent for the French Government to the Court of Shuja-ud-Daula at Faizabad, in 1770*, Delhi: Manohar, 1988.

_____ *Indian Maps and Plans from earliest times to the advent of European surveys*, Delhi: Manohar, 1989.

Gordon, Stewart, *The Marathas, 1600–1818*, Cambridge: Cambridge University Press, 1993.

—— *Marathas, Marauders, and State Formation in Eighteenth-Century India*, Delhi: Oxford University Press, 1994.

Graff, Violette, ed., *Lucknow: Memories of a City*, Delhi: Oxford University Press, 1997.

Gros, François (ed.), *Passeurs d'Orient. Encounters between India and France*, Paris: Ministère des Affaires Etrangères, 1990.

Guignard, Brice, 'Les soldats français de Pondichéry (1700–1761)', in *La lettre du CIDIF*, Paris: CIDIF, 12–13, 1995–96, pp. 1–37.

Guyon, Abbé, *Histoire des Indes orientales anciennes et modernes*, 3 volumes, Paris: Lottin, 1744.

Habib, Irfan, 'Potentialities of Capitalistic Development in the Economy of Mughal India', in *Essays in Indian History: Towards a Marxist Perception*, Delhi: Tulika, 1995, pp. 180–232.

—— 'Processes of Accumulation in Pre-Colonial and Colonial India', ibid., pp. 259–95.

—— 'Colonialization of the Indian Economy 1757–1900', ibid., pp. 296–335.

—— 'Studying a Colonial Economy—Without Perceiving Colonialism', ibid., pp. 336–66.

—— (ed.), *Confronting Colonialism: Resistance and Modernization under Haider Ali and Tipu Sultan*, Delhi: IHC and Tulika, 1999.

Hamilton, Walter, *East-India Gazetteer containing Particular Descriptions of the Empires, Kingdoms, Principalities ... of Hindostan ...*, London, 1828. [Delhi: Low Price Publications, 1993.]

Hamont, T., *Lally-Tollendal*, Paris: Plon, 1887.

Harouel, Jean-Louis, *L'embellissement des villes. L'urbanisme français au XVIIIe siècle*, Paris: Picard, 1993.

Hasan, Nurul, 'Du Jardin Papers. A Valuable Source for the Economic History of Northern India. 1778–1787', in *The Indian Historical Review*, V, 1–2, Delhi: ICHR, 1978–79, pp. 187–99.

Hatalkar, V.G., *Relations between the French and the Marathas [1668–1815]*, Bombay: Bombay University Press, 1958.

—— *French Records Relating to the History of the Marathas*, 9 volumes, Bombay: Maharashtra State Board for Literature and Culture, 1978–85.

Haudrère, Philippe, *La Compagnie française des Indes au XVIIIe siècle (1719–1795)*, 4 volumes, Paris: Librairie de l'Inde, 1989.

—— 'Quelques aspects du commerce entre la France et l'Asie à la fin du XVIIIe siècle 1765-1793', in CHEAM, *Trois siècles de présence française en Inde*, pp. 109–22.

—— 'La Compagnie des Indes', in Philippe le Tréguily, and Monique Morazé (eds), *L'Inde et la France*, pp. 11–21.

——, 'Le commerce', ibid., pp. 23–31.

Hayavadana Rao, C., *History of Mysore (1766–1799)*, volume III, Bangalore: Government Press, 1946.

Hilaire-Pérez, Liliane, *L'expérience de la mer. Les Européens et les espaces maritimes au XVIIIe siècle*, Paris: Seli Arslan, 1997.

Hobson-Jobson. A Glossary of colloquial Anglo-Indian words and phrases, and of kindred terms, etymological, historical, geographical and discursive, by Col. Henry Yule R.E., C.B. and A.C. Burnell, Ph.D., C.I.E. New edition edited by William Crooke, London: John Murray, 1903. [Delhi: Munshiram Manoharlal, 1979.]

Indo-French Relations: History and Perspectives, Delhi: MSH–Embassy of France, 1990.

Irvine, William, *The Army of the Indian Moghuls*, Luzac, 1903. [Republished, Delhi: Eurasia Publishing House, 1962.]

_____ *Later Mughals*, 2 volumes, edited by Jadunath Sarkar. Reprinted, Lahore: Universal Books, no date.

Kaye, M.M. (ed.), *The Golden Calm. An English Lady's life in Moghul India. Reminiscences by Emily, Lady Clive Bayley and her father, Sir Thomas Metcalfe*, Exeter: Web & Bower, 1980.

Keene, H.G., *The Fall of the Moghul Empire of Hindustan*, London, 1887. [Reprinted at Lahore: Al-Biruni, 1976.]

Kejarival, O.P., *The Asiatic Society of Bengal and the Discovery of India's Past*, Delhi: Oxford University Press, 1988.

Khan, Sayyid Ahmad, *Athar al-Sanadid*, translated into English and published by R. Nath under the title *Monuments of Delhi. A Historical Study*, Delhi, 1979.

Kieffer, Jean-Luc, *Anquetil-Duperron, L'Inde en France au XVIIIème siècle*, Paris: Les Belles Lettres, 1983.

Labernardie, Marguerite V., *Le vieux Pondichéry. Histoire d'une ville coloniale française*, Paris/Pondichéry: Leroux, 1936.

Lafeuillade, Lieut. Colonel Jean, *Le XVIIIe siècle. L'Evolution Militaire Organique*, Paris: Charles-Lavauzelle et Cie, 1937.

Lafont, Jean-Marie, *French Administrators of Maharaja Ranjit Singh*, second edition, Delhi: National Book Shop, 1986.

_____ *La présence française dans le royaume sikh du Penjab. 1822–1849*, Paris: EFEO, 1992. [Prix Giles 1995 of the Institut de France, Académie des Inscriptions et Belles-Lettres.]

_____ [working editor], *Reminiscences: The French in India*, Delhi: Embassy of France–Intach, 1997.

_____ *INDIKA. Essays in Indo-French Relations, 1630–1976*, Delhi: Manohar–CSH, Publications of the French Research Institutes in India, 2000.

_____ 'Sur l'Inde et sur la France. Nouveaux regards', in *Rencontre avec l'Inde*, XVII, Delhi: ICCR (Ministry of External Affairs, India), 1988, pp. 13–22. Special issue published for the International Congress of AUPELF at Delhi, December 1988. [Reprinted, ibid., 26/1, 1997, pp. 49–60.]

_____ 'L'Inde et la France en 1781–1783. Première partie: Le Rapport au Roi de 1779' [Service Historique de l'Armée de Terre (SHAT), Château de Vincennes], in *Rencontre avec l'Inde*, XVI, Delhi: ICCR, Ministry of External Affairs, 1988, pp. 58–71.

―――― 'L'Inde et la France en 1781–1783. Deuxième partie: Le Mémoire du colonel de Folnay au Ministre de la Guerre' [SHAT, Château de Vincennes], in *Rencontre avec l'Inde*, XVII, 3/4, Delhi: ICCR, 1988 (published 1990), pp. 5–30.

―――― 'L'Inde et la France en 1781–1783. Troisième partie: Expédition à faire dans l'Inde en 1781 (Projet), par O.N. Loeillot Demars' [SHAT, Château de Vincennes], in *Rencontre avec l'Inde*, XVIII, 1/2, Delhi: ICCR, 1989 (published 1991), pp. 59–96.

―――― 'Les Indes des Lumières. Regards français sur l'Inde de 1610 à 1849', in *Passeurs d'Orient. Encounters between India and France*, Paris: Ministère des Affaires Etrangères, 1991, pp. 12–33.

―――― 'Les Français au service des Etats indiens indépendants', ibid., pp. 34–40, 19 b/w illustrations, 9 colour plates.

―――― 'The Quest of Indian Manuscripts by the French in 18th Century', in *Indo–French Relations. History and Perpectives*, Delhi: MSH–Embassy of France, 1991, pp. 1–35.

―――― 'Some Aspects of the Relations between Tipu Sultan and the French. 1761–1799', presented at All India Seminar on Tipu Sultan: Modernization and Resistance, University of Bangalore, India, 18–19 January 1992; published in *Tipu Sultan. A Great Martyr*, Bangalore: University of Bangalore, 1993, pp. 77–111.

―――― 'Tableau de l'Hindoustan à la fin du XVIIIème siècle', in *L'extraordinaire aventure de Benoît de Boigne aux Indes*, Paris: Culture & Développement, 1996, pp. 8–21, 9 illustrations, 1 map.

―――― 'Benoît de Boigne. Essai de chronologie', ibid., pp. 149–50.

―――― 'Benoît de Boigne en Hindoustan. L'homme et son impact sur le Doab Gange-Jamouna. 1784-1795', in *L'Inde, la France, la Savoie. Le général de Boigne*, Chambéry: University of Savoye, 1996, pp. 157–91, 7 illustrations.

―――― 'Company Paintings ou Farenghi Paintings? Contribution française à l'émergence d'une école de peinture indienne au XVIIIème siècle', in *Cahiers de la Compagnie des Indes*, 1–1996, Lorient: Musée de la Compagnie des Indes, pp. 7–30, 11 illustrations.

―――― 'The French in Lucknow', in V. Graff (ed.), *Lucknow. Memories of a City*, Delhi: Oxford University Press, 1997, pp. 67–82, 1 illustration.

―――― 'Observations on the French military Presence in the Indian States. 1750–1849', presented at International Seminar on New Military History of South Asia, Cambridge, 15–17 July 1997; published in K.S. Mathew and J. Stephen (eds), *Indo–French Relations*, Delhi: ICHR, Monograph Series 2, 1999, pp. 198–234.

―――― 'Politics and Architecture in the French Settlements', in *Reminiscences. The French in India*, pp. 15–49, numerous colour illustrations.

―――― 'French Military Intervention in India compared to the French Intervention in North America, 1776–1785', presented at International Seminar on Tipu Sultan, Asiatic Society, Calcutta, 2–4 December 1999. Forthcoming.

_____ 'French Experts in the Indian States in 18th–early 19th Centuries', lecture at the Centre for European Studies, Jadavpur University, Calcutta, 8 December 1999. Forthcoming.

_____ 'The "Mémoires" of Lieut. Colonel Russel concerning Mysore in the Service Historique de l'Armée de Terre, Château de Vincennes, Paris', Diamond Jubilee session of the Indian History Congress, Calicut, 29–30 December 2000. Forthcoming.

La Fontaine, Jean de, *Le songe d'un habitant du Mogol et autres fables illustrées par Imam Bakhsh Lahori*, Paris: Réunion des Musées Nationaux and Imprimerie Nationale, 1989.

Lannoy, Mark de, 'A "Dutchman" in the Service of the Raja of Travancore. Eustache-Benoît de Lannoy (1715–1777)', in *Journal of Kerala Studies*, XIII, 1986, pp. 1–16.

_____ *The Kulasekhara of Travancore: History and State Formation in Travancore from 1671 to 1758*, Leiden: School of Asian, African, and Amerindian Studies, 1997.

Law de Lauriston, Jean, *Mémoire ... de l'Empire Moghol, 1756–1761*, edited by A. Martineau, Paris: Champion-Larose, 1913.

Le Bouédec, Gérard, *Activités maritimes et sociétés littorales de l'Europe atlantique, 1690–1790*, Paris: Armand Colin, 1997.

Legoux de Flaix, *Essai historique, géographique et politique sur l'Indoustan ...*, 2 volumes, Paris: Pougin, 1807.

Les relations historiques et culturelles entre l'Inde et la France. XVII–XX siècles, 2 volumes, La Réunion: AHIOI, Archives Départementales de La Réunion, France, 1987.

Le Tréguilly, Philippe and Monique Morazé (eds), *L'Inde et la France. Deux siècles d'histoire commune. XVII–XVIIIe siècles. Histoire, sources, bibliographie*, Paris: CNRS, 1995. [Some of the documents said to be in the Archives Nationales in Paris are in fact at the Centre des Archives d'Outre-Mer in Aix-en-Provence.]

Lettres édifiantes et curieuses (LEC), ed. Paris, 1781, T. X–XV (*Lettres sur l'Inde*).

Lettres et Conventions des Gouverneurs de Pondichéry avec différents Princes hindous. 1666 à 1793, Pondicherry: Société de l'Histoire de l'Inde Française, 1911–14.

Lévi, S., 'Les origines d'une chaire : l'entrée du Sanscrit au Collège de France', reprinted in *Mémorial Sylvain Lévi*, Paris: Hartmann, 1973, pp. 145–62.

Llewellyn-Jones, Rosie, *A Fatal Friendship. The Nawabs, the British and the City of Lucknow*, Delhi: Oxford University Press, 1985.

_____ *A Very Ingenious Man: Claude Martin in Early Colonial India*, Delhi: Oxford University Press, 1992.

_____ *Engaging Scoundrels. The Tales of Old Lucknow*, Delhi: Oxford University Press, 2000.

Luel, Béatrice, *Inventaire des Archives du Consulat de France à Surate. 1759–1787*, Nantes: Archives Diplomatiques, 1986.

[Maclagan, Edward], 'Four letters of Austin of Bordeaux', in *Journal of the Punjab Historical Society*, IV, Lahore, 1916, pp. 3–17.

150

Maclagan, Edward, *The Jesuits and the Great Mogul*, London: Burns Oates & Washbourne, 1932.

Madec, René, *Mémoire de René Madec, Nabab dans l'Empire Mogol, Commandant d'un Parti français au Service de l'Empereur (1736–1784)*, with notes by Max Vignes and presentation by Jean Deloche, Pondicherry: Alliance Française, 1993.

Maissin, Jacques, *Un manuscrit français du XVIIIe siècle: Recherche de la vérité sur l'état civil, politique et religieux des Hindous, par Jacques Maissin*, with introduction and notes by Rita H. Régnier, Paris: EFEO, 1975.

Malleson, G.B., Colonel, *History of the French in India from the Founding of Pondichery in 1674 to the Capture of that Place in 1761*, London, 1866. [Delhi: Gian Publishing House, 1986.]

—— *French Final Struggles in India, including an Account of the Capture of the Isles of France and Bourbon ...*, London, 1884. [Delhi: Inter-India Publications, 1977.]

Mansingh, Gurbir, Lt. Gen., 'French Military Influence in India', in *Reminiscences: The French in India*, pp. 51–87.

Manucci, Nicolao, *Histoire générale du Grand Moghol ...*, [Catroux S.J., editor], Paris, 1705–15, 2 volumes in one.

—— *Mogul India 1653–1708 or Storia do Mogor*, translated with introduction and notes by William Irvine, 4 volumes, 1907–08. [Reprint, Delhi: Low Price Publications, 1990.]

Marshall. Peter J., *Bengal: The British Bridgehead. Eastern India 1740–1828*, Cambridge: Cambridge University Press, 1987.

Martin, Claude, *Testament of the Major General Cl. Martin. Dernière volonté et Testament du Major général Cl. Martin*, Lyon, An XI-1803 (with a French translation).

Martineau, Alfred, *Les origines de Mahé de Malabar*, Paris: Champion-Larose, 1917.

—— *Le Général Perron*, Paris: Société d'Editions Géographiques, Maritimes et Coloniales, 1931.

—— *Bussy et l'Inde française. 1720–1785*, Paris: Leroux, 1935.

—— *Journal de Bussy, Commandant Général des forces de terre et de mer dans l'Inde. 13 Novembre 1781–31*, Mars 1783, Paris: Leroux, 1932.

Michaud, J., *Histoire de l'Empire de Mysore*, Paris,1801–09. [Translated into English and published in India in 1924 under the title *Michaud's History of Mysore under Hyder Ali and Tipu Sultan*. Reprint, Delhi: Asian Educational Services, 1985.]

Misra-Besnard, Kamakshi, *Le mouvement nationaliste en Inde. Le cas de Chandernagor: le premier maillon de la décolonisation française, 1905–1952*, unpublished Ph. D. dissertation, University of Nantes, France, 1998.

Mitter, Partha, *Much Maligned Monsters: History of European Reactions to Indian Art*, Delhi: Oxford University Press, 1977.

Modave, Louis-Laurent de Féderbe, Comte de, *Voyage en Inde du comte de Modave. 1773–1776*, edited by Jean Deloche, Paris: EFEO, 1971.

Mohibbul Hasan, *History of Tipu Sultan*, second revised and enlarged edition, Calcutta: The World Press, 1971.

Montalembert, Marc-René, Marquis de, *La fortification perpendiculaire, ou Essai sur plusieurs manières de fortifier la ligne droite, le triangle, le quarré, et tous les polygônes, de quelqu'étendue qu'en soient les côtés, en donnant à leur défense une direction perpendiculaire*, 10 volumes, Paris, 1776–95 (*non vidi*).

Muller, Jean-Claude, 'Recherches sur les premières grammaires manuscrites du sanscrit', in *Bulletin d'Etudes Indiennes*, 3, Paris, 1985, pp. 125–44.

Murr, Sylvia, 'Les conditions d'émergence du discours sur l'Inde au siècle des Lumières', in *Purusartha*, 7, Paris, 1983, pp. 233–84.

———— *L'Inde philosophique entre Bossuet et Voltaire*. Volume I: *Moeurs et coutumes des Indiens (1777)*, volume II: *L'indologie du père Coeurdoux. Stratégies, apologétique et scientificité*, Paris: EFEO, 1987.

Omont, Henri, *Missions archéologiques françaises en Orient aux XVIIe et XVIIIe siècles*, 2 volumes, Paris: Imprimerie Nationale, 1902.

Parker, Geoffrey, *La révolution militaire: La guerre et l'essor de l'Occident. 1500–1800*, Paris: NRF–Gallimard, 1993. [Original edition, Cambridge, UK, 1988.]

Piveron de Morlat, *Mémoire sur l'Inde. Guerre des Indes, 1778–1786*, edited and annotated by J.-M. Lafont. English edition forthcoming.

Plans en relief. Villes Fortes des Anciens Pays-Bas Français au XVIIIe S., Lille: Musée des Beaux-Arts, 1989.

Pluchon, Pierre, *Histoire de la colonisation française. Tome I. Le premier empire colonial. Des origines à la Restauration*, Paris: Fayard, 1991.

———— 'Bussy: stratégie et politique', in *Trois siècles de présence française en Inde*, Paris: CHEAM, 1994, pp. 37–55.

Polier, Antoine-Louis, *Le Mahabarat et le Bhagavat du colonel Polier, présenté par Georges Dumézil*, Paris: NRF-Gallimard, 1986.

———— *Mythologie des Indous travaillée par Mdme la Chanoinesse de Polier sur des manuscrits authentiques apportés de l'Inde par feu Mr. le Colonel de Polier*, 2 volumes, Roudolstadt et Paris, 1809 (posthumous).

———— *Ijaz-i Arsalani*, translated into English and introduced by Muzaffar Alam and S. Alavi, volume I, Delhi: Oxford University Press, forthcoming 2001.

Porcher, Marie-Claude (ed.), *Inde et Littératures, Purusartha 7*, Paris, 1983.

Prakash, Om, *European Commercial Enterprise in Pre-Colonial India*, Cambridge: Cambridge University Press, 1998.

Prost, Philippe, *Les forteresses de l'Empire. Fortifications, villes de guerre et arsenaux napoléoniens*, Paris: Editions du Moniteur, 1991.

Ray, Himanshu P., *Monastery and Guilds: Commerce under the Satavahanas*, Delhi: Oxford University Press, 1986.

———— *Winds of Change: Buddhism and the Maritime Links of Early South Asia*, Delhi: Oxford University Press, 1994.

———— 'A Resurvey of "Roman" Contacts with the East', in M.-F. Boussac and J.-F. Salles (eds), *Athens, Aden, Arikamedu. Essays on the interrelations between India, Arabia and the Eastern Mediterranean*, Delhi: Manohar–CSH, 1995, pp. 97–114.

———— and Jean-François Salles (eds), *Tradition and Archaeology: Early Mediterranean Contacts in the Indian Ocean*, Delhi: Manohar–CSH, 1996.

Richard, Francis, 'Les manuscrits persans d'origine indienne à la Bibliothèque Nationale', in *Revue de la Bibliothèque Nationale*, 19, Paris: Bibliothèque Nationale, 1986, pp. 30–45.

———— *Catalogue des manuscrits persans*, volume I: *Ancien fonds*, Bibliothèque Nationale, Département des manuscrits, Paris: Bibliothèque Nationale, 1989.

———— 'Jean-Baptiste Gentil collectionneur de manuscrits persans', in *Dix-huitième Siècle*, 28/1996, Paris, pp. 91–110.

———— 'Les missions catholiques', in Le Tréguilly *et al.*, *L'Inde et la France*, pp. 65–73, 149–51, and 213–17 (bibliography).

Richards, John F., *The Mughal Empire*, Cambridge: Cambridge University Press, 1993.

Rinckenbach, Alexis, *Dépôt des fortifications des Colonies*, I: *Indes*, Aix-en-Provence: Archives Nationales, Centre des Archives d'Outre-Mer, 1998, 8 colour plates.

———— '"Le dernier soupir de Dupleix": les cartes et plans des ingénieurs géographes en Inde', in *Cahiers de la Compagnie des Indes*, 2, 1997, Port-Louis: Musée de la Compagnie des Indes, pp. 63–72.

———— *Les Villes Fleurs. Aventures et cartographie des Français aux Indes aux XVIIe et XVIIIe siècles. Petit Journal de l'Exposition*, Port-Louis (France): Musée de la Compagnie des Indes.

———— and Ch. Beyeler, *Les Indes belliqueuses. Aventures et cartographie des Français aux Indes*, CD-ROM, Aix-en-Provence: Archives Nationales, Centre des Archives d'Outre-Mer, 1999. [English edition forthcoming.]

Roberts, P.E., *History of British India under the Company and the Crown*, completed by T.G.P. Spear, third edition (with corrections), Oxford: Oxford University Press, 1958.

Roche, Daniel, *Le siècle des lumières en province. Académies et académiciens provinciaux, 1680–1789*, 2 volumes, Paris: Editions de l'Ecole des Hautes Etudes en Sciences Sociales, 1978.

Roux, A. de, N. Fauchère, G. Monsaingeon, *Les plans en relief des places du Roy*, Paris: Adam Biro, 1989.

Said, Edward, *Orientalism*, London: Routledge & Kegan Paul, 1978; revised edition, 1987.

Saint-Genis, Victor de, *Le général de Boigne. 1751–1830*, Poitiers: Dupré, 1873.

Saint Venant, Marie-Gabrielle de, *Benoît de Boigne (1751–1830). Du général au particulier*, Chambéry: Mémoires et Documents de la Société Savoisienne d'Histoire et d'Archéologie, T. XCVIII, 1996.

Sardesai, G.S., *The New History of the Marathas*, 3 volumes, Bombay: Phoenix Publications, 1948.

Sarkar, Sir Jadunath, *Fall of the Mughal Empire*, 5 volumes, Delhi: Orient Longman, 1972. [First edition, 1950.]

Schwab, Raymond, *La Renaissance orientale*, Paris: Payot, 1950.

―――― *Vie d'Anquetil-Duperron*, Paris, Payot, 1934, translated into English and introduced by Devika Chandrashekar, Delhi: Manohar–CSH, forthcoming.

Sen, S.P., *The French in India. First Establishment and Struggle*, Calcutta: University of Calcutta, 1947.

―――― *The French in India. 1763–1816*, Delhi: Munshiram Manoharlal, 1958. [Second edition, 1971].

Sharma, Y. D., *A Guide to the Buildings and Gardens: Delhi Fort*, Delhi: Archaeological Survey of India, 1937.

Siddiqi, Jamal Moh, 'Aligarh (1791–1803). Quartier général administratif des généraux de Boigne et Perron', in *L'extraordinaire aventure de Benoît de Boigne aux Indes*, Paris: Culture & Développement, pp. 61–66, 6 illustrations.

Sources de l'Histoire de l'Asie et de l'Océanie dans les Archives et Bibliothèques françaises ... I: Archives, München/New York/London/Paris: K.G. Saur, 1981.

Sources de l'Histoire de l'Asie et de l'Océanie dans les Archives et Bibliothèques françaises. II: Bibliothèque Nationale, München/New York/London/Paris: K.G. Saur, 1981.

Sources de l'Histoire de l'Asie et de l'Océanie dans les Archives et Bibliothèques françaises. III: Autres Bibliothèques, München/New York/London/Paris: K.G. Saur, 1992.

Stephen, S. Jeyaseela, 'Urbanism and the chequered Existence of the Indo-French Town of Pondicherry (AD 1674–1793)', in *Revue Historique de Pondichéry*, XIX, Pondicherry, 1996, pp. 29–64.

Subrahmanyam, Sanjay (ed.), *Merchants, Markets and the State in Early Modern India*, Delhi: Oxford University Press, 1990.

Suffren, Bailli de, *Journal de Bord du Bailli de Suffren dans l'Inde. 1781–1784*, Paris: Challamel et Cie, 1888. [Reprinted in Rennes, La Découvrance, 1995.]

Taillemite, Etienne and Denis Lieppe (eds), *La percée de l'Europe sur les océans, vers 1690-vers 1790*, Paris: Presses de l'Université de Paris–Sorbonne, 1997.

Tavernier, Jean-Baptiste, *Travels in India*, 2 volumes, translated by V. Ball, edited by William Crooke. First Indian edition, Delhi: Oriental Reprint, 1977.

The Dutch in Malabar, being a Translation of Selections Nos 1 and 2 with Introduction and Notes, by A. Galletti, A.-J. Van Der Burg and P. Groot, Madras, 1911. [Selections from the records of the Madras Government. Dutch Records no. 13.]

Thornton, E., *A Gazetteer of the Countries adjacent to India on North-West, including Sindh, Afghanistan, Beluchistan, the Punjab and the Neighbouring States*, 2 volumes, London, 1844.

Toussaint, Auguste, *L'océan indien au XVIIIe siècle*, Paris: Flammarion, 1974.

Tramond, Joannès, *Manuel d'histoire maritime de la France*, Paris: Société d'Editions Géographiques, Maritimes et Coloniales, 4th edition, 1942.

Vergé-Franceschi, Michel, *La marine française au XVIIIe siècle*, Paris: SEDES, 1996.

Vigié, Marc, 'La politique de Dupleix 1742–1754', in *Trois siècles de présence française en Inde*, Paris: CHEAM, 1994, pp. 17–35.

———— *Dupleix*, Paris: Fayard, 1993.

Vincent, Rose (ed.), *Pondichéry 1674–1761. L'échec d'un rêve d'Empire*, Paris: Editions Autrement, 1993.

Weber, Jacques, *Les Etablissements français en Inde au XIXe siécle (1816–1914)*, 5 volumes, Paris: Librairie de l'Inde, 1988.

Weber, Jacques (ed.), *Compagnies et Comptoirs. L'Inde des Français, XVII–XXe siècles*, Paris: Denoël, 1991.

Weinberger-Thomas, Catherine (ed.), *L'Inde et l'Imaginaire, Purusartha*, 11, Paris, 1988.

———— 'Les Mystères du Veda: Spéculations sur le texte sacré des anciens brames au siècle des Lumières', in *Purusartha*, 7, 1983, pp. 177–231.

Weller, Jac, *Wellington in India*, Napoleonic Library, London: Greenhill Books and Pennsylvania: Stackpole Books, 1993. [First edition, Longman Group, 1972.]

Wendel, François-Xavier, S.J., *Les Mémoires de Wendel sur les Jat, les Pathan et les Sikh*, edited by J. Deloche, Paris: EFEO, 1979.

Young, Desmond, *Fountain of the Elephants*, London: Collins, 1959.

Zaidi, Inayat A., 'French Mercenaries in the Armies of South-Asian States, 1499–1803', in *Indo-French Relations: History and Perspectives*, Delhi: MSH–Ambassade de France, 1990, pp. 51–78.

Index

Abul Fazl 9, 10, 32

Academy of Sciences, Paris 5

Achem 7

Agra 12, 21, 114, 130, 132

Ahmed Shah Abdali 10, 15

Aimable, L' (ship) 114

Ain-i-Akbari 9, 32

Akbar 132

Akbarabadi Gate, Red Fort, Delhi 125

Ala ud-Din Khilji 32

Albuquerque 44

Alfonso VI of Portugal 34

Ali Raja of Cannanore 42, 46, 48

Aligarh 12, 88

Ambur, battle of 84

America 25, 66, 95

American colonies, *see* North America

American War of Independence 66, 100

Amiens, Treaty of 92

Ananda Ranga Pillai 82

Anglo–French relations 100

Anglo–Mughal relations 100

Angria 3, 28, 40, 48

Anquetil de Briancourt 30–31 Plate 2 (Surat)

Anquetil Duperron 9, 13, 21–22, 30, 54, 58, 70, 116

Anville, d' 32

Anwar ud-Din 84, 124

Arabia 44

Arabic manuscripts 13

Arabic shores 42

Arabs 36

Arcate/Arcot 3, 16, 50, 52, 96–97 Plate 34 (plan), 100, 124

Arcati rupee 96

Armenians 5, 98, 112, 118

Arras 78

Asaf Jah 32, 124; *see also* Nizam ul-Mulk

Athar al-Sanadid 133

Augustin Hiriard of Bordeaux 21

Aurangabad 9, 32, 124

Aurangzeb 2, 12, 32, 70, 96, 102, 130, 132–33 Plate 49 (Mahtab Bagh)

Aurobindo Ghosh 112

Austrian 112

Austro–Hungarian Empire 104

Auteuil 84

Awadh 6, 8, 9–11, 13, 16, 22, 26, 108, 134–35 Plate 50 (Residence of Shuja ud-Daula)

Ayodhya 134

Babur 128, 132

Bagh-i-Hayat Bakhsh, Delhi 132

Bagnols 13

Bahadur Shah of Gujarat 34

Bahadur Shah (Shah Alam I) 11

Balassore 104, 118

Baldaeus 44

Bali 7

Bamongatty 118

Bandar Abbas 114

Bandel 104

Bandra, Jesuit college of 34

Bangalore 74
Bankibazar 104, 115
Bantam 98
Banvali Das 10
Bassein 34
Batavia 62
Batterie des Roches, Mahé 46, 48
bayanor 46, 48
Beaulieu 84
Bednore 42, 96
Belgium 4, 78
Bellanger 48–49 Plate 10 (Mahé)
Bellecombe 88, 90
Belnos 26
Benaras 10, 116
Bengal 10, 15, 18, 66, 112, 114, 116, 134
Bengal coast 104–05 Plate 38 (map)
Bengali goods 17
Bengali manuscripts 13
Bengali silk 118
Beri Timmana 98
Béringhen, Marquis de 25
Bernier, François 32, 130
Bhonsle 40
Bibliothèque Nationale, Paris 25–26
    (Département des Estampes), 116
    (Sanskrit manuscripts)
Bignon, Abbé 25
Bihar 112
Bijapur 70
Birendra Nath Banerji 112
Blanchisserie 2, 5, 84–85 Plate 28 (plan)
Blanquet de la Haye, 64
Bohras 34
Boigne, de 12, 88, 131
Boissieu, de 77
Bombay 2, 7, 28–29 Plate 1 (map), 34–35
    Plate 4, 36–39 Plate 5, 40, 44, 100
Bourcet, François 4, 88–89 Plate 30
    (fortifications)
Bourcet, Jean 4, 84–85 Plate 28
    (*Blanchisserie*), 86, 87, 90
Bourquien, Louis 12
Bouthenot 42
Braddyth 115

Brest 38
Brillant, Le (ship) 7, 40
bullion 14–15, 66, 84, 96
Burgundy wine 115
Bussy, Marquis de 5, 9, 11, 13, 18, 19, 32,
    38, 42, 58, 66, 68, 70, 84, 86, 92, 94, 95,
    100, 106, 124
Buxar, Battle of 10, 134

Caillaud 50
Calcutta 2, 15, 30, 88, 92, 100, 104, 108–11
    Plate 40 (plan), 112, 114
Cambay, Gulf of 28
Canaple 8, 12, 134, 135
Canimère, temple of 60
Cannanore 48
Cape, the 7
Capuchin mission 116
cardamom 48
Carnatas 36
Carnatic 3, 5, 68, 70, 76, 96, 100, 106
Caron 64
cartaz 40
Carvas 36
Cassimbazar, *see* Kasimbazar
Castries, de 5
Catherine of Braganza 34
Cattel 70
Cauvery river 3, 54, 64
Caveripatnam 72
Central Asia 132
Centre des Archives d'Outre-Mer 1, 2, 21,
    23–24 (DFC)
Ceylon 4, 34, 62, 92, 94, 98
chahar bagh 132
Challe, Robert 64, 76, 86
Chambéry 12
Champie de Fontbrun 4, 80–81 Plate 26
    (Governor's Palace, Pondicherry)
Chanda Sahib 50, 52, 96
Chandernagor 2, 16, 18, 24, 80, 100, 104,
    106, 112–13 Plate 41 (plan), 114–5 Plate
    42 (plan), 116–7 Plate 43 (view), 118
Chandni Chowk, Delhi 12, 124, 130, 132
Chandra Dourgam, *see* Chandraine

Chandraine 3 (Ginji), 72–73 Plate 22 (view)
Charles II of England 34
Charlotte, Queen of England 96
Cherbourg 4
Chevalier, 6, 108, 116
Chidambaram, temple of 60, 70
China 7, 25, 34, 112
China, temple of, Coromandel coast 60
Chinglepet, 3, 102–03 Plate 37 (plan)
Chinsurah 66, 104, 115, 118
Chiringam, *see* Srirangam
Chittagong 2
Choiseul 5, 18
Christian VII of Denmark 62
Circars, the Four 106
Clive, Marguerite 106
Clive, Robert 15, 28, 40, 50, 68, 96, 106,
    108, 112
Cochin 2, 44–45 Plate 8 (plan), 114
Coconut Tree Island (Ile des Cocotiers) 90
Coeurdoux, S.J. 84
Colbert 23, 25
Compagnie d'Ouvriers de la Mer 7
Compagnie des Indes Orientales 21, 26
Conajee Angria 40
Concan, *see* Konkan
Confiance, La (ship) 62
Constantinople 26
Cordier 120
Cornwallis 17, 19
Coromandel coast 15, 38, 42, 58, 60–61
    Plate 16 (map), 64, 66, 76, 94
Corps de Français de Raymond 124
Corps Royal d'Artillerie 4
Cossigny 42
Courcelles 8
Cromwell 34
Cuddalore 2, 5, 19, 38, 50, 60, 68–69 Plate
    20 (plan), 70, 102

Dacca 2, 118
Dalliens (Switzerland) 50
Daman 28
Dane/Danish 2, 15, 21, 58, 62–63 Plate 17
    (Tranquebar), 98, 104, 112

Dansborg (Tranquebar) 62
Dara Shikoh 10, 11, 12, 13, 30, 123, 130
Dargah Quli Khan 124
Daud Khan 98
Daulatabad, fort of 9, 32–33 Plate 3 (plan)
De Boigne, *see* Boigne
Decaen 92
Deccan 5, 8, 9–10 (Gentil), 28–29 Plate 1
    (map), 84, 124
Delhi 6, 8, 10, 12, 20, 21, 112, 114, 116,
    124–25 Plate 46 (Palace of Nizam ul-
    Mulk), 126–29 Plate 47 (Palace of Salim
    Shah Suri), 130–31 Plate 48 (Palace of
    the Great Mughal), 132–33 Plate 49
    (Mahtab Bagh)
De Mello de Castro 34
Denmark 62
Denyon, *see* Nyon
Deogir 32
Dépôt des Fortifications des Colonies 23–24
Desclaisons 4, 86, 88, 90
Desvaux 42
détroits 7
Deydier 46, 86
Dabhol 28
diamonds 26 (Sancy), 54 (Orlov), 96
    (Arcot), 96 (Pigot)
Din Panah, Delhi 128
Diu 28
Diwan-i-Khas, Red Fort, Delhi 125
diwanat 17
Doab 12, 131
Dravidian languages 62
Drugeon 12
Duchemin 58, 68
Dulac 88
Dumas 5, 78, 80, 96
Dumont 4, 5, 58, 82–83 Plate 27
    (Governor's Palace, Pondicherry)
Dupleix, Jeanne 80, 115
Dupleix, Joseph 5, 13, 18, 32, 52, 64, 68, 80,
    82, 84, 96, 100, 112, 114
Duplessis 112
Du Quesne 76
Dutch 2, 21, 30, 32, 44–45, 58, 64–65 Plate

18 (Negapatnam), 76, 77, 92, 98, 104,
    106, 112; *see also* VOC

East India Company 5, 17, 34, 36, 48, 58,
    62, 68, 86, 96, 98, 100, 102, 106, 115, 135
Edict of Nantes 64
Egypt 42
Elias, Catherine 5
Ellora caves 9
England 64
English pirates 36
European military technology 16

Faizabad 8, 9–12, 108, 134, 135
Faiz Bazaar, Delhi, 130
Flamicourt 58
Folnay 36
Fort Agoado, Goa 28
Fort Barlong, Pondicherry 76, 78
Fort-Louis, Pondicherry 2, 4, 23, 76, 77,
    78–79 Plate 25 (plan), 90
Fort Mahé 2, 48
Fort d'Orléans, Chandernagor 2, 80, 112
Fort Saint-David, Cuddalore 5, 7, 50, 60,
    68–69 Plate 20 (plan), 102
Fort Saint-George, Madras 7, 98
Fort William, Calcutta 2, 88, 108–11 Plate
    40 (plan), 134
Fourcroy de Ramecourt 90
France des Lumières 18
Franco–Dutch rivalry 64, 98
François-Marie de Tours 116
Fraser, William 129
French
    Agents in India 18–19
    brigades of Hindustan 92
    cartographers 2, 22, 26
    curiosity towards India 21–22
    Hussards in Mysore 74
     Arcot 96
    in Chinglepet 102
    in Cochin 44
    in Cuddalore 68
    in Surat 30
    military brigades in Indian states 16–17

officers in Bombay 36
policy towards North America 19–20, 94
policy towards India 18, 94
refugees at Tranquebar 62
Revolution 4, 25
settled in Madras 98
trade in Bengal 114
trade in India 84
Frischmann 50

Gaignères 25
Ganesha temple (Trichinopoly) 52
Ganga river 104
Garcia de Orta 34
Garneray 62
Gaston d'Orléans 25
Gaupp 50
Geitapour 28
Gentil 6, 8, 9–11 (biography and
    collections), 11, 22, 26, 30, 32, 106, 108,
    124–25 Plate 46 (Palace of Nizam ul-
    Mulk), 126–29 Plate 47 (Palace of Salim
    Shah Suri), 130–31 Plate 48 (Palace of
    the Great Mughal), 132–33 Plate 49
    (Mahtab Bagh), 134–35 Plate 50
    (Residence of Shuja ud-Daula)
Gérard 4, 54–55 Plate 13 (Great
    Srirangam), 56–57 Plate 14 (Small
    Srirangam)
Gerbault 4, 80
Gergelin coast 104–05 Plate 38 (map)
Germain 70
German 62, 98
Germany 64
Geslin 12
Ghaghra river 8, 12, 134
ghats (western) 40
Ghautis 36
Ghazi al-Din Khan 125
Gheria 3, 28, 40–41 Plate 6 (plan)
Ghulam Qadir 125
Gingins 50
Ginji 3, 5, 15, 60, 64, 70–71 Plate 21 (plan),
    72, 74, 76, 96
Glatignac 5

Goa 2, 28, 34
Golconda 66, 96, 102, 106
Golden Mosque, Chandni Chowk, Delhi 124
Goptipara 116
Goretty 114, 116
Great Seignor 26
Grenadiers 6, 74
Gujarat 28–29 Plate 1 (map of the coast), 34
Gujarati 34
Gurgin Khan 118

Halle 62
Harny 28
Hassan Abdal (Pakistan) 132
Heptanesia (Bombay) 34
Hindu religion 3, 54–57
Hiriard, Augustin de Bordeaux 21
Hoffelize, d' 70
Holkar 16
Hoogly, river 66, 112, 114, 116, 118, 121
Hugel 74
Hughes 42, 68
Hungary, *see* Austro–Hungarian Empire
    and Ostende
Huguenots 50, 64, 100
Huguier 82
Humayun 34, 128, 132
Hussards 74
Hyder Ali Khan 3, 4, 8, 16, 42, 46, 48, 50,
    58, 68, 70, 74, 96
Hyderabad 6, 8, 16, 18, 124

Ibrahim Khan 112
Ile Bourbon (La Réunion) 92
Ile de France (Mauritius) 8, 92, 94
Indes Orientales 24
India 26
Indian
    economy 14, 15, 17 (silver), 19–20
    (colonial)
    states 15, 16–17
Indian Ocean 5, 66, 68, 94, 100
Indological studies in France 13
Indore 16
Indranarayan Chowdhury 112

Irish brigade 100
Italian 98, 116 (missionaries)
Izdruk (Vijaydurg) 3, 7, 40–41 Plate 6
    (plan)
Jagannath temple 54, 104
Jahanara, Princess 132
Jaipur 14, 116
Jaisingh 116
Jama Masjid, Delhi 125, 130, 131
Jambukeshwara temple 54
Jamuna river 12, 124, 131, 132
Janjira-i-Mahrub 28, 40
Jantar Mantars 116
Japan 66
Jeddah 114
Jesuits 34, 44, 46, 72, 116
Jesuit Island (Bombay) 34
Jews 5, 44–5
Jugdia 118
Juliana 11

Kabul 132
Kamran Mirza 132
Karikal 5, 24, 58, 60
Kashmir 14
Kasim Ali Khan 118
Kasimbazar 2, 104, 116, 118–19 Plate 44
    (plan), 120–1 Plate 45 (cross-section)
Khojas 34
Konkan 28–29 Plate 1 (map), 40
Kremlin 54
Krishnagiri (Ginji) 72
kumedan 16
Kunvee river 40

La Bourdonnais 100
La Fayette 19
Lafitte de Brassier 5, 6–7 (biography),
    36–39 Plate 5 (Bombay), 40–41 Plate 6
    (Izdruk), 42–43 Plate 7 (Mangalore),
    44–45 Plate 8 (Cochin), 62–63 Plate 17
    (Tranquebar), 66–67 Plate 19
    (Negapatnam), 100–01 Plate 36
    (Madras), 102–03 Plate 37 (Chinglepet),
    108–11 Plate 40 (Calcutta)

Lahore 14, 21, 132
Lahori, Muhammad Salih Kambo 14
Lallée 42
Lally 4, 5, 7, 13, 18, 68, 82, 100, 102
La Lustière 4, 92–93 Plate 32 (fortifications)
Lavabre 118, 120–21 Plate 45 (cross-section,
    Kasimbazar)
Law de Lauriston 4, 5, 48, 86
Lawrence, Stringer 50, 102
Le Gentil 80, 86
Le Goux de Flaix 8, 84 (textiles)
Legris 70
Le Marchand 12
Lenoir 86
Leyrit 5
Lille 23, 78
London 20, 58, 92
Lord Lake 12
Louis XIV 23, 25, 77, 80
Louis XV 25, 116
Louis XVI 13, 24, 25
Louisbourg (North America) 100
Lucknow 9–12

McLean 80
Madec 10, 12, 74
Madras 2, 6, 7, 19, 30, 44, 50, 60, 66, 68, 72,
    90, 96, 98–99 Plate 35 (plan), 100–01
    Plate 36 (plan), 102
Madurai 58, 102
Mahé 2, 24, 46–47 Plate 9 (plan), 48–49
    Plate 10 (plan), 86, 94, 114
Mahim 36
Mahtab Bagh 12, 14, 132–33 Plate 49 (plan)
*Maison du Raja Bahadur, hors Dely, au bord du
    Gemna* (Raja Bahadur's Residence at
    Delhi, on the banks of the Jamuna) 125
Maissin 3, 5, 52, 54, 56
Maistre de la Tour 46
Malabar (Bombay) 36
Malabar coast 7, 40, 46, 94
Malborough (ship) 106
Maldive Islands 42, 46, 114
Mangalore 3, 4, 7, 42–43 Plate 7 (plan), 96,
    114

159

Mangicoupam 68
Manila 114
Manucci 98
Manusmriti 116
Marathes 3, 7, 12, 18, 28, 30, 36, 38, 40, 50, 56, 58, 70, 72, 76, 96
Marchant 58
Maridas Pillai 58
Marolles 25
Mars 12
Martin, Claude 8, 11 (with portrait), 108
Martin, François 30, 34, 64, 70, 72, 76, 84
Mascarenas Islands 94
Mascate 114
Masulipatnam 60, 106
Mattancherry 44
Mazagong 36
Mazarin 25
Mendece, Lucia 11
Metcalfe, Thomas 129
Middle East 25, 112, 114
Mihr Chand 11
Mir Kasim Ali 10
Modave 9, 12, 108, 119, 128, 130, 134, 135
Mahan Singh (Mounsingue) 11
Moluccas 62
Montagne Verte (Mahé) 46, 48
Montalembert 90
Montigny 6, 131
Moscow 54
Montigny 6, 11
Morse 100
Moulut 118
Mozac 116
Mughal
    armies 72, 76, 102, 124
    empire 66, 96, 134
    art 10–11, 22, 114 (Dupleix), 132
Mughals 30
Muhammad Ali/Mehemet Ali 50, 52, 58, 96, 102
Muhammad bin Tughlaq 32
Muhammad Shah 96, 124, 133
Muraqqa-i-Delhi 124
Murshidabad 17, 104, 118, 119

Museum d'Histoire Naturelle, Paris, 84
Muzaffar Khan 125
Muziris 42
Mysore 6, 7, 8, 16, 44, 46, 50, 74, 94, 95
Nadir Shah 10, 15, 124
Nandi Raja 56
Nantes 30, 64
Napoleon 13
nahr i-bihisht 132, 133
Nathamuni 54
National Archives of India 24
Nawab of Arcot 50, 52, 58; family at Pondicherry 16, 96
Nawab of Bengal 118
Nawab of Carnatic 77
Nayak 42 (Bednore), 50 (Madurai)
Negapatnam 2, 7, 58, 64–65 Plate 18 (print), 72
Nepal 13
Netherlands 64
Nevasilal 11
Nicobar Islands 7
Nicolas Nicolay 25
Nizam 6, 8, 16, 17, 18, 32, 100, 106
Nizam Ali Khan 124
Nizam ul-Mulk 11, 50, 124–25 Plate 46 (Palace, Delhi)
North America 5, 6, 17–19, 38, 40
Nyon (de Nyon/Denyon) 4, 76–77 Plate 24 (Pondicherry), 78–79 Plate 25 (Fort-Louis), 80

opium trade 34
Orissa coast 104–05 Plate 38 (map), 112
Ostende Company 104, 112

Paliacat 60, 66
Pallava 70
Palmas 118
Panja Sahib (Pakistan) 132
Paradise 132
Pareil (Bombay) 36
Paris 5, 18, 23, 38, 44, 90, 94
Parsis 34, 36
Partab Singh of Tanjore 58

Paschoud 50
Patna 2, 112, 118
Patparganj, battle of 12
Pays de Vaud 50
Peacock Throne 124
Pegu 7
pepper trade 46, 48
Perron 12, 92, 131
Persia 26, 128
Persian Gulf 42
Persian manuscripts 10, 13
Persians 36, 125
Pettapoli 60
Picot de la Motte 46
Pigot, George 80, 100
Piply river 104
Piveron de Morlat 6, 42, 70, 94
Pluche, Abbé 114
Pointe de Godvarin 60, 104
Pointe des Géants 28
Pointe des Palmiers 104
Poivre, Pierre 84
Polier, Antoine-Louis 8, 12, 14, 50, 108, 135
Polier, Paul-Philippe 50, 68, 102, 108
Pompadour, Madame de 82
Pondi island 7
Pondicherry 1 (map), 2, 4, 7, 16, 18, 24, 30, 46, 48, 60, 64, 68, 72, 74, 76–77 Plate 24 (plan), 80–81 Plate 26 (Governor's Palace, drawing), 82–83 Plate 27 (*idem*), 84–85 Plate 28 (*blanchisserie*), 86–87 Plate 29 (Villenour Gate), 88–89 Plate 30 (fortifications, drawing), 90–91 Plate 31 (fortifications), 92–93 Plate 32 (ramparts), 94–95 Plate 33 (ramparts), 97, 100, 102, 112 (Union Territory)
Poona 6
Porcher Desoulches 58
Porte ou Terpolin á Dely (Gate of Terpolin at Delhi) 125
Port Louis (Mauritius) 90, 94, 95
Porto Novo 66, 102
Portuguese 21, 30, 34, 36, 40, 46, 64, 98, 112
Praslin, de 88
Pré carré 23

Préfets de Delhi 12
Preston 102
printing press 44, 62
Propaganda Fide 116
Protestant mission (Tranquebar) 62
Provence 115
Ptolemeus 34
Punjab 15, 100
Purana Qila, Delhi 128
Puranas 116

Quelci 28
Qudsia Begum 124
Quimper 131

Rajagiri (Rasegadou, Ginji) 3, 72, 74–75
  Plate 23 (drawing)
Ram Raja of Ginji 64, 76
Ramanuja 54
Ramayana 116
Ranganatha Swami, temple of 54
Ranger 4, 46–47 Plate 9 (Mahé), 48
Ranjit Singh of Punjab 100
Rasegadou, *see* Rajagiri
Ravi river 132
Raymond 17, 124
Réaumur 114
Red Fort, Delhi 124, 131
Régiment de l'Ile de France 42
Régiment de Meuron 92
regiment of Lorraine 7
Riftièrre 112–13 Plate 41 (Chandernagor),
  116–17 Plate 43 (*Loge* of Chandernagor)
Rochambeau 19, 38
Rock Fort (Trichinopoly) 52
Rohilla Afghans 125
Royal Navy (English) 19, 92, 94, 100
Ryswick, Treaty of 64

Sadat-Ullah Khan of Carnatic 70, 96
Sa'dulla Khan 125, 132
Sabor, sandbanks 104
Sadras, temples of 60
Safdar Jang 11, 124, 125
Saint-David, Fort, *see* Fort Saint-David

Saint-Helen Island 7
Saint-Louis church (Pondicherry) 78
Saint-Paul College (Goa) 34
Salabat Jang 124
Salim Shah Suri 11, 128–29 Plate 47 (Palace
  in Delhi)
Salimgarh Fort, Delhi 128, 130, 131
Salsette, island 28
Sambhaji 68
San Thomé 64, 98
Sangueser 28
Sanskrit manuscripts for France 10, 13, 116
Sanskrit studies in India 70, 116
sapan wood 48
Sarala Devi Ghosal 112
Sartine 6
Sayyid Ahmad Khan 133
Schonamille 115
Schulze 62
Schwartz 58, 62
Sepoy Mutiny (Great Revolt of 1857) 26
Serampore 62, 104
Serres, Dominique 114
Seurden 28
Seven Year War 8, 96, 100
Seychelles, archipelago 7
Shah Alam I 11
Shah Alam II 12, 13, 16, 17, 18, 102, 125,
  131
Shah Jahan 14, 32, 125, 130–31 Plate 48
  (Palace of the Great Mughal in Delhi),
  132
Shajahanabad 131
Shalimar Gardens 132
Shergarh, Delhi 126
Sher Shah Suri 127, 128, 130
Schinglepet, *see* Chinglepet
Shuja ud-Daula 8, 10–12 (Gentil), 11
  (portrait), 16, 108, 134–35 Plate 50
  (Residence in Faizabad)
Siam 25
Sichtermann 115
Sidi 28, 36, 40, 48
Silver 17
Sinan, Jeanne-Madeleine 5

Sinan, Joanis 5
Sindhia (Daulatrao) 92
Sindhia, Madhavrao 12, 16, 17, 88, 100, 131
Sion 36
Siraj ud-Daula 108, 112
Shiva temple at Srirangam island 54
Shivaji 40, 68
Skinner, James 129
Snake Island 28
Sobha Singh 112
Solvyns 28
Sombre (Reinhardt) 10
Sornay, Pierre Basile 5
Souillac 38, 86, 94–95 Plate 33
  (Pondicherry, ramparts)
Spain 34
Sri Ranga temple (Ginji) 74
Sri Ranganatha, temple of 72
Srirangam island 3, 4, 50, 70
Srirangam temple (great) 54–55 Plate 13
  (plan)
Srirangam temple (small) 56–57 Plate 14
  (plan)
Srirangapatnam 15, 18 (illustration), 46
Stockhouse 115
Strasbourg 13
Stuart 68
Suffren 4 (portrait with Hyder Ali Khan), 5,
  19, 38, 66, 68, 94, 100
Sumatra 7
Surat 2, 7, 28, 30–31 Plate 2, 36, 40, 64, 114
Surcouf 62
Swali (port of Surat) 28
Swiss in the English East India Company's
  service 50, 68, 92, 102
Switzerland 64

Taj Mahal 12, 131 (painting in France), 132
Tangiers (Morocco) 34
Tanjore 3, 15, 58–59 Plate 15 (plan), 62, 70
Tavernier 32
Ternay 6
textiles 15, 84
Thiagar 74
Tiinzch 4, 9, 32–33 Plate 3 (Daulatabad)

161

Tipu Sultan 3–4, 8, 11 (portrait), 13, 16, 42, 44, 50, 58, 70, 74, 94, 95, 96, 100
Topas 58, 98
Touchant de la Lustière, *see* La Lustière
Tournai (Belgium) 4, 23, 78
Trade 14–15, 66, 84, 98, 114 and *passim*
Tranquebar (Turangaburi) 2, 58, 60, 62–63 Plate 17 (plan), 72
Trichinopoly (Tiruchirapally) 3, 50–51 Plate 11 (plan), 52–53 Plate 12 (view), 54–57 Plates 13 and 14 (temples of Srirangam island), 70
Trimliwash 102
Trinquemale (Ceylon) 66, 68, 86, 92, 94
Tronjoly 7, 40, 44
Turkish sultans 25
Turkey 25

Ujjain 116
Union (ship) 7
Union Territory (Pondicherry) 113
Upanishads 13, 30
Urdu dictionary 116
United States of America 17, 68, 92, 94–95, 100

Vaishnava movement 54
Valory 5, 6, 96–97 Plate 34 (Fort of Arcot)
Vandivash 7
Vauban 23, 78, 90
Vedas 116
Velho, Thérèse 11
Versailles 13 (Tipu's embassy), 18, 25, 86, 87, 90, 94
Versailles, Treaty of 17–18, 66, 68, 92, 94, 100
Victoria and Albert Museum, London, 130
Vijaya Ranga Naik of Tanjore 70
Vijayanagar 70, 102
Vijaydurg (Izdruk, Gheria) 40–41 Plate 6 (plan)
Villejuif (Cochin) 2, 44–45
Villenour (Gate of, Pondicherry) 2, 86–87 Plate 29
Villenour 4, 5

Vincent, Jeanne (Mrs Dupleix) 115
Virena temple (Madras) 98
Vishnu temple Vizagapatnam 2, 106–07 Plate 39 (plan)
VOC (Dutch East India Company) 19, 34, 64–65 Plate 18 (Negapatnam, view), 66–67 Plate 19 (Negapatnam, plan), 76, 77
Volton 12

Wah gardens (Pakistan) 132
Walpole 100
Washington 19
Watson 28, 40, 68, 106, 108, 112
Wellesley, Arthur 15
Wellesley, Richard 92
Westminster tiara, London, 96

Xavier, François S.J., 44

Yale, Governor of Madras 98
Yale University (USA) 98
Yamunacharya 54
Yanaon 24, 104 (river), 106
Yavada kingdom 32
Yorktown (USA) 17, 19, 94
Yusuf Khan 50, 58, 62, 102

Zeigenbalg 62
Zeigler 50
Zend Avesta 9, 30, 70
Zoroastrian studies 13
Zulfikar Khan 70